John Freely is one of the most widely respected writers of travel books, histories and guides about Greece and Turkey. He is the author of *The Grand Turk*, *Storm on Horseback*, *Children of Achilles*, *The Cyclades*, *The Ionian Islands*, *The Western Shores of Turkey*, *Strolling through Athens* and the bestselling *Strolling through Istanbul* (all I.B.Tauris). He lives in Istanbul.

'Whenever I'm asked to recommend a book about Turkey, I reply, "Anything by John Freely".'
Stephen Kinzer, former *New York Times* correspondent

'Freely abounds in colourful details …'
Philip Mansel, *Independent*

'[*The Western Shores of Turkey* is an] enchanting guide …
a work of genuine scholarship, lightly worn and charmingly conveyed. I fell in love with the book and stayed enamoured until the final page.'
Paul Bailey, *The Sunday Times*

'… a man effortlessly able to convey in depth the meaning of what he sees.'
Marlena Frick, *Scotsman*

'[*Strolling through Istanbul* is] a classic.
The best travel guide to Istanbul.'
The Times

'Freely reveals a superb eye for the telling detail.'
Independent

'He makes [writing] look easy and does so with great style and charm, seeing the big picture and writing with a novelist's eye for the telling detail.'
Victoria Holbrook

'John Freely is a virtuoso of cultural narration.'
Talat S. Halman, Dean of the Faculty of Humanities and Letters at Bilkent University

A TRAVEL GUIDE TO HOMER

*On the Trail of Odysseus through
Turkey and the Mediterranean*

JOHN FREELY

I.B. TAURIS

LONDON · NEW YORK

Published in 2014 by I.B.Tauris & Co Ltd
6 Salem Road, London W2 4BU
175 Fifth Avenue, New York NY 10010
www.ibtauris.com

Distributed in the United States and Canada
Exclusively by Palgrave Macmillan
175 Fifth Avenue, New York NY 10010

ISBN: 978 1 78076 197 8
eISBN: 978 0 85773 494 5

A full CIP record for this book is available from the British Library
A full CIP record is available from the Library of Congress

Library of Congress Catalog Card Number: available

Printed and bound by CPI Group (UK) Ltd, Croydon, CR0 4YY

For Toots, my Penelope

Contents

List of Illustrations

Note from the Author

This book is meant to be a guide to Homer's *Iliad* and *Odyssey*, which will lead the traveller from Troy along the Aegean coast of Turkey and then around the shores of the Mediterranean, following in the footsteps of Odysseus as he goes off to fight in the Trojan War and, after many adventures, makes his way back to his home and family in Ithaca.

I first crossed the wake of Odysseus in October 1945 on a US Navy troopship coming back to New York from the Pacific and China-Burma-India theatres of war. I had read the *Iliad* and *Odyssey* before going off to war, and I reread them several times during the half-century that I have lived in Greece and Turkey, when my travels shadowed those of Odysseus, although some imagination is often needed, for our hero was known as 'the man of many ways'. I have woven my own account together with Richmond Lattimore's translations of the *Iliad* and the *Odyssey*, one or another of which I have always had with me in all my Homeric journeys, and through them and other reading I think I have learned something of the world of Homer himself, which I have tried to pass on in this book of travels.

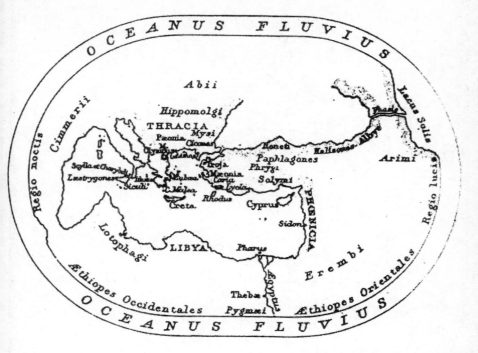

1   The World according to Homer in 1000 BC

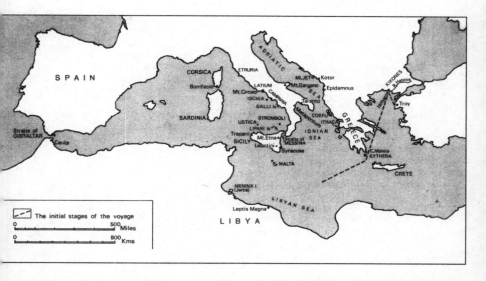

2   The Odyssey: Initial stages of the voyage

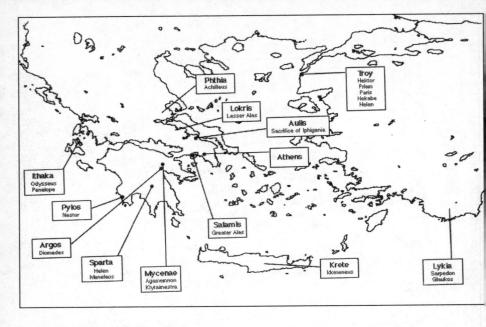

3 The Catalogues of Greeks and Trojans

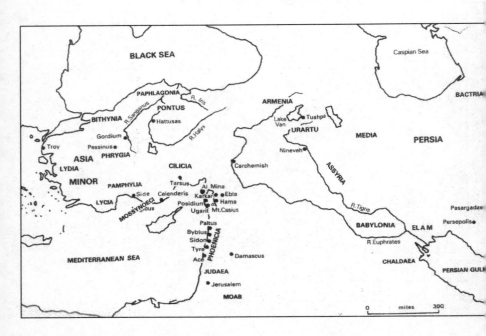

4 The Near and Middle East

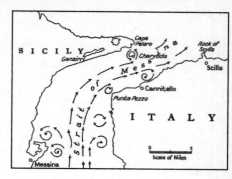

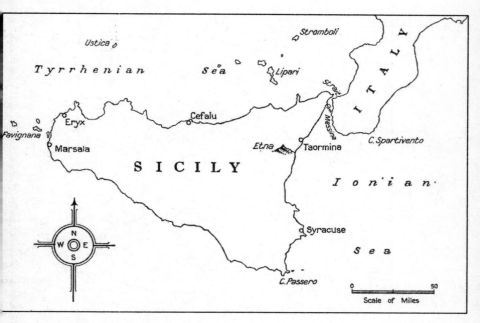

5   Italy and Sicily

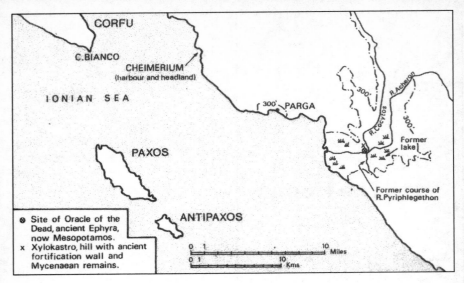

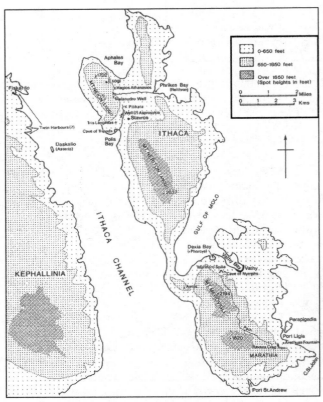

6 (above) Site of Oracle of the Dead, ancient Ephyra
(below) Homeric sites on Ithaca

The Homeric World

Greek literature begins with Homer's two epic poems, the *Iliad* and the *Odyssey*, whose enormous literary influence still endures today, nearly 3,000 years after they were composed.

The *Iliad* is set in the plain of Troy, a great fortress city on the Asian side of the Dardanelles (Hellespont) near its Aegean end. The Dardanelles, together with the Sea of Marmara (Propontis) and the Bosphorus, forms the historic strait between the Aegean and the Black Sea (Pontus) that separates Europe and Asia in what is now north-western Turkey. The European side of the strait has since antiquity been called Thrace. The other side is known in Turkish as Anatolia, which in times past was generally called Asia Minor. The word '*anatolia*' means 'east' in Greek, more literally 'the land of sunrise'. The name 'Asia' may have had the same meaning as this in both the Indo-European and Semitic families of languages, while 'Europe' may have meant 'sunset' or the 'land of darkness'. The distinction would have been evident to the first Greek mariners making their way through the Hellespont from the Aegean, with Asia to the East and Europe to the West, the waters of the strait clearly dividing the 'land of sunrise' from the 'land of darkness'.

The background of the story told in the *Iliad* can be summarized thus: Paris, also called Alexandros, son of King Priam of Troy, is a guest of the Greek warlord Menelaus at Sparta. Paris seduces Helen, wife of Menelaus, who returns with him to Troy. Menelaus appeals for help to his brother Agamemnon, King of Mycenae in the Argolid, who calls on warlords throughout the Greek world to join him in an expedition against Troy, their fleet assembling at Aulis in Boeotia before making their way to the Hellespont. The Greeks attack Troy but are unable to take it and put the city under siege, sacking several places in the Troad, the huge peninsula south of the Hellespont.

The *Iliad* begins during the final year of the siege, which lasted for ten years, going on to describe a period of fifty-two days, ending before the capture and sack of Troy by the Greeks. The story of the actual capture of the city and its aftermath is told partly in episodes of the *Odyssey*, and partly in the latter poems of the post-Homeric Epic Cycle, the first of which tell of what happened before the beginning of the *Iliad*.

The Greeks after Homer's time considered the Trojan War to be one of the early episodes in the history of the Hellenes, as they called themselves thenceforth, referring to their country as Hellas. (The word 'Greek' comes from the Roman 'Graeci', stemming from a tribe in Epirus.) It was the opinion of Thucydides that the Greeks first acted together as a people in the Trojan War. As he writes in Book I of his *History of the Peloponnesian War*:

> We have no record of any action taken by Hellas as a whole before the Trojan War. Indeed my view is that at this time the whole country was not even called 'Hellas' ... it took a long time before the name ousted all the other names. The best evidence for this can be found in Homer, who, though he was born much later than the time of the Trojan War, nowhere uses the name 'Hellenic' for the whole force. Instead he keeps this name for the followers of Achilles who came from Phthioti and were in fact the original Hellenes. For the rest in his poems he uses the words 'Danaans', 'Argives', and 'Achaeans' ... because in his time the Hellenes were not yet known by one name, and so marked off as something separate from the outside world.

The Greeks first appear as a people in what is now Greece midway through the Bronze Age (*c.* 2000–1600 BC). They apparently came by land and from the north, speaking a form of what became the Greek language, bringing with them their gods, presumably Zeus and the other Olympian deities known from the historical period. They left no written records and are known only from archaeological evidence.

The Mycenaean period, *c.* 1550–1100 BC, takes its name from the Bronze Age fortress-city of Mycenae in the Argolid. Mycenaean pottery similar to that unearthed at Troy has been found at twenty-four other sites along the Aegean coast of Anatolia or its immediate hinterland. There were Mycenaean coastal settlements at Miletus and Iasus, as well as on the nearby islands of Chios, Samos, Cos and Rhodes, and there is some evidence that the Greeks traded up the two main rivers flowing down from the Anatolian plateau, the Hermus and the Maeander. Mycenaean pottery has also been found at Clazomenae, Ephesus and Sardis, and a Mycenaean burial ground has been unearthed near Bodrum, Greek Halicarnassus.

The Mycenaean period is the Heroic Age of Greek myth, including the legends of Heracles, Oedipus, Perseus, and Theseus, along with Minos and the Labyrinth on Crete, the first kings of Athens, the expeditions of the Seven against Thebes, Jason and the Argonauts, and the Trojan War. Herodotus, referring to the birth of Pan, says that this 'was after the Trojan War and about eight hundred years before my time', or *c*. 1250 BC. He also writes that Homer and Hesiod lived 'four hundred years before my time', that is, *c*. 850 BC. He writes of both the Argonauts and the Trojan War, saying that the siege of Troy began 'in the third generation after Minos', and that the war occurred 'in the next generation after' the voyage of the Argonauts. According to Homer, several of the Greek heroes who fought at Troy were sons of men who had sailed with Jason, including his son Euneos, lord of Lemnos.

Greek tradition held that their eponymous ancestor was Hellen, father of Doris, Aeolus, and Xuthus, whose sons were Ion and Aechaeus, thus giving a common ancestry to the Dorians, Ionians, Aeolians and Achaeans, the principal Greek tribes in the late Bronze Age. Homer refers to Hellas and the Hellenes in the *Iliad*, where the men of Agamemnon's army as a whole are described variously as Danaans, Argives and Achaeans, or sometimes as sons of the Achaeans.

According to Homer, at the time of the Trojan War Mycenae was ruled by Agamemnon, 'far the greatest of all the Achaians'. Book 2 of the *Iliad* ends with two lists, the Catalogue of Ships and the Catalogue of Trojans, the first of which lists the warships in the armada of Agamemnon, whose contingent was the largest in the Greek fleet. There were contingents from all over the Greek world, the most distant being those from the Ionian Islands, in the Adriatic Sea between Greece and southernmost Italy. There were two contingents from the Ionian Islands, one of them led by Odysseus. There was also a large contingent from Crete, a powerful Bronze Age kingdom with its capital at Knossos. The Cretan contingent was co-commanded by Idomeneus, a grandson of King Minos, a son of Zeus who, according to mythology, founded the Minoan dynasty.

The oldest of the Greek heroes at Troy was Nestor, King of Pylos, in the north-western corner of the Peloponnesos. Nestor was accompanied by his son Antilochus, a close friend of Achilles, who is described in Book 4 as 'first to kill a chief man of the Trojans', and who would himself die in battle later in the siege.

Following the Catalogue of Ships Homer recites the much shorter Catalogue of Trojans, those who fought in defence of Troy. The catalogue includes groups from five geographical areas, beginning with the Troad, with contingents of Trojans, Dardanians, Zelians and Pelasgians. The Trojans were led by Hector, son of King Priam of Troy. The Dardanians were from the region just to the east of the Trojans in the Troad, taking their name from Dardanos, ancestor of the Trojan kings. They were led by Aeneas, the mythical founder of Rome, who was the son of the goddess Aphrodite and Anchises, a second cousin of Priam.

The second group was made up of three peoples from across the Hellespont in Thrace, namely Thracians, Ciconians and Paeonians. The third group comprised two tribes on the Black Sea coast of Asia Minor: Paphlagonians and Halizones. The fourth group was made up of two contingents from north-western Asia Minor, the Mysians and Phrygians. The latter were a people who had migrated from south-eastern Europe and eventually supplanted the Hittites, an Indo-European people who dominated Anatolia in the late Bronze Age from their capital at Hatussa. The fifth group included three units from south-western Asia Minor: Maeonians, Carians and Lycians.

Mysia, Caria and Lycia have all been identified with regions in western Anatolia mentioned in the Hittite tablets. It appears that the people from these regions, and perhaps the Trojans themselves, spoke an Indo-European language known as Luwian, closely related to Hittite.

There are several references in Hittite texts to the Land of Assuva, which was probably the region in western Asia Minor known to the Greeks as Lydia. It is generally agreed that the Greek word 'Asia' derives from the Hittite 'Assuva'. The earliest Greek reference to Asia is in Book 2 of the *Iliad*, where the poet writes of 'the Asian meadow beside the Kaystrian waters', referring to the River Cayster, which flows into the Aegean through the ruins of the ancient Ionian city of Ephesus.

Hittite texts mention two place names – Taruisa and Wilusa – which are believed to be references to Troy and Ilium, the two names which Homer uses interchangeably in referring to the Trojan capital. One text gives the details of a treaty between the Hittite king, Muwatallis (*c.* 1300 BC) and the king of Wilusa, Alaksandros, who may be the prince of Ilios (Troy) Alexandros (Paris). Mention is also made of a people called Dardany, which may refer to the Dardanians, the name coming from Dardanus, the legendary ancestor of the Trojan kings.

Hittite records also make several references to Arzawa, an aggressive state, possibly Troy, that seems to have controlled north-western Anatolia. There are also references to the Ahhijava, a powerful seafaring people who have been identified as the Achaeans, or Mycenaean Greeks. The Ahhijava princes corresponded with the Hittite rulers from a coastal city named Millawanda, probably Miletus.

Miletus was first settled *c.* 1600 BC by mariners from Minoan Crete, who established in the Aegean what Thucydides called a *thalassocracy*, or 'empire of the sea'. The Minoan Empire came to an end *c.* 1450 BC, when the Mycenaeans took control of Crete.

During the Middle Minoan period, *c.* 2000–1700 BC, palace records on Crete were kept in a pictographic script known as Linear A, which has never been deciphered. During the Mycenaean period the palace archives in Crete were written in a syllabic script called Linear B, an early form of Greek which has also been found in Mycenaean sites in Greece.

Near the beginning of his *History of the Peloponnesian War*, Thucydides remarks that 'the country now called Hellas had no settled population; instead there was a series of migrations, as the various tribes, being under the constant pressure of invaders who were stronger than they were, were always prepared to abandon their own territory'. He goes on to say that 'the period of shifting populations ended' only many years after the Trojan War, followed by the 'period of colonization', when 'Ionia and most of the islands were colonized by the Athenians'.

The great migration that brought the Hellenes across the Aegean to Ionia and the other regions on the Aegean shore of Asia Minor occurred during the Dark Ages of the Greek world, a period of several centuries following the catastrophic end of the Bronze Age. This catastrophe seems to have occurred within a period of less than fifty years at the end of the thirteenth and beginning of the twelfth century BC, when almost every important city or palace in the eastern Mediterranean world was destroyed, many of them never to be occupied again. Among the places destroyed were Mycenae, Tiryns, Pylos and seven other Mycenaean strongholds in what is now mainland Greece; the Minoan cities of Knossos and Cydonia in Crete; four cities in Cyprus; thirteen cities in Anatolia, including Troy and the Hittite capital at Hattusa; nine cities in Syria; and nine cities in the southern Levant. A number of alternative explanations of the catastrophe have been proposed, including earthquakes, droughts or other ecological disasters, widespread revolutions, mass migrations such as the invasion by the mysterious 'Sea Peoples' mentioned in Egyptian inscriptions, new methods of warfare, or 'systems collapse' due to one or more of the previously mentioned factors or to the introduction of ironworking, which led to the era that followed the Bronze Age being called the Iron Age. Whatever the cause, the effect was a drastic depopulation of the Greek world, with many places, particularly the Aegean islands, being totally abandoned, the surviving communities scattered and isolated from one another.

Ancient tradition held that the Greek migration to Anatolia was due to the invasion of Dorians, a tribe from Macedonia, though modern scholars have rejected this idea. The Dorians were in any event part of the migration, along with the Aeolians and Ionians, a mass movement which probably began *c.* 1040 BC. The Ionians settled in the central sector of the Aegean coast of Anatolia and its offshore islands, with the Aeolians to their north, with some overlapping, and the Dorians to the south. The Aeolian settlements were, with one exception, between the Hellespont and the River Hermus, as well as on the islands of Lesbos and Tenedos. The cities founded by the Ionians were between the valleys of the rivers Hermus and Maeander, as well as on Chios and Samos. The Dorian colonies were on Cos and Rhodes and in Caria, the south-western corner of Anatolia, where the Aegean merges with the Mediterranean.

The eighth century BC is known in Greek history as the 'age of colonization', for it was then that the Greeks began establishing colonies all around the Mediterranean and the Black Sea as well as in the straits connecting the two seas. These were not colonies in the modern sense, but city-states in their own right, independent of the city that had founded them. They also founded *emporia*, or trading-posts, which did not have colonial status.

Chalcis and Eretria on the island of Euboea, who together had sent forty ships to join Agamemnon's army in the siege of Troy, founded eight of the twenty-two Greek colonies in Sicily and southern Italy, which became known as Magna Graecia, or 'Great Greece'. The earliest of the Greek colonies in Magna Graecia was the Euboean emporium of Pithacusae, now known as Ischia, founded *c.* 770–760 BC on an island off the north-western reach of the Bay of Naples. A decade or so earlier the Euboean cities had taken a leading role in founding the emporium of Potamoi Karon, now called Al Mina, beside the estuary of the River Orontes in north Syria, now the Turkish province of Hatay, as well as two other nearby emporia at Posidium and Paltus.

Corinth cooperated with Chalcis in founding two colonies in Sicily, and five in north-western Greece and its offshore islands in the Ionian Sea (southern Adriatic), including Kerkyra (Corfu) and Leucas (Lefkada). Kerkyra has been identified as Homeric Scheria, home of the Phaiakians, who entertained Odysseus royally on the penultimate stage of his long voyage back to Ithaca. Leucas would be one of the islands ruled by Meges, whose contingent of forty vessels is described in the Catalogue of Ships just before that of Odysseus.

The Ionian city of Phocaea in Asia Minor established colonies on the coasts of south-east Italy, Corsica and France, the latter including Massalia, the ancestor of Marseilles, as well as on the Hellespont, the Sea of Marmara and the Black Sea.

The most active of all the colonizers was the Ionian city of Miletus, founded on the site of the earlier Mycenaean colony that had sent a contingent to fight as allies of the Trojans in the defence of Troy. Miletus founded at least forty colonies, mostly on the Hellespont, the Sea of Marmara and the Black Sea, as well as the fortified port of Milesionteichos, part of the great Greek emporium of Naucratis on the Nile delta.

These colonies put the Greeks in conflict with the Phoenicians, who are mentioned in both the *Iliad* and the *Odyssey*. The Phoenician city-states were led by Tyre and Sidon in Syria, who themselves founded Carthage and many other colonies in the Mediterranean. The Euboean cities were in contact with the Phoenicians at their emporia in north Syria, where they acquired both goods and ideas from Phoenicia and elsewhere in the East, transmitting them to other Euboean emporia, principally Pithecusae, which sent wine and oil in exchange.

The most important cultural acquisition of the Greek traders was the Phoenician alphabetic script, which Herodotus calls *phoinikeia*. The Phoenicians had transformed and simplified earlier syllabic scripts into a standard alphabetic writing with twenty-two characters. The Greeks adapted the Phoenician system to create an alphabet with twenty-four letters, including six vowels. Originally there were several versions of the Greek alphabet, most notably western (Chalcidian) and eastern (Ionic). The Chalcidian version gave rise to the old Italic alphabet and thence to the Latin, while the Ionic developed into the present Greek alphabet. The Athenians adopted the Ionic script as their standard in 403 BC, and the other versions disappeared soon afterwards. Thus the Greeks became literate again, some four centuries after the collapse of Mycenaean civilization and the disappearance of Linear B script during the Dark Ages.

The earliest inscribed example of the new script is dated *c*. 740–720 BC. This was found on Ischia in 1953 on a fragment of a pottery drinking vessel known as Nestor's Cup, with a three-line inscription in the Chalcidian alphabet, a single iambic verse followed by two hexameters: 'Nestor had a certain cup, good to drink from./But whoever drinks from this cup, will immediately/be seized with desire for Aphrodite of the beautiful crown.'

Nestor's Cup is described in Book 11 of the *Iliad*, and thus the discovery of the inscription led most scholars to date the Homeric epics to the second half of the eighth century. The dating and history of the poems, the dates and identity of the poet himself, and the dates when the oral poems were first written down in their present form, are all parts of what has come to be known as the Homeric Question.

Most scholars now agree that the poems attributed to Homer stem from the collective inheritance of many ancient bards, known in Greek as *aoidai*, who sang their songs to the accompaniment of the lyre. This tradition seems to have begun in Ionia in the eighth century BC, when the *aoidai* performed in the courts of the aristocracy, singing of the glorious deeds of the great heroes of times past, songs that their predecessors had brought over from the Greek mainland at the time of the great migration. The earlier *aoidai* are believed to have had an established place in Mycenaean courts, and their successors in Ionia sang songs in the same epic tradition, passed along through succeeding generations.

Most modern scholars place the birth of Homer's poems in the latter half of the eighth century BC, although a few date them to 680–660 BC. The consensus is that there was one Homer, who composed the *Iliad c.* 740 BC and the *Odyssey c.* 720 BC. Shortly after 700 BC scenes from the Homeric epics began to appear in Greek vase-painting, many of them depicting episodes involving Odysseus, lending support to dating the *Iliad* and the *Odyssey* to the latter half of the eighth century BC.

Ancient writers were almost unanimous in dating the first standard texts of the *Iliad* and *Odyssey* to *c.* 550 BC, when the Pisistratids, the Athenian tyrant Pisistratus and his sons, are supposed to have had them written down and recited at the festival of the Greater Panathenaia. This view is rejected by several modern scholars, most notably Gregory Nagy, who has proposed an evolutionary model with at least five consecutive phases of Homeric transmission, ranging in time from the Mycenaean era to *c.* 150 BC, when Aristarchus of Samothrace, head of the Library of Alexandria, produced recensions of the *Iliad* and the *Odyssey*, dividing each of them into twenty-four books designated with the twenty-four letters of the Greek alphabet, which in modern editions were replaced by numerals.

The evolution of the Homeric epics gave rise to a change in the traditional profession of the singer, who originally was called an *aiodos* and later a *rhapsodos*. The *aiodos* was a bard who improvised as he sang, as contrasted with the *rhapsodos*, who recited from a fixed text, their profession safeguarded by associations or 'guilds' of rhapsodes.

The rhapsodes on the island of Chios called themselves *Homeridae*, or Sons of Homer, claiming that they were descended from the poet. The first mention of the Homeridae is in Pindar's *Nemean Odes*, written *c.* 485 BC. As Nagy notes: 'Starting from the very point where the *Homeridae*, singers of sewn-together utterances, most often take their start from the prelude of Zeus.'

The scholia to Pindar's *Nemean Odes* explains what he means by 'sewn-together':

> But some say that – since the poetry of Homer had not been brought together under one thing, but rather had been scattered about and divided into parts – when they performed it rhapsodically, they would be doing something that is similar to sequencing or sewing, as they produced it into one thing.

Since the *Iliad* and the *Odyssey* both begin in the penultimate year of the ten-year stories, there must have been some earlier epic or epics that told the whole tale. Homer and his audience knew the details of the full story of the Trojan War, but the *Iliad* and the *Odyssey* became so popular that earlier versions of the epics were neglected and lost. The lost epics make up the so-called Trojan Cycle, those that dealt with the Trojan War and related events. This cycle is made up of six epics along with the *Iliad* and the *Odyssey*. There is almost no overlapping in the epics of the cycle, which are written around the *Iliad* and the *Odyssey* so as to tell the whole story of the Trojan War. It has been suggested that the final version of the Trojan Cycle was created early in the Hellenistic period, by taking originally independent poems and combining them with *Iliad* and the *Odyssey* so that together they told the whole story. The poems themselves are lost, and we know of them mostly from a summary of their plots by Proclus, who may be the Neoplatonist philosopher of the fifth century AD.

The epics of the cycle are, in chronological order: the *Cypria*, in eleven books, describing the background of the Trojan War and the siege of Troy down to the point where the *Iliad* begins; the *Iliad*, twenty-four books, with revisions at the beginning and end which link it with the *Cypria*; *Aethiopus*, five books, a continuation of the story of the Trojan War down to the death of Achilles and the quarrel over his armour between Odysseus and Telamonian Aias; *Little Iliad*, four books, from the quarrel of Odysseus and Aias down to the stratagem of the Wooden Horse; *Iliupersis*, two books, from the Trojan Horse down through the sack of Troy; *Nostoi* (Returns), five books, homeward journeys of Agamemnon and other Greek heroes, not including Odysseus; *Odyssey*, twenty-four books; the return of Odysseus; *Telegonia*, in two books, the life of Odysseus from the end of the *Odyssey* up to his death.

There are also a collection of post-Homeric poems known as the *Homeric Hymns*, the earliest of which is dated to the seventh century BC. There are thirty-three hymns, four of which are long, 294–580 lines, and twenty-one short, 3–59 lines. There are three hymns each to Dionysus and Aphrodite; two each to Demeter, Artemis, Apollo, Athena, Hermes, Hestia, and the Dioscuri, the twin sons of Zeus, Castor and Polydeuces (Latin Pollux), brothers of Helen; and one hymn each to Ares, Hera, the Mother of the Gods, Heracles the Lion-hearted, Asclepius, Pan, Hephaestus, Poseidon, the Son of Chronus, Most High (Zeus), the Muses and Apollo, Earth the Mother of All, Helios, and Selene.

The two hymns to Apollo are to Delian Apollo and Pythian Apollo, the first named for his shrine on the sacred isle of Delos in the Cyclades, the second for the one at Delphi.

The *Hymn to Delian Apollo* tells of the god's birth on Delos, originally called Ortygia, in the Cyclades. He and his twin sister Artemis were children of Leto, mistress of Zeus, banished by the jealous Hera, who forbade everyone in the world from offering her shelter where she might give birth. Leto wandered all over the Greek world without finding a place that would welcome her, until finally the barren isle of Ortygia in the Cyclades agreed to receive her. Artemis was born first and helped Leto deliver Apollo. After his birth the name of the island was changed to Delos, 'the Shining', since one of Apollo's epithets was Phoebus, 'the Shining One'.

The poet addresses Apollo at the beginning of the hymn's second stanza:

> How, then, shall I sing of you who in all ways are worthy of a song?
> ... shall I sing of how at first Leto bare you to be the joy of men, as
> she rested against Mount Cynthus in that rocky isle, in sea-girt Delos
> – while on either hand a dark wave rolled on landwards driven by
> shrill winds – whence arriving you rule over all men.

The festival of Delian Apollo was attended by the Ionians from Athens and the Cyclades, the 'encircling isles' around the sacred centre of Delos, as well as those from the Greek colonies on the Aegean coast of Asia Minor and the offshore islands of Samos and Chios. The penultimate stanza of the hymn gives a lyrical description of the Ionians celebrating the festival:

> And you, O lord Apollo, god of the silver bow, shooting afar, walked
> on craggy Cynthus, and now keep wandering about the islands and
> the people in them. Many are your temples and wooded groves, and
> all peaks and towering bluffs of lofty mountains and rivers flowing

to the sea are dear to you, Phoebus, yet in Delos do you most delight your heart, for all the long-robed Ionians gather in your honour with their children and shy wives, mindful, they delight you with boxing and dancing and song, so often as they hold their gathering. A man would say that they were deathless and unaging if he should then come upon the Ionians so met together. For he would see the graces of them all, and would be blessed in heart gazing at the men and well-girded women with their swift ships and great wealth. And there is this great wonder besides – and its renown shall never perish – the girls of Delos, hand-maidens of the Far-shooter: for when they have praised Apollo first, and also Leto and Artemis who delights in arrows, they sing a song telling of men and women of past days, and charm the tribes of men. Also they can imitate the tongues of all men and their clattering speech: each would say himself was singing, so close to truth is their sweet song.

The *Hymn to Delian Apollo* has been attributed by a scholiast on Pindar to Cynaethus of Chios, one of the late and spurious *Homeridae*, who composed it in 522 BC for performance at the unusual double festival held by the tyrant Polycrates of Samos to honour both Delian and Pythian Apollo. The poet refers to Homer in the last stanza of the hymn, addressing the maidens singing in the choir:

And now may Apollo be favourable and Artemis; and farewell all you maidens. Remember me in after time whenever any one of men on earth, a stranger who has seen and suffered much, comes here and asks of you: 'Whom think ye, girls, is the sweetest singer that comes here, and in whom do you most delight?' Then answer, each and all, with one voice: 'He is a blind man, and dwells in rocky Chios; his lays are ever more supreme.' As for me, I will carry your renown as far as I roam over the earth to the well-placed cities of men, and they will believe also; for indeed this thing is true. And I will cease to praise far-shooting Apollo, god of the silver bow, whom rich-haired Leto bare.

This reference to the poet being a blind man living in Chios is part of the legend of Homer, the earliest versions of which probably date back to the latter half of the sixth century BC, when the *Iliad* and the *Odyssey* as written texts first became extremely popular throughout the Greek world. There is not a single contemporary document about Homer's personal life, and so any biography of the poet is pure speculation. There are seven extant Greek-language *Lives of Homer*, as well as a curious work called *The Contest of Homer and Hesiod*. All of these date from the imperial Roman era, but it has been shown that parts of these texts date back to the seventh century BC.

Studies of these texts suggest that Homer probably lived and worked in the Aeolian and Ionian Greek colonies on the Aegean coast as well as on the island of Chios. Among the many places that claimed to be Homer's birthplace, the most likely is Smyrna, where he would have been born *c.* 770 BC on the River Meles, which still flows into the Gulf of Izmir past the recently excavated remains of the ancient city.

When writing about the Trojan War and other events of the Heroic Age, Greek historians from Herodotus and Thucydides onwards did not distinguish between this legendary past and the known events of history. Thucydides was aware that Homer's epics date from a time much later than that of the Trojan War, but he does not doubt the historicity of Homer and of Agamemnon and his expedition against Troy.

Later Greek authors give dates for the fall of Troy ranging from 1334 BC to 1150 BC. The generally accepted date of 1184 BC was that of Eratosthenes of Cyrene, head of the Library of Alexandria in the mid-third century BC, who introduced a systematic chronology based on the Olympic Games. The first modern scholar to draw a line in the chronology between myth and history proper was the English historian George Grote. Grote, in his great multivolume *History of Greece*, published in 1845–56, suggested that the inauguration of the Olympic Games in 776 BC marked the beginning of Greek history, for he could find no historical authority for the Heroic Age described by Homer, whose epic poems were relegated to the spectral status of myths.

But soon afterwards the new science of archaeology would push back that line, when it showed that the world described by Homer in the *Iliad* had actually existed, bringing the Heroic Age from behind the veil of myth into the light of history.

2

The Catalogues of Ships and Trojans

The second book of the *Iliad* begins with an account of how Zeus sent Agamemnon a dream in which Nestor, oldest and most eminent of the Achaeans, told him that 'Zeus bids you arm the flowing-haired Achaians for battle/in all haste, since now you might be able to take the wide-wayed city of the Trojans.'

Agamemnon is convinced by the dream, not knowing that Zeus was trying to trick him into disaster. But in any event he decided that, after consulting Nestor and the other Argive leaders, he would first test the morale of his army by telling them that it was time for them to 'run away with our ships to the beloved land of our fathers/since no longer shall we capture Troy of the wide ways.'

Hearing this, the Achaeans raced to their ships and prepared to head homewards, leading Hera to send Athena down from Olympos to stop them. Athena did so and 'There she came to Odysseus, the equal to Zeus in counsel,/standing still; he had laid no hand on his black, strong-benched/vessel, since disappointment touched his heart and his spirit.' Athena told him to go and persuade the Achaeans not to flee, and 'So he went through the army marshalling it, until once more/they swept back into the assembly place and the shelters.' Then, after eating and sacrificing to the gods, Agamemnon marshalled his men and led them in divisions out into the valley of the River Scamander on the Trojan plain:

so of these the multitudinous tribes from the ships and
shelters poured to the plain of Skamandros, and the earth beneath
their feet and under the feet of their horses thundered horribly.

They took up position on the meadow of Skamandros,
thousands of them, as leaves and flowers appear in their season.

Toward the end of Book 2 Homer invokes the Muses by asking them 'Who then of all those were the chief men and lords of the Danaans?' He then describes what came to be called the Catalogue of Ships, saying 'I will tell you the lords of the ships, and the ships numbers.' The catalogue describes every contingent in Agamemnon's army, naming each of the leaders and their cities and enumerating their ships.

The catalogue lists 164 contingents under 46 commanders, representing more than a score of tribes or peoples, including the Boeotians, Minyans, Phoceans, Locrians, Abantes of Euboea, Athenians, Argives, Mycenaeans, Lacedaemonians, men of Pylos and its environs, Arcadians, Epeans of Elis, men of Dulichium and the Echinean isles, Cephallians, Aetolians, Cretans, Rhodians, Symians, men of the smaller islands of the south-west Aegean, Myrmidons, men of Methone and its environs, Lapiths, and Magnetes. They were all of them ultimately under the command of Agamemnon, 'far the greatest of all the Achaeans'.

The first of the contingents listed in the catalogue is that of the Boeotians: 'Of these there were fifty ships in all, and on board/ each of these a hundred and twenty sons of the Boeotians.' The 6,000 Boeotians came from 29 towns, the best known being Aulis, the port from which Agamemnon's fleet set sail. The number of vessels in each contingent is given, ranging from 100 ships from Mycenae commanded by Agamemnon to three ships from Syme led by Nireus.

The catalogue gives a total of 1,186 vessels in Agamemnon's armada. It is generally assumed that there were 120 men in each ship, as in the case of the Boeotians, although the ships from Methone and its vicinity, number unknown, had only 50 oarsmen each, all of them archers. Using the Boeotian figure gives a grand total of 142,320 warriors in Agamemnon's forces, obviously a highly inflated number, as was generally the case in ancient estimates of the sizes of armies.

Thorough studies have been made of the Catalogue of Ships, in antiquity as well as by modern scholars, and it is now generally agreed that it was originally composed earlier than the *Iliad*, though they were given their present form by Homer. Denys Page concludes that the Catalogue of Ships 'offers a truthful, though selective, description of Mycenaean Greece'.

According to J. V. Luce, the catalogue was originally compiled no earlier than *c.* 1150 BC, that is, soon after the fall of Troy. It survived during the Dark Ages through the oral tradition of epic poetry, and eventually became part of Homer's *Iliad*. Since the Catalogue of Ships is a Late Mycenaean compilation and the *Iliad* the final form of an epic poem that developed during the centuries after the fall of Troy, it is inevitable that there are discrepancies involved.

The Catalogue of Ships describes the islands in the Ionian Sea as having two kingdoms, one ruled by Odysseus, who commands twelve ships, and Meges, who commands forty. Though Odysseus had a relatively small contingent, he was one of the leaders in the Achaean forces at Troy, whereas Meges is of little importance:

> But Odysseus led the high-hearted men of Kephallenia,
> those who held Ithaka and leaf trembling Neriton
> those who dwelt about Krokyleia and rigged Aigilips
> those who held Zakynthos and those who dwelt about Samos,
> those who held the mainland and the places next to the crossing.
> All these men were led by Odysseus, like Zeus in counsel.
> Following with him were twelve ships with bows red-painted.

The kingdom of Agamemnon is much diminished in the Catalogue of Ships. Earlier in Book 2 of the *Iliad* Agamemnon addresses the assembled Achaeans, as 'lord of many islands and all Argos'. But later in Book 2 the catalogue has Diomedes ruling over the Argolid and the island of Aegina, while Agamemnon's kingdom extends north-westward from Mycenae and Corinth to Aegion on the Corinthian Gulf:

> They who hold Argos and Tiryns of the huge walls,
> Hermione and Asine lying down the deep gulf,
> Troizen and Eïone, and Epidauros of the vineyards,
> they who held Aigina and Mases, sons of the Achaians,
> of these the leader was Diomedes of the great war cry
> ...
> But the men who held Mykenai, the strong-founded citadel,
> Korinth the luxurious, and strong-founded Kleonai
> ...
> of their hundred ships the leader was powerful Agamemnon,
> Atreus' son, with whom followed far the best and bravest
> people; and among them he himself stood armoured in shining
> bronze, glorying, conspicuous among the great fighters,
> since he was greatest among them all, and led the most people.

According to the catalogue, the kingdom of Agamemnon's brother Menelaus was in the south-western Peloponnesos, extending southward from Sparta to Messe, near the tip of Cape Taenaron:

> Those who held the swarming hollow of Lakedaimon,
> Pharis, and Sparta, and Messe of the dove cotes
> ...
> of these his brother Menelaos
> of the great war-cry
> was leader, with sixty ships marshalled apart from the others,
> He himself went among them in the confidence of his valour,
> driving them battleward, since above all his heart was eager
> to avenge Helen's longing to escape and her lamentations.

The kingdom of Nestor, who commanded one of the largest contingents in Agamemnon's armada, was in the south-west Peloponnesos, with its capital at Pylos:

> They who dwelt about Pylos and lovely Arene,
> and Thryon, the Alpheios crossing, and strong-built Aipy;
> they who lived in Kyparisseeis and Amphigeneia,
> Pteleos and Helos and Dorion
> ...
> of these the leader was the Gerenian horseman, Nestor,
> to whose command were marshalled ninety hollow vessels.

The contingent of Salamis, a tiny island kingdom ruled by Telamonian Aias, the Greater Ajax, took its place next to that of the Athenians: 'Out of Salamis Aias brought twelve ships and placed them/next to where the Athenian battalions were drawn up.'

Locrian Aias, the Lesser Ajax, commanded the contingent from Locris, a small kingdom on the shore of the Thermaic Gulf, just south of the realm of Achilles:

> Swift Aias, son of Oïleus led the men of Lokris,
> the lesser Aias, not great in size like the son of Telamon,
> but far slighter. He was a small man armoured in linen,
> yet with the throwing spear surpassed all Achaians and Hellenes
> ...
> Following along with him were forty black ships
> of the Lokrians, who dwell across from Euboia.

Euboea is separated from the kingdoms of Locris and Boeotia by the long channel known as the Europos, the narrowest stretch of which, between Aulis on the mainland and Chalcis on the island, is now spanned by a bridge. The catalogue lists the Euboean contingent directly after that of the Locrians.

> They who held Euboia, the Abantes, whose wind was fury,
> Chalkis, and Eretria, the great vineyards of Histaia
> …
> of these the leader was Elephenor, scion of Ares,
> son of Chalkodon and lord of the great Abantes.
> And the running Abante followed with him, their hair grown
> long at the back, spearmen furious with the out-stretched ash spear
> to rip the corslets girt about the chests of their enemies.
> Following along with him were forty black ships.

The last contingent described in the Catalogue of Ships was that of the Magnesians, also known as Magnetes, a people of Thessaly who lived in the Pelion, the inhospitable coast north of the Gulf of Volos: 'Prothoös son of Tenthredon was leader of the Magnesians,/ Those who dwelt about Peneios and leaf-trembling/Pelion. Of these Prothoös the swift-footed was leader./Following along with him were forty black ships.'

The catalogue also lists contingents from Crete and the islands between it and the south-westernmost promontories of Asia Minor. The largest of these contingents by far was that of the Cretans, led by Idomeneus, grandson of King Minos:

> Idomeneus the spear-famed was leader of the Kretans
> those who held Knosos and Gortyna of the great walls,
> Likros and Miletus and silver-shining Lykastos,
> and Phaistos and Rhytion, all towns well established
> and others who dwelt beside them in Krete of the hundred cities.
> Of all these Idomeneus the spear-famed was leader,
> with Meriones, a match for the murderous Lord of Battles.
> Following along with these were eighty black ships.

The next largest of the Aegean island contingents was led by Pheidippos and Antiphos, grandsons of Heracles, who commanded ships from Nisyrus, Krapathos (Carpathos), Kasos, Cos and the Calydnian isles:

> They who held Nisyros and Krapathos and Kasos,
> and Kos, Eurypylos' city, and the islands called Kalydnai,
> of these again Pheidippos and Antiphos were the leaders,
> sons both of Thessalos who was born to the lord Heracles.
> In their command were marshalled thirty hollowed vessels.

A son of Heracles, Tlepolemus, commanded a small contingent from Rhodes, including warriors from each of the island's three cities:

> Herakles' son Tlepolemos the huge and mighty
> led from Rhodes nine ships with the proud men of Rhodes aboard
>   them,
> those who dwelt about Rhodes and were ordered in triple division,
> Ialysos and Lindos and silver-shining Kameiros.
> Of all these Tlepolemos the spear famed was leader,
> he whom Astyocheia bore to the strength of Herakles.

All three of the Rhodian cities are known to have had Mycenaean colonies, and these were probably the centres from which the Mycenaeans spread their influence through the smaller islands between Crete and the mainland of Asia Minor.

Following the Rhodians in the Catalogue of Ships were the warriors from Syme, the smallest contingent in Agamemnon's fleet, with only three warships:

> Nireus from Syme led three balanced vessels,
> Nireus son of Aglai and the king Charapos,
> Nireus, the most beautiful man who came beneath Ilion
> beyond the rest of the Danaans next after perfect Achilleus.
> But he was a man of poor strength and few people with him.

Syme, one of the smallest of the inhabited Greek islands, has always been noted for its intrepid mariners, who since antiquity have sailed all around the Aegean as sponge fishermen. Their little island and Rhodes are just off the tip of the Cnidos peninsula, the south-westernmost promontory of Asia Minor. Pindar writes of this beautiful and historical seascape in one of his poems: 'Sea-girt Rhodes, child of Aphrodite and bride of Helios ... nigh to a promontory of spacious Asia.'

The Catalogue of Ships is followed by the much shorter Catalogue of Trojans, which lists a dozen places that sent contingents to aid Priam, in contrast to the 164 in the Catalogue of Ships. It makes no mention of numbers of men, but is a mere enumeration of tribes and their leaders. Luce points out that the Catalogue of Trojans, like the Catalogue of Ships, shows marked discrepancies with the rest of the *Iliad*. Luce concluded that the Trojan Catalogue probably represents what was known at the end of the Mycenaean era about the Troad, Thrace and some regions of Asia Minor, particularly in places like Miletus that had Mycenaean colonies.

Walter Leaf's conclusion was that 'the Trojan Catalogue ... seems to represent accurately a state of things which must have existed at the time of the Trojan War, and could not have existed after it, nor for long before.' He goes on to say that 'It would seem to follow that there existed from the first some sort of a metrical narrative of the war, of which the Trojan Catalogue has survived in something like its original form.'

> Tall Hektor of the shining helm was leader of the Trojans,
> Priam's son; and with him far the best and the bravest
> fighting men were armed and eager to fight with the spear's edge.
> The strong son of Anchises was leader of the Dardanians,
> Aineias, whom divine Aphrodite bore to Anchises
> in the folds of Ida, a goddess lying in love with a mortal.

The Dardanians were followed in turn by three or four other groups from the Troad. The first of these were the men who lived in the lower valley of the Aesepus, the river that forms the western boundary of the Troad, flowing from the foothills of Mt Ida into the Sea of Marmara: 'They who dwelt in Zeleia below the foot of Mount Ida,/men of wealth, who drank the dark water of Aisepos,/Trojans: of these the leader was the shining son of Lykaon,/Pandaros, with the bow that was actual gift of Apollo.' (There is an inconsistency here, for in Book 5 of the *Iliad* Pandaros is referred to as a Lycian.)

The second contingent from the Troad came from the Marmara coast between the Aesopus and the entrance to the Hellespont, led by two sons of the seer Merops, both of whom were subsequently killed by Diomedes:

> They who held Adresteia and the countryside of Apaisos,
> they who held Pityeia and the sheer hill of Tereia,
> these were led by Adrestos and Amphios armoured in linen,
> sons both of Merops of Perkote, who beyond all men
> knew the art of prophecy, and tried to prevent his sons
> from going into the battle where the men die. Yet these would not
> listen, for the spirits of dark death were driving them onward.

The third group of warriors from the Troad came from the shore of the Hellespont just above the Narrows, where their border marched with that of the Dardanians. They were led by Asius, who was later killed by Idomeneus: 'They who dwelt in the places about Perkote and Prakticon,/who hold Sestos and Abydos and brilliant Arisbe,/their leader was Asios, son of Hyrtakos, whom huge and shining/horses carried from Arisbe and the river Selleëis.'

The next contingent were Pelasgians from a town named Larisa. They were led by the brothers Hippothoös and Pylaeus, the first of whom was later killed by Telamonian Aias: 'Hippothoös led the tribes of spear-fighting Pelasgians,/they who dwelt where the soil was rich about Larisa;/Hippothoös and Pylaios, scion of Ares, led these,/sons alike of Pelasgian Lethos, son of Teutamos.'

The Pelasgians were believed to be one of the indigenous peoples who inhabited Hellas and western Asia Minor before the arrival of the Greeks, the Lelegians being another, both of them referred to in the *Iliad* as allies of the Trojans.

There are three towns named Larisa in western Asia Minor. One of them is north of Cape Lekton in the Troad, the second is near Cyme in Aeolia, and the third is within the territory of Ephesus in Ionia. Leaf believed that Homeric Larisa was in the Troad, but Strabo was of the opinion that Aeolian Larisa is the one referred to in the Catalogue of Trojans.

As Walter Leaf points out, the first part of the catalogue described the contingents on a circular tour through the Troad, but then the arrangement changes, so that the tribes named are all along lines converging upon Troy, with the extremity of each line radius marked by the words 'far away'. He notes that 'These four lines I take to represent the four trade routes which converged on Troy as a common emporium, so long as Troy closed the mouth of the Hellespont.'

Taking the arrows in the order in which they appear in the Catalogue of the Trojans, the first leads north-west across the Hellespont into Europe, to the regions inhabited by the Thracians, the Cicones, and the Paionians:

> Akamas led the men of Thrace with the fighter Peiroös,
> all the Thracians held within the hard stream of the Hellespont.
> Euphemos was leader of the Kikonian spearmen,
> son of Troizenos, Keas' son, the king whom the gods loved.
> Pyraichmes in turn led the Paionians with their curved bows,
> from Amydon far away and the broad stream of Axios,
> Axios, whose stream on all earth is the loveliest water.

All three of the peoples mentioned along this route can be located with certainty in the regions they occupied in the Heroic Age.

The Thracians inhabited the whole region from the Hellespont to the northern reaches of the basin of the River Hebrus, which flows into the Aegean at Aeneus, whose harbour was just

70 kilometres from Troy across the Melas Gulf, 'an easy day's sail', according to Leaf. Aenus is mentioned by Homer in Book 4 of the *Iliad*, where he says that it was the home of Peirus, son of Imrasus, a Trojan ally. Herodotus says that it was an Aeolian Greek settlement. The city is also mentioned in a poem by Alcaeus of Lesbos (b. *c.* 620 BC), in praise of the Hebrus:

> Hebros, loveliest of rivers, you issue
> hard by Ainios into the dark blue waters
> of the sea where, passing by Thrace, you end your turbulent passage;
> there, where young girls, passing by Thrace, and bathing
> with light hands their ravishing thighs, enjoy you
> all as if some magical salve were in your wonderful waters.

The Cicones occupied the coast west of Aenus, under Mt Ismaros, which, according to Leaf, 'separated them from the basin of the Hebrus'. Homer mentions them in Book 17 of the *Iliad*, where he mentions a leader of the Cicones, Mentes, who is impersonated by Apollo in a battle scene. They are also mentioned in the *Odyssey*, where Odysseus raids and sacks Ismaros, their city.

The Paeonians were to the west of the Cicones and occupied the coast between the rivers Nestos and Axios, their power extending through all of what later became the Macedonian kingdom. Their leader Pyraichmes was slain by Patroclus and was replaced by Asteropaius, the ambidextrous, who later fought and wounded Achilles before he was killed by him.

The second arrow leads north-east to the Black Sea coast of Asia Minor, to the regions inhabited by the Paphlagonians and Halizones:

> Pylaimenes the wild heart was leader of the Paphlagones,
> from the land of the Enetoi where the wild mules are engendered,
> those who held Kytoros and those who dwelt about Sesamos,
> those whose renowned homes were about the Parthenios river,
> and Kromna and Aigialos and high Erythinoi.
> Odios and Epistrophos led the Halizones
> from Alybe far away, where silver was first begotten.

Strabo puts the Paphlagonians on what is now the Turkish coast eastward from Ereğli, ancient Heracleia Ponticus, to Kerempe Burnu, the Greek Cape Karambis. He places the Halizones farther to the east, stretching from Samsun, ancient Amisus, almost as far as Trabzon, the Greek Trebizond.

The identity of Eneti has always been somewhat of a mystery, with some saying that it was a tribe and others a city. Leaf tentatively

identified Eneti with Heracleia, while he placed Sesamon and
Kytoros in and somewhat to the east of Amasra, ancient Amastris,
with Aigailos still farther to the east near Cape Carambis, which he
identified as 'high Erythinai'.

The names Halizones and Alybe have been a puzzle for scholars
both ancient and modern, their only clue being that the latter was
said to be the original source of silver in antiquity. Strabo says that in
earlier times there had been silver mines above the Pontic coast west
of Trebizond in the Taurus Mountains, probably near the present
town of Gümüşhane, which means 'Silver House' or 'Mint'. Marco
Polo remarked upon these mines when he passed this way in 1296,
when they were known in Greek as Argyropolis, or 'Silver City', a
name that was used up until the nineteenth century, when it came to
be known to the Turks as Gümüşhane.

Leaf says that 'This part of the coast, too, the natural outlet of
the Hittite kingdom, may have been the source from which inland
silver was exported westwards', in support of which he quotes the
classicist A. H. Sayce:

> The silver mines of the Taurus, which were worked by the Hittites,
> were the chief source of the silver supplied to the early oriental
> world; hence the metal was a special favourite with the Hittites, from
> whom the rest of the world obtained it.

The third arrow points to the regions in north-western Asia Minor
south of the Sea of Marmara, home of the Mysians, Phrygians, and
Maeonians:

> Chromis, with Ennomos the auger, was lord of the Mysians;
> yet his reading of birds could not keep off dark destruction
> but he went down under the hands of swift-running Aiakides
> in the river, as he slew other Trojans beside him.
> Phorkys and godlike Askanios were lords of the Phrygians
> from Askania far away, eager to fight on the onfall.
> Mesthles and Antiphos were leaders of the Maionians,
> sons of Talaimenes, who were born of the lake Gygaian:
> these led the Maionian men whose home was beneath Mount
>   Tmolos.

Mysia lies immediately east of the Troad, the valley of the Aesepus
forming the boundary between the two regions. The eastern and
southern boundaries of Mysia are unknown, but it seems at one time
to have included the plain at the head of the Gulf of Adramyttene as
well as the Caicus valley with Pergamum.

The boundary between Mysia and Phrygia was probably the River Rhyndacus, now known as the Mustafakemalpaşa, which flows into the Marmara about halfway along its southern shore. The western frontier of Phrygia was the River Sangarius, Turkish Sakarya, which changes direction from north-west to north-east near the town of Lefke (Yenişehir), after which it flows into the Black Sea 130 kilometres east of the mouth of the Bosphorus. The bend in the river is 32 kilometres east of the eastern end of Lake Ascania, at the western end of which was ancient Nicaea, Turkish Iznik. The 'Askania' mentioned in the Trojan Catalogue was undoubtedly the district around the lake.

Archaeological evidence indicates that by the middle of the ninth century BC, the Phrygians were well established in the highlands at Gordion, at the conflux of the rivers Sangarius and Tembris, some 100 kilometres south-west of what is now Ankara, capital of the Turkish Republic. Within another century Gordion would be capital of the Phrygian kingdom, which comprised most of west-central Anatolia and lasted until *c.* 600 BC.

The Maeonians can be definitely located by the reference in the catalogue to the Gygaean Lake and Mt Tmolos, which are in the basin of the River Hermus and the plain of Sardis. Sardis became capital of the Lydian kingdom under Gyges (r. *c.* 685–652 BC), founder of the Mermnadae dynasty, who exploited the gold washed down from Mt Tmolos by the River Pactolus, minting it to make the world's first coins. Gyges and his successors are buried under huge tumuli near the Gygaean Lake, which is in the upper Hermus valley. The last and most famous king of Lydia, Croesus, met his end in 546 BC, when 'golden Sardis' was conquered by the Persian king, Cyrus.

Shards of Mycenaean pottery of the thirteenth century BC found at Sardis suggest a possible conquest of the Lydian capital at about the same time as the fall of Troy. Other shards unearthed at Sardis indicate that it was occupied by an Hellenic people during the period 1200–900 BC and perhaps for another two centuries afterwards. This would support Greek tradition, which held that the first Hellenes to rule at Sardis were the Heraclidae, the self-proclaimed sons of Heracles, who supplanted a native dynasty that had originated before the Trojan War in the time of the Maeonians. According to Herodotus, the Heraclidae 'held sway for two and twenty generations of men, or five hundred and five years, son succeeding father in the rule, until Candaulus, son of Myrsus'. Candaulus was killed by Gyges, who usurped the throne to become King of Lydia, beginning the Mermnadae dynasty.

The fourth and last arrow led off to south-western Asia Minor, where dwelt the Carians and Lycians:

The Karians of the outland speech were led by Nastes,
they who held Miletos and the leaf-deep mountain of Phthiron,
the waters of Maiandros and the headlong peaks of Mykale;
of these the two leaders were Amphimachos and Nastes
...
Sarpedon with unfaulted Glaukos was lord of the Lykians
from Lykia far away, and the whirling waters of Xanthos.

The places mentioned in the catalogue's description of the Carian homeland include the city of Miletus, the River Maeander, and Mt Mycale, which are actually in southern Ionia, although in earlier times they were probably inhabited by the Carians, who were forced up into the highlands to the south of the Maeander valley after the Greek migration. Phthiron is probably Mt Latmos, which marks the boundary between the Maeander valley and the Carian highlands in south-westernmost Asia Minor.

The Carians originated in Minoan Crete, according to Herodotus, and they seem to have migrated to south-western Asia Minor in the latter half of the second millennium BC, well before the Greek migration, probably crossing through the chain of islands mentioned in the Catalogue of Ships.

Herodotus' account has been generally confirmed by excavations at Miletus, which reveal evidence of a Minoan settlement much predating the Ionian migration. This settlement appears to have been taken over by the Mycenaeans in the late Bronze Age, c. 1400 BC. This would have been at about the same time that the Mycenaeans became the dominant power on Crete itself, ending the Minoan era.

Scholars have deciphered correspondence between the Hittites and the Achaeans found at Boğazkale, the ancient Hittite capital of Hattusha. There reference is made to a city on the south-west coast of Anatolia known as Millawata or Millawanda, which has been identified as Miletus. Miletus was known to the Mycenaeans as Milwatos, which is also the name of a Minoan site that has been excavated on Crete, probably the place of origin of the Cretan settlers of Miletus in Asia Minor.

The description in the catalogue of the Lycian contingent, led by Sarpedon and Glaucus, mentions the River Xanthus, which flows into the sea at the south-western corner of Asia Minor, where the Aegean gives way to the Mediterranean.

Archaeologists have excavated a number of Lycian sites and found evidence of human habitation dating back to the late Bronze Age. Hittite archives of the mid-fourteenth century BC refer to a rebellious people called the Lukki, undoubtedly the Lycians. The

Lukki are also referred to in tablets of about the same period found at Tel-al-Amarna in Egypt, where they are described as a warlike nation of sea-raiders.

Scholars now tend to agree with Herodotus that the Lycians were a non-Hellenic people who, like the Carians, originated in Crete and crossed the Aegean to Asia Minor.

Lycia represents the end of the fourth and last of the arrows radiating from Troy, representing the trade routes between the Trojans and their European and Asian partners, who came to help them when they were besieged by the Achaeans. Before that the allies would have gathered on the Trojan plain outside the citadel, exchanging goods in an annual summer fair, their trade and toll fees enriching Priam and his people.

3

The Anger of Achilles

Sing, goddess, the anger of Peleus' son Achilleus
and its devastation, which put pains thousandfold upon the Achaians,
hurled in their multitudes to the house of Hades strong souls
of heroes, but gave their bodies to be the delicate feasting
of dogs, of all birds, and the will of Zeus was accomplished
since that time when first there stood in division of conflict
Atreus' son the lord of men and brilliant Achilleus.

Such are the opening lines of the *Iliad*, which begins in the tenth
and last year of the siege of Troy, when Agamemnon quarrelled
with Achilles, who withdrew from the fighting along with his men
and sulked in his tent. The quarrel concerned Chryseis, daughter
of Chryses, priest of Apollo at his shrine in Chryse south of Troy,
which the Greeks had plundered and given the girl to Agamemnon
as his concubine. Their father came to the Greek camp to request the
return of Chryseis, but Agamemnon harshly refused and drove him
away. Chryses prayed to Apollo to avenge him, whereupon the god
inflicted a deadly plague upon the Greeks.

When the plague went on and the Greeks continued to perish
for nine days, Achilles called an assembly and the prophet Teiresias
told them that they will all die unless they propitiate Apollo by
returning Chryseis to her father. Agamemnon reluctantly agreed,
but he demanded that Achilles compensate him by giving up his
own captive concubine Briseis. Agamemnon had his herald take
Chryseis from Achilles and sent Odysseus with a ship to return her
to her father, who thereupon prayed to Apollo and had the god end
the plague.

Achilles had by then withdrawn in anger from the Greek camp
with his men, as he prayed to his mother, the sea-goddess Thetis.

He asked her to use her influence with Zeus and the other gods to have the Achaeans defeated in his absence, so that Agamemnon in particular realized the importance of the hero he has dishonoured. Thetis passed on her son's prayer to Zeus, who reluctantly agrees to carry out Achilles' request, despite the objection of his wife Hera.

Meanwhile Achilles 'still sat in anger beside his swift ships/ ... Never now would he go to assemblies where men win glory/never more into battle, but continued to waste his heart out/sitting there, though he longed always for the clamour and the fighting.'

As soon as Agamemnon's army began their march, the goddess Iris brought a message from Zeus to Hector that the Achaeans were advancing across the plain toward the city: 'She spoke, nor did Hektor fail to mark the word of the goddess./Instantly he broke up the assembly; they sprang to their weapons./All the gates were opened and the people swept through them/on foot, and with horses, and a clamour of shouting rose up.'

When the two armies approached one another on the Trojan plain, Paris (Alexandros) went forward to challenge the best of the Achaeans to do battle with him. His challenge was immediately accepted by Menelaus, who was eager to take revenge on the man who had stolen his wife Helen and brought on the war. On seeing him Paris became frightened and withdrew, but the scorn of Hector shamed him into confronting his rival, offering to engage Menelaus in single combat, 'to fight together for the sake of Helen and all her possessions'.

Agamemnon called out to his men to put down their arms, as Hector stood between the two armies to proclaim that Paris and Menelaus would 'fight alone for the sake of Helen and all her possessions./That one of them who wins and is proved stronger, let him/take the possession fairly and the woman, and lead her homeward/while the rest of us cut our oaths of faith and friendship.'

Agamemnon and Hector then sent for two lambs each to be sacrificed to the gods, while they prepared the ground for the single combat between Paris and Menelaus. Meanwhile the goddess Iris had informed Helen that 'Menelaos the warlike and Alexandros will fight/with long spears against each other for your possession.'

Helen immediately went with two of her handmaidens to the tower in the citadel walls above the Skaean gates, where Priam and other Trojan elders were looking out at the drama now unfolding on the plain below. The old men were chattering 'as cicadas' do, and as they saw Helen approaching they murmured softly to each other:

Surely there is no blame on Trojans and strong-greaved Achaians
if for a long time they suffer hardship for a woman like this one.

Terrible is the likeness of her face to immortal goddesses.
Still, though she be such, let her go away in the ships, lest
she be left behind, a grief to us and our children.

Priam called out to Helen: 'Come over where I am, dear child,
and sit down beside me,/to look at your husband of time past, your
friends and your people./I am not blaming you: to me the gods
are blameworthy/who drove on me this sorrowful war against the
Achaians.'

Paris is defeated by Menelaus, but he is rescued by Aphrodite and
miraculously brought back to Helen's bed. Menelaus raged up and
down the battlefield searching for his enemy, but when Paris could
not be found Agamemnon declared victory for his brother:

Listen to me, O Trojans, Dardanians and companions:
clearly the victory is with warlike Menelaos.
Do you therefore give back, with all her possessions, Helen
of Argos, and pay a price that shall be befitting,
which among people yet to come shall be as standard.

Zeus then managed to have the Trojan archer Pandorus break
the truce by treacherously wounding Menelaus and thus the fighting
resumed, so 'on that day many men of the Achaians and Trojans/lay
sprawled in the dust face downward beside one another'.

Athena then gave to Diomedes such added strength and daring
that he killed many Trojans and defeated Aeneas, who is rescued
by his mother Aphrodite. Diomedes then attacked and wounded
Aphrodite, only to be confronted by Apollo and warned against
warring with the gods. During the fighting several of the gods joined
in on one side or the other, trying to influence the outcome of the
battle, including Ares, who was wounded by Diomedes and put out
of action.

Hector rallied his army and prevented a total rout, but their
situation had now grown so dire that salvation could only come
through divine intervention. The Trojans would have closed
themselves inside the citadel 'wall, subdued by terror before the
warlike Achaians,/had not Priam's son Helenos, best by far of the
augurs,/stood beside Aineias and Hektor and spoken a word to
them'.

Helenos told them that they must hold their men fast by the
citadel gates, after which Hector should tell their mother Hecuba to
assemble all the ladies of honour at the temple of Athena. There she
should take her finest robe 'and lay it along the knees of Athene, the
lovely haired. Let her/promise to dedicate within the shrine twelve

heifers,/yearlings never broken, if only she will have pity/on the town of Troy, and the Trojan wives, and their innocent children.'

Hector then summoned Paris to return with him to the army, after which he bade farewell to his wife Andromache and their infant son Astyanax on the citadel wall, and finally returned to rejoin his army.

Hector and Paris led the Trojans into battle, each of them killing his first opponent, as did their Lycian ally Glaucus. Seeing this, Athena sped down from Olympos to Ilion, where she was met by Apollo, who 'planned that the Trojans should conquer'. They conferred on how they might put a stop to the fighting at least for the moment, and Apollo suggested that they might put in the mind of Hector to battle in single combat against one of the Achaean heroes, winner take all. They succeeded in doing so, and Hector challenged the Achaeans, who chose Telamonian Aias, by lot, to do battle with him. The two of them fought furiously until they were interrupted by nightfall, whereupon they agreed a temporary truce and exchanged presents before the Achaeans and Trojans retired to their own camps.

Later, after the Achaeans had their evening feast, Nestor suggested that at dawn they should declare a truce so that they could cremate and bury their comrades 'whose dark blood has been scattered beside the fair waters of the Skamandros'. He also said that they must also build a wall with ramparts and a deep ditch around their camp and ships, 'that we may not be crushed under the attack of these proud Trojans'. 'So he spoke and all the kings approved him.'

Meanwhile the Trojans and their Dardanian allies were meeting in their citadel, where Priam's counsellor Antenor proposed that they give back Helen and all her possessions to the Achaeans so that they would end the war and leave. Paris objected strenuously: 'I refuse, straight out. I will not give back the woman./But the possessions I carried away to our house from Argos/I am willing to give all back, and to add to these from my own goods.'

Priam rose to say that they should take their supper and then retire, mindful of their watch duties during the night, and at dawn they should send the herald Idaeus to the Achaean camp, to say that the Trojans would return Helen's possessions if a truce was called so that they could bury their dead. When Idaeus delivered the message to the Achaeans, they refused to take back either Helen or her possessions, but they readily agreed on a truce so that both sides could inter their fallen comrades.

At dawn on the day following the truce, Zeus assembled all the immortals on the highest peak of Olympos and strictly forbade them to help either the Trojans or the Achaeans as they had in the past, after which he flew down to Mt Ida on the Troad, where he sat 'looking out over the city of Troy and the ships of the Achaians'.

The two armies advanced across the Trojan plain, both on foot and in chariots. When they collided,

> they dashed their shields and their spears, and the strength of
> armoured men in bronze, and the shields massive in the middle
> clashed against each other, and the sound grew huge of the fighting.
> There the screaming and the shouts of triumph rose untogether
> of men killing and men killed, and the ground ran blood.

Around noon the tide of battle turned sharply against the Achaeans and they fled headlong back to their walled camp, pursued closely by the Trojan army under Hector, who was determined to set fire to the Greek fleet. But once the Achaeans reached the ditch outside their walls, Agamemnon rallied his men and they counterattacked furiously, killing many Trojans before Hector continued the assault and forced the Greeks to seek safety within the walls of their camp.

By that time night had fallen, and so Hector decided to encamp his army outside the Achaean camp and renew the attack in the morning. And so the Trojans unharnessed their horses, sacrificed oxen to the gods and with high hearts enjoyed a great feast under the stars beside their watchfires: 'A thousand fires were burning there in the plain, and beside each/one sat fifty men in the flare of the blazing firelight./And standing each beside his chariot, champing white barley/and oats, the horses waited for the dawn to mount to her high place.'

Meanwhile Agamemnon summoned his men to an assembly, and in tears he said that since Zeus had set his heart against him they should give up their attempt to take Ilion: 'Come then, do as I say, let us all be won over; let us/run away with our ships to the beloved land of our fathers/since no longer shall we capture Troy of the wide ways.'

Diomedes objected vigorously, saying that if Agamemnon did not have the heart to continue he should sail off with his own ships, leaving the rest of them to go on fighting till they sacked Troy. The Achaeans acclaimed Diomedes, and Nestor suggested that Agamemnon invite the Achaean princes to a feast and then deliberate, saying 'Here is the night that will break our army, or else will preserve it.'

Agamemnon led the Achaean lords to his shelter and set before them an abundant feast, after which Nestor spoke and told him that he had made a grievous error in dishonouring Achilles, whose friendship they should now try to regain. Agamemnon readily admitted his mistake, pleading madness, and he offered to return his slave-girl Briseis to Achilles along with lavish presents. Nestor suggested that they send this offer with an embassy led by Phoinix, the old tutor and companion of Achilles, along with Odysseus, Telamonian Aias and two heralds.

Achilles greeted them hospitably, telling his beloved companion Patroclus to bring wine for his guests, 'since those who have come beneath my roof are the men that I love the best'. Odysseus then lifted a toast to Achilles telling him of the extravagant offer of retribution made by Agamemnon. But Achilles refused outright, saying that there was no way in which Agamemnon could right the wrong he had done him. He went on to say that his mother Thetis told him that he had his choice of one or another fate:

> If I stay here and fight beside the city of the Trojans,
> my return home is gone, but my glory shall be everlasting;
> But if I return home to the beloved land of my fathers,
> the excellence of my glory is gone, but there will be a long life
> left for me, and my end will not come quickly.

Phoinix made an emotional appeal to his old pupil, but Achilles was adamant. Thereupon Odysseus and Telamonian Aias returned to their camp, leaving Phoinix to remain as a guest of Achilles. When they returned Odysseus told Agamemnon that Achilles had rejected his offer, wherepon everyone remained silent until Diomedes spoke, telling them that they should pay no more attention to Achilles, saying that

> He will fight again, whenever the time comes
> that the heart in his body urges him to, and the god drives him.
> ...
> So he spoke, and all the kings gave him their approval,
> acclaiming the word of Diomedes, breaker of horses.
> Then they poured a libation, and each man went to his shelter,
> where they went to their beds and took the blessing of slumber.

But Agamemnon was unable to sleep, and so he rose and armed himself. So, likewise, did Menelaus, who went to his brother's shelter and found Agamemnon putting on his armour beside the stern of his ship. They learned that they both had the idea of getting some of their comrades to organize a spying expedition against the Trojans, and eventually Odysseus and Diomedes volunteered, after which the two of them set out toward the Trojan camp.

Meanwhile Hector had called a nocturnal meeting of the Trojan leaders and advisors to organize a spying expedition into the Achaean camp. Dolon, son of the sacred herald Eumedes, volunteered on the promise of a rich reward and set off into the night, only to be caught by Odysseus and Diomedes, who first forced him to divulge all of the Trojans' military dispositions and then beheaded him. Immediately afterwards they entered the encampment of Hector's Thracian allies, twelve men and their king, all sound asleep, each with a team of horses tethered in their communal shelter. Diomedes silently killed all thirteen men in turn with his sword, while Odysseus dragged each of them away by the feet, so as to clear a way for the horses, which they untied and headed back to their own lines, stopping briefly to pick up Dolon's armour so they could dedicate it to Athena.

After they returned to the Achaean camp and were congratulated by their comrades, the two of them tied up the Thracian horses at Diomedes' shelter and laid down the bloody arms of Dolon to be dedicated to Athena. Then 'after they had bathed and anointed themselves with olive oil/they sat down to dine, and from the full mixing bowl drawing/the sweet-hearted wine poured out an offering to Athene'.

So ends Book 10, the prelude to a great daylong battle which does not end until Book 18.

Next morning the revitalized Achaeans, encouraged by Athena, followed Agamemnon as he led then out of the camp, where they were confronted by Hector and his army.

> And the men, like two lines of reapers, who, facing each other,
> drive their course all down the field of wheat or of barley
> for a man blessed in substance, and the cut swathes drop showering,
> so Trojans and Achaians driving in against one another
> cut men down, nor did either side think of disastrous panic.

Agamemnon led the Achaean charge, killing everyone who opposed him, as the Trojans retreated as far as the Skaean gates before they stood their ground. Agamemnon went on killing even after a spear-thrust wounded him in the arm. But then when the pain became too great he was forced to order his charioteer to drive him back to the Achaean camp, calling out to his men to continue fighting. The charioteer lashed the horses, and the 'foam ran down their chests ... as they carried their stricken king away from the fighting'.

When Hector saw Agamemnon withdrawing he rallied his men and charged into the fray, killing all of the Achaeans he came upon as they fled back to their camp, only Diomedes and Odysseus standing their ground. Diomedes was struck in the foot by an arrow, leaving Odysseus alone in the midst of the Trojans, one of whom wounded him in the ribs with a spear-thrust. Menelaus heard him calling out and alerted Telamonian Aias, whereupon the two of them went out to rescue their comrade. Menelaus called in his charioteer and they took Odysseus back to the camp, while Aias fought a rear-guard battle to cover their retreat.

Meanwhile Achilles had been observing the battle from his ship, and when he saw Nestor helping a wounded man into his tent he asked Patroclus to see if it was the aged seer Machaon, son of Asclepius, the great healer. He saw that it was in fact Machaon, and then, before he left, Nestor suggested that he speak to Achilles and persuade him to rejoin the Achaeans, or at least 'let him give you his splendid armour to wear to the fighting,/if perhaps the Trojans might think you were he and give way'.

Meanwhile the battle continued, as Hector 'fought on like a whirlwind' and drove his men on toward the Achaean camp, but their horses held back from crossing the deep ditch outside the walls. Hector jumped to the ground from his chariot, and his companions did the same, but they were unable to force their way through the gates. 'Everywhere the battlements and the bastions were awash/ with men's blood shed from both sides, Achaian and Trojan.'

Then finally Hector took a great boulder and hurled it against the gate, smashing it in. He burst through the gateway, carrying a spear in each hand, and none of the Achaeans could stand up against him.

> Whirling, he called out across the battle toward the Trojans
> to climb over the wall, and they obeyed his urgency.
> Immediately some swarmed over the wall, while others swept in
> through the wrought gateways, and the Danaans scattered in terror
> among the hollow ships, and clamour incessant rose up.
> ...
> [The Trojans] came on after Hektor, the son of Priam, raging
>   relentless,
> roaring and crying as one, and their hopes ran high of capturing
> the ships of the Achaians, and killing the best men beside them,
> all of them. But Poseidon who circles the earth and shakes it
> rose up out of the water to stir on the Argives,
> likening himself in form and weariless voice to Kalchas [the augur].

Nestor now took counsel with Agamemnon, Diomedes and Odysseus, the three Achaean leaders who had been wounded and were thus unable to take part in the battle around their ships. Agamemnon suggested that they might haul down the ships closest to the shore and row them some distance out to sea and anchor them there, and then under the cover of night 'we might haul down all the rest of our vessels./There is no shame in running, even by night, from disaster.' But Odyssey and Diomedes rejected this plan outright, and so they all went back to rejoin their comrades, as Poseidon swept down 'and in the heart of every Achaian implanted/great strength, to carry the battle on, and fight without flinching'.

Looking down from Olympos, Hera was happy to see this, for, she too favoured the Achaeans. But Zeus, who was now sitting on Mt Ida looking down on Troy, favoured the Trojans and had forbidden the other immortals from interfering, might see what Poseidon was doing and stop him. So she asked Aphrodite's help in beautifying herself and flew down to Ida with the god Sleep, her intention being to seduce Zeus and have him put to sleep long enough for Poseidon to help the Achaeans to defeat the Trojans.

Zeus was surprised to see Hera, but he was immediately filled with desire for her, and, after assuring her that he would surround them with a golden cloud so that not even Helios could see them, they made love on the peak of Ida:

> So speaking, the son of Kronos caught his wife in his arms. There,
> underneath them the divine earth broke into young, fresh
> grass, and into dewy clover, crocus and hyacinth
> so thick and soft it held the hard ground deep away from them.
> There they lay down together and drew about them a golden
> wonderful cloud, and from it the glimmering dew descended.

The god Sleep then quickly made his way to the ships, where he told Poseidon that he could go on helping the Achaeans only until Zeus awoke. Poseidon, again crying out in the voice of Kalchas, urged the Achaeans to make a renewed effort, with Agamemnon, Odysseus and Diomedes joining in even though they were wounded. Telamonian Aias hurled a huge rock that stunned Hector and forced him to withdraw from the field, which so stirred the Achaeans that they 'remembered once again their warcraft and turned on the Trojans'.

Meanwhile Zeus awoke, and when he saw that the Achaeans had put the Trojans to flight he realized that he had been duped and he threatened to punish Hera, but she laid the blame on Poseidon and he was appeased. After Hera returned to Olympos Zeus summoned Iris and sent her with a message for Poseidon, ordering him to stop interfering in the war. Poseidon objected, saying that he was equal in rank to Zeus, but in the end he 'left the Achaian people,/and went, merging in the sea, and the fighting Achaians longed for him'.

Zeus then sent Apollo down to treat Hector, who recovered quickly and led his army in a counterattack that drove the Achaeans back to their ships, which the Trojans began to set on fire.

Meanwhile Patroclus had rejoined Achilles, 'and stood by him and wept warm tears'. When Achilles asked him why he wept, Patroclus told him that the Achaeans were suffering grievously, 'For all those who were before the bravest in battle/are lying up among the ship with arrow or spear wounds', including Agamemnon, Odysseus and Diomedes. He asked Achilles to lend him his armour so that he could join in the fighting, 'so perhaps the Trojans might think I am you, and give way'. Achilles could see that the Trojans were setting the Achaean ships afire, and so he allowed Patroclus to borrow his armour along with his horses and chariot and charioteer, Automedon, also putting the men of his fifty ships, the Myrmidons, under the command of his beloved companion.

When the Trojans saw Patroclus and the Myrmidons they thought that Achilles had rejoined the Achaeans, and then 'each man looked about him for a way to escape the sheer death'. Inspired by the presence of Patroclus, the Achaeans drove the Trojans out of their camp and all the way up the Trojan plain to the walls of Troy. Among those whom he killed was Sarpedon, a son of Zeus who was one of the leaders, along with Glaucus, of the Lycian contingent, who had himself just been wounded by an arrow shot by Teukros, half-brother of Telamonian Aias. When Glaucus heard Sarpedon's death-cry he prayed to their patron Phoibos Apollo, pleading for help against Patroclus. Apollo immediately eased the pain of Glaucus' wound and then, after urging Hector to stop the Achaeans, he went down into the battlefield, from where he carried Sarpedon's body away so that he could be buried 'within the broad countryside of Lycia'.

Patroclus tried to scale the tower beside the Skaean Gate, but 'three times Phoibos Apollo battered him backward'. The god again urged Hector to emerge from the Skaean gates and attack the Achaeans, which soon brought him head to head against Patroclus. Apollo, moving unseen on the battlefield, stunned Patroclus with a blow from behind and knocked off his helmet, after which Euphorbus, a Dardanian warrior, 'hit him between the shoulders with a sharp javelin'.

Hector then moved in and speared Patroclus through the belly, so that he fell 'thunderously, to the horror of all the Achaian people'. As soon as Patroclus fell Menelaus rushed over and stood astride his dead body with his shield and spear, 'raging to cut down any man who might come forth against him'. The first to do so was Euphorbus, the Dardanian warrior who had first speared Patroclus, and who now told Menelaus that he was going to win glory by taking away the body as his trophy. As he spoke he thrust his spear at Menelaus, whose shield turned it away, after which Menelaus speared him through the throat and killed him instantly. Menelaus then went to summon Telamonian Aias to help him carry the corpse of Patroclus back to Achilles, but when they returned the body had been stripped of the armour of Achilles by Hector, who then put it on himself.

Hector now returned to retrieve the body of Patroclus from Menelaus and Aias, who had by then gathered reinforcements. Thus a fierce battle developed around the corpse of Patroclus, and in the midst of it Menelaus sent Antilochus on the run to inform Achilles. Meanwhile he and the other Achaeans eventually 'carried the dead man out of the battle and back to the hollow ships' as the battle raged around them.

When Antilochus reached the Achaean camp he found Achilles waiting in front of the ships. Antilochus wept as he delivered the sad news:

> Patroklos has fallen, and now they are fighting over his body
> which is naked. Hektor of the shining helm has taken his body.
> ...
> He spoke, and the dark cloud of sorrow closed on Achilleus.
> In both hands he caught up the grimy dust, and poured it
> over his head and face, and fouled his handsome countenance,
> and the black ashes were scattered over his immortal tunic.
> And he himself mightily in his might, in the dust lay
> at length, and took and tore at his hair with his hands and defiled it.

Hera sent the goddess Iris to tell Achilles that he should show himself at the ditch, where the Trojans were still fighting to take the body of Patroclus from the Achaeans. He did so and shouted out three times, so terrifying the Trojans that the Achaeans were able to rout them and bring the body of Patroclus back into their camp. They 'set him upon a litter, and his own companions about him/ stood mourning, and along with the swift-footed Achilleus/went, letting fall warm tears as he saw his steadfast companion/lying there on a carried litter and torn with the sharp bronze'.

The Trojans gathered in assembly before their supper, and the first to speak was Poulydamas, Hector's close friend and counsellor, who said that they should immediately withdraw to Troy to avoid being slaughtered by Achilles in the morning. But Hector rejected his proposal outright, and ordered everyone to stand their night watches and prepare to do battle in the morning.

The Achaeans spent the night mourning for Patroclus, and Achilles 'led the thronging chant of their lamentation'. Addressing Patroclus directly, Achilles vowed that 'I will not bury you till I bring to this place the armour/and the head of Hector, since he was your great-hearted murderer.'

Meanwhile Thetis went to Hephaestus, god of the forge, and had him fashion a new set of armour for Achilles, to replace the set that Hector had stripped from Patroclus. She brought the armour the next morning to Achilles, who then 'walked along by the seashore/crying his terrible cry, and stirred up the fighting Achaians'.

The Achaeans then gathered, including Diomedes and Odysseus, limping and

> leaning on spears, since they had the pain of their wounds yet upon
> them,
> and came and took their seats in the front row of the assembled.
> And last of all came in the lord of men Agamemnon
> with a wound on him, seeing that Koön, the son of Antenor
> had stabbed him with the bronze edge of the spear in the strong
> encounter.

Achilles addressed them, speaking directly to Agamemnon about their quarrel over the slave girl Briseis, saying 'we will let all this be a thing of the past, though it hurts us'. Agamemnon responded in kind, saying that he had been deluded by Zeus, and he gave back Briseis to Achilles, swearing before Zeus that he had never laid a hand on her.

Achilles thereupon broke up the assembly, saying 'Go now and take your dinner, so that we may draw on the battle.' He himself refrained from eating, mourning beside the body of Patroclus along with the other Achaean leaders. Then he donned the armour made for him by Hephaestus, arming himself with the ash spear of his father Peleus.

As the moment of battle approached, Zeus called a council of the immortals, telling the other gods that 'I shall stay here upon the fold of Olympos/sitting still, watching, to pleasure my heart. Meanwhile all you others/go down, wherever you may go, among the Achaians and Trojans/and give help to either side, as your own pleasure directs you.'

At the outset the Achaeans dominated the battlefield, for the Trojans were terrified by the presence of Achilles, 'shining in all his armour, a man like the murderous war god'. But once the immortals joined in the conflict became more evenly balanced, as 'gods went on to encounter gods; and meanwhile Achilleus/was straining to plunge into the combat opposite Hektor'.

But Apollo inspired Aeneas to engage Achilles, and would have been killed by him if not for the intervention of Poseidon, who plucked him from the battlefield and left him in the rear ranks of the Trojans.

Achilles was amazed at the sudden disappearance of Aeneas, and 'gathering the fury upon him, sprang on the Trojans/with a ghastly cry'. He killed three Trojans in turn, the third being Polydoros, brother of Hector, who then hurled a spear at Achilles, but Athena deflected its course and it missed him. Achilles charged furiously against him, 'but Phoibos Apollo caught up Hektor/easily, since he was a god, and wrapped him in thick mist'.

Achilles raged on, killing one Trojan after another, 'harrying them as they died, and the black earth ran blood'. When the fleeing Trojans reached the crossing place of the Scamander, Achilles 'split them and chased some back over the flat land toward the city' and there 'Hera let fall a deep mist to stay them'.

Meanwhile the other half of the fleeing Trojan army were crowded into the deep and swift-flowing river fleeing from Achilles, who left his spear on the bank and plunged in with his sword in hand, slashing around him in a circle so that soon 'the water was reddened with blood'. He went on slaughtering Trojans until the river-god Skamandros finally complained to him in a deep voice rising from the depths of the stream: 'the loveliness of my waters is crammed with corpses, I cannot/find a channel to cast my waters into the bright sea/since I am congested with the dead men you kill so brutally./Let me alone, then; lord of the people, I am confounded.'

Achilles said in answer that he would not let off slaughtering the Trojans till he had penned them up inside their city and come to terms with Hector, 'until he has killed me or I have killed him'. Skamandros then tried to drown Achilles, who was finally saved when Hera had Hephaestus create a fire storm that forced the river-god to abate his fury.

The tensions created by the battle now brought on a civil war among the gods: Ares v. Athena; Athena v. Aphrodite; Apollo v. Poseidon; Artemis v. Hera; Hermes v. Leto; and Artemis v. Zeus on Olympos. After the immortals ceased their fighting,

> Phoibos Apollo went into the sacred city of Ilion,
> since he was concerned for the wall of the strong-founded city
> lest the Danaans storm it on that day, before they were fated.
> The rest of the gods who live forever went back to Olympos,
> some in anger and others glorying greatly, and sat down
> at the side of their father the dark haired.

Meanwhile Achilles continued to slaughter the Trojans, as those who escaped him fled into the citadel. Apollo inspired the brave warrior Agenor to make a stand at the gate against Achilles, and the two of them hurled spears at one another without effect. Apollo then enclosed Agenor in a dense mist and sent him into the citadel, while he himself took on the Trojan's form, and when Achilles sprang at him he ran away, keeping slightly ahead of his pursuers. Meanwhile,

> all this time the rest of the Trojans fled in a body
> gladly into the town, and the city was filled with their swarming.
> They dared no longer outside the wall and outside the city
> to wait for each other and find out which one had got away
> and who had died in the battle, so hastily were they streaming
> into the city, each man as his knees and feet could rescue him.

As Achilles vainly pursued the supposed Agenor far from the gates of Troy, Phoibos Apollo finally revealed his true identity. The frustrated Achilles then raced back to the city, where Hector stood firm outside the Skaean gates despite the tearful pleas of his parents Priam and Hecuba. But when Achilles came running toward him, shaking his ash spear,

> the shivers took hold of Hektor ... and he could no longer
> stand his ground, but left the gates behind, and fled, frightened,
> and Peleus' son went after him in the confidence of his quick feet.
> ...
> [Achilles] went straight for him in fury, but Hector
> fled away under the Trojan wall and moved his knees rapidly.
> They raced along by the watching point and the windy fig tree
> always away from under the wall and along the wagon-way
> and came to the two sweet-running spring wells
> ...
> where the wives of the Trojans and their lovely
> daughters washed the clothes to shining, in the old days
> when there was peace, before the coming of the sons of the Achaians.

When for the fourth time they came to the well springs, Athena, appearing in the form of Hector's brother Deïphobus, persuaded him to stand and fight with Achilles. The two faced one another and Achilles hurled his spear at Hector. It flew over his shoulder and stuck in the ground, but Athena retrieved it and gave it back to Achilles. Hector in turn threw his spear but it was driven back by Achilles' shield, after which he drew his sword and swung it as his opponent lunged at him with his spear. Hector was well protected by the armour he had stripped from Patroclus, but Achilles drove the spear through the soft part of his neck.

With his last breath, Hector reminded Achilles that he too was fated to die in the war. 'Now though he was a dead man brilliant Achilleus spoke to him:/"Die: and I will take my own death at whatever time/Zeus and the rest of the immortals choose to accomplish it".'

Achilles stripped the bloody armour from Hector's body, which was stabbed repeatedly by the Achaeans who now came to look at the corpse of the man who had killed so many of their comrades. Achilles then tied the body of Hector to the back of his chariot, feet first, and dragged him around under the walls of Troy, as Priam and Hecuba and Andromache wailed in lamentation for him, joined in their mourning by all the women of Troy.

Meanwhile, after Achilles had dragged Hector's body back to the ships, the Achaeans began arranging for the last rites of Patroclus. That night Patroclus appeared to Achilles in a dream, saying 'Bury me as quickly as may be, let me pass through the gates of Hades.' He also asked that his remains be buried together with those of Achilles, because they had been beloved companions since their childhood: 'Therefore, let one single vessel, the golden two handled urn the lady your mother gave you, hold both our ashes.'

The following day they began cutting down trees for the funerary pyre and gathering the sacrificial animals who would be consumed in the fire along with the remains of Patroclus. The Achaeans then carried Patroclus in procession and laid him down in the place that Achilles had chosen, after which they piled up the timber for the pyre. They placed the body of Patroclus on top of the pyre and committed it to the flames, as Achilles said farewell to his beloved companion: 'Good-bye, Patroklos, I hail you even in the house of the death-god.'

But the pyre did not light until Achilles prayed to Boreas and Zephyros, the north wind and the west, which then began to blow against the pyre, 'and a huge inhuman blaze rose', roaring through the night. The next day Agamemnon convened an assembly, and when Achilles awoke he joined in and addressed the Achaeans, telling them that they must gather the bones of Patroclus from the ashes of the pyre and out them in a golden jar. 'And I would have you build a grave mound which is not very great/but such as will be fitting, for now, afterwards, the Achaians/will make it broad and high – such of you Achaians as may/be left to survive me here by the benched ships, after I am gone.'

After they had done what he asked, Achilles kept all of the Achaeans there and held athletic games in honour of Patroclus, bringing out rich prizes from his ships for the winners. After the games ended the Achaeans

> scattered to go away
> each man to his fast-running ship, and the rest of them thought of
>   their dinner
> and of sweet sleep and its enjoyment; only Achilleus
> wept still as he remembered his beloved companion, nor did sleep
> who subdues all come over him, but he tossed from one side to the
>   other
> in longing for Patroklos, for his manhood and his great strength.

At dawn Achilles yoked horses to his chariot and tied Hector's body behind it, dragging it three times around the tomb of Patroclus before throwing the corpse face downwards in the dust. Seeing this, most of the gods took pity on Hector, who had now remained unburied for twelve days, all of them except Hera, Athena and Poseidon, who had always favoured the Achaeans over the Trojans. Zeus sent Iris to summon Thetis, and when she arrived he told her to convince her son to accept ransom from Priam so that he could bury Hector. When she did so, saying that Zeus had sent her, Achilles answered her at once, saying, 'So be it. He can bring the ransom and take off the body, if the Olympian himself so urgently bids it.'

Zeus then sent Iris to Ilion, to tell Priam that he should go alone to see Achilles, bringing gifts 'which might soften his anger'. Against the strong objection of his wife Hecuba, Priam gathered gold and other rich gifts for the ransom, and set off in his chariot along with a mule wagon driven by his herald Idaeus. Seeing them set out, Zeus sent Hermes to guide Priam, having him pretend that he is a henchman of Achilles. Hermes took the reins of the chariot and drove it past the sentries directly to the imposing shelter of Achilles, where he unloaded the gifts that Priam had brought as ransom. Hermes returned to Olympos, while Priam entered Achilles' shelter, leaving Idaeus outside.

Priam entered unseen and went straight to Achilles, embracing his knees and kissing his hands. The old man identified himself as the father of one

> you killed a few days ago in defense of his own country,
> Hektor; for whose sake I come now to the ships of the Achaians
> to win him back from you, and I bring you gifts beyond number.
> Honour then the gods, Achilleus, and take pity upon me, remembering
> your father, yet I am still more pitiful;
> I have gone through what no other mortal on earth has gone through;

I put my lips to the hands of the man who has killed my children.
...
So he spoke, and stirred in the other a passion of grieving
for his own father. He took the old man's hand and pushed him
gently away, and the two remembered, as Priam sat huddled
at the feet of Achilleus and wept close for manslaughtering Hektor
and Achilleus wept now for his own father, now again
for Patroklos. The sound of their mourning moved in the house.

Priam asked that the body of Hector be given back to him in exchange for the ransom, and as quickly as possible, for his son had now been twelve days without burial. Achilles readily agreed and went outside to the mule-wagon with two of his companions to carry in the gifts, bringing the herald Idaeus back inside with them. After he had his serving maids wash Hector's corpse and anoint it with oil, Achilles and his companions put it on a litter and carried it outside and laid it in the wagon, covering it over with two great cloaks and a tunic from among the presents brought by Priam. They then slaughtered a sheep which they ate together with Priam and Idaeus for their evening meal, after which Achilles had his servants prepare beds for his guests.

After the meal Achilles asked Priam how long a truce he would need for the burial of Hector. Priam answered him directly, saying,

If you are willing that we accomplish a complete funeral
for great Hektor, this, Achilleus, is what you could do and give
me pleasure: For you know surely how we are penned in our city,
and wood is far to bring in from the hills, and the Trojans are
    frightened badly.
Nine days we would need in our palace to mourn him,
and bury him on the tenth day, and the people feast by him,
and on the eleventh day we would make the grave barrow for him,
and on the twelfth day fight again; if so we must do.

In turn Achilles answered him: 'Then all of this, aged Priam, shall be done as you ask it./I will hold off our attack for as much time as you bid me.'

They each went off to their beds, 'Priam and the herald who were both men of close counsel,/slept in the place outside the house, in the porch's shelter;/but Achilles slept in the inward corner of the strong-built shelter./And at his side lay Briseis of the fair colouring.'

Hermes had been pondering 'in his heart the problem of how to escort King Priam/from the ships and not to be seen by the devoted gate-wardens'. So he appeared to Priam and warned him of the danger he faced, for if Agamemnon recognized him he would surely hold him for ransom. 'He spoke, and the old man was afraid, and wakened his herald,/and lightly Hermes harnessed for them the mules and the horses/and himself drove them through the encampment. And no man knew of them.'

It was dawn when they came to the ford of the Scamander, where Hermes departed from them and returned to Olympos, leaving Priam and Idaeus to drive on to Troy with the body of Hector. The first to spot them was Priam's daughter Cassandra, who saw Hector drawn by the mules on a litter, whereupon she cried out in sorrow and told the entire city of their arrival.

Priam told the men of Troy that Achilles had promised that he would not attack the city again until the twelfth day, and so they should hasten to bring timber into the city for Hector's funerary pyre. 'Nine days/they spent bringing in an endless supply of timber. But when/the tenth dawn had shown forth with her light upon mortals,/they carried out bold Hektor, weeping, and set the body/ aloft a towering pyre for burning. And set fire to it.'

When the dawn came they all assembled around the pyre, where first they put out the remaining fire with wine, and

> the brothers and companions of Hektor gathered the white bones
> up, mourning, as the tears swell and ran down their cheeks. Then
> they laid what they had gathered up in a golden casket
> and wrapped this about with soft robes of purple,
> and presently put it away in the hollow of the grave

Then over the grave they quickly laid huge stones together to form the base of Hector's tumulus:

> they piled up the grave-barrow, and on all sides were set watchmen,
> for fear the strong-greaved Achaians might too soon set upon them.
> They piled up the grave-barrow and went away, and thereafter
> assembled in a fair gathering and held a glorious
> feast within the house of Priam, king under God's hand. Such was the
> burial of Hektor, breaker of horses.

And such is the end of the *Iliad*, though not of the Trojan War. As Richmond Lattimore notes: 'In fact, Achilleus did not, in the *Iliad* or anywhere else, take Troy; he died first, but his death is not told in the *Iliad*, though it is foreseen.'

I was thinking of these things when I first stood on the mound that now covers the site of ancient Troy. Looking out over the Trojan plain, I could see the tumuli that tradition has identified as the last resting-places of the two heroic protagonists in the last epic battle of the *Iliad*, the tomb of Achilles near the Aegean coast and that of Hector on the Hellespontine shore, the memories of their exploits still fresh more than 3,000 years after the Trojan War.

4

Mixed Multitudes and the Great Migration

The Trojan War, like all great wars, produced a seismic shift in the geopolitics of its era, the late Bronze Age, which was followed by some four centuries of darkness that Thucydides called the 'period of shifting populations'. This population movement included the great migration of the Hellenes across the Aegean to the western shores of Asia Minor and its offshore islands, as well as the earlier 'mixed multitudes' of Strabo. According to Strabo, these were the hordes of peoples, including Greeks and others, who left Troy after the city fell, following the seers, Kalchas, Amphilochus and Mopsus, who led them over the Taurus Mountains to the shores of the eastern Mediterranean, to the regions known as Pamphylia and Cilicia, continuing through Syria as far as Phoenicia.

Herodotus mentions two of the three seers in his description of the Pamphylian contingent in the fleet of Xerxes when he invaded Greece during the Persian wars: 'The Pamphylians furnished thirty ships; they themselves were armed with Greek arms. These Pamphylians are descended from those Greeks who scattered from Troy with Amphilochus and Kalchas.'

Amphilochus and Kalchas were famous Greek seers associated with the wanderings of the mixed multitudes, another being the former's brother Mopsus. Kalchas figures prominently in the *Iliad*, but Amphilochus and Mopsus are not mentioned by Homer. All three of them appear together in Hesiod's *Melampodia*, a lost poem whose contents are summarized in the Loeb edition of *Hesiod, the Homeric Hymns and Homerica*. The subject seems to have been the histories of famous seers, including Mopsus' mother Manto and his grandfather Teiresias. The poem begins at Colophon, one of the ancient Ionian cities: 'It is said that Kalchas the seer returned from Troy with Amphilochus the son of Amphiaraus and came on foot to this place. But happening to find near Clarus a seer greater than himself, Mopsus, the son of Manto, Teiresias' daughter, he died of vexation.'

Kalchas, Amphilochus and Mopsus are mentioned by Strabo in his account of the Pamphylian migration, where he quotes Herodotus in telling much the same story. Strabo also quotes the archaic poet Callinus of Ephesus in saying that Kalchas died before crossing the Taurus, and that Mopsus and Amphilochus led some of the refugees on to Cilicia and beyond to Syria and Phoenicia.

But other versions of the story of the mixed multitudes say nothing about the death of Kalchas in Claros, and have him joining Amphilochus and Mopsus to lead their followers over the Taurus Mountains to Pamphylia and Cilicia.

Teiresias, the legendary blind Theban seer, is mentioned in Book 10 of the *Odyssey*, where Odysseus, at the bidding of the nymph Circe, journeys to Hades 'there to consult with the soul of Teiresias the Theban,/the blind prophet, whose senses stay unshaken within him,/to whom Persephone has granted intelligence/even after death, but the rest of them are flittering shadows.'

Kalchas, a grandson of Apollo, was the most gifted soothsayer of his time, and he had been of invaluable help to the Achaeans at every stage of the Trojan War, starting from the time that Agamemnon assembled his fleet at Aulis. Kalchas makes his first appearance in the *Iliad* near the beginning of Book 1, where, in answer to a plea by Achilles, he tells him and the other assembled Achaeans the reason for the anger of Apollo, who has set a plague upon them. Kalchas tells the Achaeans that Apollo is angry at them because they have dishonoured his priest Chryses by taking his daughter Chryseis, and that the god will lift the plague until the girl is returned to the god's shrine at Chryse.

It was Kalchas who devised the stratagem of the wooden horse, and he himself was one of the Achaeans hidden within it. After the sack of Troy, when the rest of the Achaeans prepared to return to Greece, Kalchas predicted that their homeward voyages would be difficult, since Athena was angry with them. Thus Kalchas decided not to join them and, along with his fellow prophet Amphilochus, set out on foot across Asia Minor, leading the throng of Greek and Trojan refugees that Strabo called the 'mixed multitudes'.

Amphilochus was a son of the prophetess Manto and thus a grandson of Teiresias. Mopsus was also a son of Manto and grandson of Teiresias. Mopsus is said to have founded the Ionian city of Colophon and was also the soothsayer at the oracular shrine of Apollo at Claros. He and his brother Amphilochus are credited with founding several cities in Pamphylia and Cilicia.

The wanderings of the mixed multitudes took place about a century before the beginning of the great Hellenic migration across the Aegean to the coast of Asia Minor and its offshore islands, with the Aeolians moving first, followed by the Ionians and then the Dorians.

According to Herodotus, all three groups of Greek colonists formed political confederations, originally twelve cities each of the Aeolians and Ionians and six of the Dorians. These confederations were loosely knit, and the individual cities were entirely autonomous, as were the other Greek settlements that never joined any of the three leagues.

Tradition held that the Aeolian cities were founded by colonists from eastern Thessaly and Boeotia, who sailed across the northern Aegean to the islands of Lesbos and Tenedos and on to the Anatolian coast, where they established their settlements between the Hellespont and the Gulf of Smyrna. Protogeometric pottery found in Lesbos and Smyrna indicates that the first Aeolian settlers arrived there *c.* 1000 BC or even earlier.

The cities of the Aeolian confederation were between the rivers Caicus and Hermus, separated from those of Lesbos, Tenedos and the northern coast by the territory of the Mysians. The Mysians lived between the River Caicus and the Adramyttene Gulf, the deep indentation of the Aegean bounded on its north by the Troad, the huge peninsula formed by Mt Ida, flanked on its north by the Hellespont. The Greek settlements on Lesbos, Tenedos and the Troad never joined the Aeolian confederacy, which seems to have been founded before the end of the eighth century BC.

Farther inland in the highlands of Anatolia were the Phrygians, an Indo-European people who supplanted the Hittites in central Asia Minor early in the first millennium BC. As noted earlier, the Phrygians are mentioned in the *Iliad*, where they are listed along with the Leleges, Pelasgians and Mysians among the allies of the Trojans.

Cyme was by far the most important city in the confederation, renowned for its maritime enterprises. Aeolian Cyme, along with the Euboean cities of Chalcis and Eretria, joined together in 757 BC to found Cumae, the first Greek colony on the Italian mainland. The Cymeans on their own later founded Side on the Mediterranean coast of Anatolia. Strabo writes that 'The largest and best of the Aeolian cities is Cyme; and this with Lesbos might be called the metropolis of the rest of the cities, about thirty in number, of which not a few have disappeared.'

Strabo goes on to say that Cyme was the birthplace of Hesiod's father, Dius, who emigrated from there to Boeotia in Greece. Strabo notes that the Cymeans claimed that their city was the birthplace of Homer, but he says that 'it is not agreed that Homer was from Cyme, for many people lay claim to him'.

Herodotus says that the Aeolians also had settlements on Lesbos and Tenedos as well as around Mt Ida on the Troad, but these were not members of the confederation. There were originally six cities on Lesbos, of which the most important were Mytilene, across the stretch of the Anatolian coast occupied by the Mysians, and Methymna, which was just across the strait from Cape Lekton, the south-western promontory of the Troad. Colonists from Methymna founded the city of Assos on the coast of the Adramyttene Gulf west of Cape Lekton, probably by the end of the eighth century BC. An expedition from Mytilene founded a small settlement on the northern coast of the Troad called Achilleion, which Strabo says included the tomb of Achilles.

There was just one city on Tenedos, but it controlled a number of settlements along the coast of the mainland opposite, the so-called Tenedaean Peraea. One of the settlements on the Tenedaean Peraea was Chryse, site of the sanctuary of Sminthian Apollo.

Other Aeolian colonies were founded in the Troad at sites ranging from the shore of the Adramyttene Gulf to the Hellespont, including Antandrus, Polymedion, Hamaxitus, Larisa, Colonae and Sigeum. Around 750 BC Aeolian colonists also founded a settlement on the site of ancient Troy called Ilion.

At some time in the second half of the eighth century BC Ionians from Colophon seized control of Smyrna from the Aeolians, an incident described by Herodotus in Book 1 of his *Histories*. The work called *Of the Origin of Homer and Hesiod, and of their Contest*, in discussing the origins of the two poets, says that Smyrna and Chios as well as Colophon claimed to be the birthplace of Homer, although Homer does not mention any of these places in the *Iliad* and only Chios in the *Odyssey*:

> But, as for Homer, you might almost say that every city with its inhabitants claims him as son. Foremost are the men of Smyrna who say that he was the Son of Meles, the river of their town, by a nymph Cretheïs, and that he was at first called Melesigenes.

The site of Colophon is some 30 kilometres south of Smyrna. As noted earlier, Colophon was near the oracular shrine of Apollo at Claros, where Kalchas and Amphilochus led the mixed multitudes from Troy. During the early history of the Dodekapolis or Twelve

Cities of the Ionians, Colophon was the largest and most powerful city in the confederation. Besides taking control of Smyrna, the Colophonians also annexed the nearby Aeolian city of Notium, which thenceforth became the port of Colophon. This enabled Colophon to become a naval power, and *c.* 700 BC the Colophonians established colonies at Myrleia on the Sea of Marmara and at Siris in southern Italy.

The site of the oracular shrine of Apollo is about 13 kilometres to the south of Ionian Colophon and some three kilometres north of Aeolian Notium. The impressive ruins of the shrine date to as far back as the sixth century BC, and it remained in use until AD 392, when it was closed by Emperor Theodosius I. The shrine is mentioned in one of the Homeric *Hymns to Artemis*:

> Muse, sing of Artemis, sister of the Far-shooter, the Virgin who delights
> in arrows, who was fostered with Apollo. She waters her horses from
> Meles deep in reeds, and swiftly drives her all-golden chariot through
> Smyrna to vine-clad Claros where Apollo, god of the silver bow, sits
> waiting for the far-shooting goddess who delights in arrows.

Recent excavations at Claros have found Greek pottery dating to *c.* 900 BC, indicating that Hellenic visitors made pilgrimages to the sacred spring even before the first buildings were erected there. The spring was originally within the bounds of Aeolian Notium but was also claimed by Ionian Colophon. The people from Notium seem to have believed that the original oracle at the shrine was Mopsus, who had Aeolian Greek roots, whereas the Colophonians claimed that the first prophet there was Kalchas, who was from the Argolid. This was the basis for the legendary quarrel between Kalchas and Mopsus. When the Colophonians eventually absorbed Notium they took possession of the shrine of Apollo. They also maintained that their hero Kalchas had not died at Claros, but had gone off with the Colophonians who had founded Siris in southern Italy, where they still preserved his tomb.

Miletus, the only one of the Ionian cities mentioned by Homer, was the most important of the mainland cities in the Dodekapolis, renowned as the oldest of the Ionian settlements and their greatest maritime power. The Milesians proudly called their city 'the first settled in Ionia, and the mother of many and great cities in the Pontus and Egypt, and in various other parts of the world'.

During its early years Miletus founded a far greater number of colonies than any other city-state in the Greek world, including more than thirty around the shores of the Pontus Euxinos (Black Sea) and its approaches in the Hellespont and the Sea of Marmara. The Milesian colonies founded on the Anatolian shore of the Pontus, beginning in the eighth century BC, included Sinope (Sinop), Amisus (Samsun) and Trebizond (Trabzon), which are today the three most important Turkish cities on the Black Sea. Besides its colony of Abydos on the Hellespont, the Milesians also established a settlement at Cyzicus on the Asian shore of the Sea of Marmara.

Miletus also had a privileged position at Naucratis, the great emporium on the Nile delta founded by the Greeks *c.* 610 BC, in which the Milesians established a fortified trading station known as Milesionteichos. They were joined at Naucratis by eleven other Greek cities, including Ionians from Samos, Chios, Teos, Phocaea and Clazomenae; Dorians from Rhodes, Aegina, Cnidos, Halicarnassus and Phaselis; and Aeolians from Mytilene.

Miletus was rivalled in its maritime ventures by Phocaea, the northernmost of the Ionian cities, founded beyond the River Hermus on the peninsula that forms the northern horn of the Smyrnaic Gulf. It was settled later than the other cities in the Dodekapolis, founded by colonists from the Ionian cities of Erythrae and Teos, probably in the eighth century BC. The site was chosen for its excellent natural harbour, the finest on the Aegean coast of Anatolia.

The Phocaeans took full advantage of their superb location to send colonizing expeditions overseas, and in their first venture they joined the Milesians in founding Amisus on the Black Sea coast of Anatolia. Then in 654 BC the Phocaeans on their own founded Lampsacus, on the Asian shore of the Hellespont. Around 600 BC they established Massalia, the present Marseilles, with colonists going on from there to found Nicaea and Antipolis, now known as Nice and Antibes. Then in 560 BC the Phocaeans founded Alalia on Corsica, and at the same time they established a short-lived colony on Sardinia. They even sailed out into the Atlantic and founded a colony at Tartessus, on the present site of Seville.

The Ionian and Aeolian cities traded with the Lydians, whose capital was at Sardis, some 80 kilometres east of Smyrna in the Hermus valley. Mycenaean pottery found at Sardis indicated that the Hellenes had penetrated into Lydia in the late Bronze Age, though the Ionians and Aeolians do not seem to have reached Sardis until the seventh century BC.

Two settlements named Magnesia were founded somewhat inland of the Ionian colonies. One of them, Magnesia ad Sipylum, was north-east of Smyrna under Mt Sipylus; the other, Magnesia ad Maeandrum, was south-east of Ephesus in the Maeander valley. The founders of these two cities were said to be Aeolians from Magnesia in northern Greece, the so-called Magnetes, who are supposed to have stayed on in Asia Minor after the Trojan War, and were probably among the mixed multitudes who came this way with Kalchas and Amphilochus. An inscription found in Magnesia ad Maeandrum states that the founders of the city were the first Greeks to cross into Anatolia.

The site of Magnesia ad Sipylum is now occupied by the Turkish city of Manisa, whose name is a corruption of 'Magnesia'. The upper part of the city is on the lower slope of Mt Sipylus, where there is a curious rock figure known as 'weeping Niobe'. This was first identified as such by Pausanias, who apparently lived in Magnesia ad Sipylum at one time: 'I myself have seen Niobe when I was climbing up the mountains to Sipylos. Niobe from close up is a rock and a stream, and nothing like a woman either grieving or otherwise; but if you go further off you see a woman downcast and in tears.'

According to the myth, Niobe had six sons and six daughters. All of her children were killed by Apollo and Artemis, the twin offspring of Leto, who were angered because Niobe had mocked their mother for only bearing two children, while she herself had a dozen. Homer tells the story in Book 24 of the *Iliad*, where Priam is grieving over the death of his son Hector, killed by Achilles, who is trying to persuade the old man to pause in his mourning and have something to eat. Achilles reminds Priam that Niobe had mourned her slain children for nine days before they were finally buried:

> But she remembered to eat when she was worn out with weeping.
> And now somewhere among the rocks, in the lonely mountains,
> in Sipylos, where they say is the resting place of the goddesses
> who are nymphs, and dance beside the waters of Acheloios,
> there, stone still, she broods on the sorrows that the gods gave her.

The migration of the Dorians took them from Lacedaemon in the central Peloponnesos across the Aegean to Crete, Rhodes, Cos and the south-western coast of Anatolia in Caria. The Dorians founded a confederacy, originally called the Hexapolis, or Six Cities, comprising three cities on Rhodes – Lindus, Ialysus and Camirus – one on Cos and two in Caria, namely Halicarnassus and Cnidus. The mainland cities were established on the south-westernmost extensions of Anatolia, with Cnidus on the peninsula between Rhodes and Cos, and Halicarnassus on the one just north of Cos.

The cities of the Dorian League had their religious centre and meeting-place at the Triopium, on the same peninsula as Cnidus. Halicarnassus eventually came under the influence of the Ionian cities to its north, principally Miletus, which led to its expulsion from the Hexapolis, thereafter called the Pentapolis, or the Five Cities.

There was also a Dorian settlement at Iasus, midway along the coast between Miletus and Halicarnassus. Excavations

have revealed that the site was inhabited as early as the third
millennium BC. Minoan pottery and houses have been found from
the period *c.* 1900–1550 BC, as well as Mycenaean pottery dated
c. 1400–1200 BC. According to tradition, the first Dorian settlers
were Argives from the Peloponnesos, who arrived in the ninth
century BC.

Caria and Lycia appear in Book 2 of the *Iliad*, in the last lines of
the Catalogue of Trojans, which notes that Sarpedon and Glaucus
led the contingent 'from Lykia far away, and the whirling waters
of Xanthos'. The River Xanthus rises in the Lycian mountains and
flows into the Mediterranean near the town of Kalkan. Three of the
most important cities of the ancient Lycian League are in the lower
valley of the river – Tlos, Pinara and Xanthus – all of which survive
as impressive ruins.

Tlos is probably the earliest settlement in the Xanthus valley. The
city was known in the Lycian language as Tlawa, identified as Dalawa
in the Lukka lands mentioned in Hittite archives of the fourteenth
century BC. This early date has been verified by the discovery here of
a bronze hatchet dating from the second millennium BC.

The most remarkable monument in Tlos is a funerary monument,
in the form of an Ionic temple, carved into the side of the acropolis
cliff known as the Tomb of Bellerophon. The tomb takes its name
from the relief carved on the wall of its porch. The relief shows the
Corinthian hero Bellerophon riding on his winged horse Pegasus,
given to him by his father Poseidon. The tomb was probably built
for a prince of the royal line at Tlos who claimed descent from
Bellerophon, known in Greek as Bellerophones, grandfather of the
Lycian leaders Sarpedon and Glaucus. According to mythology,
Bellerophon first came to Lycia during the reign of King Iobates,
who set him the series of tasks described in Book 6 of the *Iliad*, the
first being to kill the Chimaera:

> first he sent him away with orders to kill the Chimaira
> none might approach; a thing of immortal make, not human,
> lion-fronted and snake behind, a goat in the middle,
> and snorting out the breath of the terrible flame of bright fire.
> He killed the Chimaira, obeying the portents of the immortals.

The ruins of the ancient Greek city of Olympos lie half-
submerged at the mouth of a river on the east coast of Lycia. The site
is 20 kilometres south of Mt Olympos of Lycia, Turkish Tahtalı Dağ,
from which the city of Olympus takes its name. Strabo, describing
the eastern coast of Lycia in Book 14 of his *Geography*, writes of
'Olympos, a large city and a mountain of the same name.'

The most impressive monument in the city is the portal of a Roman temple; there is no indication of the deity to whom it was dedicated, but it was probably Hephaestus, god of the forge. Hephaestus was the patron deity of Olympos, associated with the city because of the unquenchable fire that since antiquity has burned above on a foothill of Mt Olympos that Pliny calls Mt Chimaera. Pliny writes: 'In Lycia ... we have ... Mt. Chimaera, which sends forth flames at night, and the city-state of Hephaestum, which also has a mountain range that is often on fire. The town of Olympus stood here.'

The Chimaera has since antiquity been identified with the unquenchable fire that still burns on one of the foothills of the Lycian Mt Olympos. The mountain is mentioned in Book 5 of the *Odyssey*, where Poseidon, returning from the country of the Ethiopians, catches sight of Odysseus approaching the land of the Phaeacians on the penultimate stage of his long voyage back to Ithaca.

The fire, known in Turkish as Yanar, is in a burnt-out area about 50 metres in diameter, the flame issuing from a deep hole about a metre wide and hardly rising above ground level. A team of Turkish scientists studied the Yanar and found traces of methane, which emerges under pressure already on fire, and if any attempt is made to quench the flame it reignites itself within seconds.

The Rhodians also established a settlement at Phaselis, on the eastern coast of Lycia under Mt Olympos, across the Gulf of Antalya from Pamphylia. According to tradition, Phaselis was founded *c.* 690 BC by Dorians from Rhodes led by an Argive hero named Lacius. The men of Phaselis were renowned maritime traders, and theirs was one of the nine cities which together founded on the Nile delta the emporium known as Naucratis, 'Queen of the Sea'.

Pamphylia is a Greek word that means 'land of all the tribes'. This stems from the tradition that the first settlers were the mixed multitudes who came this way under the leadership of Kalchas, Mopsus and Amphilochus. The principal Pamphylian cities in antiquity were, from west to east, Antalya, Perge, Aspendos and Side. Antalya was founded in the second century BC, while the other three are much older.

The citizens of Perge believed that their city had been founded by Kalchas and Mopsus. Around the periphery of the courtyard within the inner gateway there are niches that once contained statues of the city's founders. Excavation in 1953 recovered the bases of nine of these statues, dating from the second century AD, which included Kalchas and Mopsus along with five mythological figures, all of them obscure, as well as a Roman senator and his son. The inscriptions on the first two of these are dedications to 'the founder Kalchas of

Argos, son of Thestor,' and 'the founder Mopsus of Delphi, son of Apollo'.

Perge has been identified as the 'Parha' of Hittite texts. A fragmentary Hittite royal letter, long known to scholars, refers to a ruler in south-western Asia Minor known as 'Muksus', a name that might refer to Mopsus. Inscriptions on a Neo-Hittite gateway in both Luwian and Phoenician discovered in 1946 at Karatepe in north-eastern Cilicia records that a prince named Azitawattas was from the royal house of 'Mukas' and ruled at Adana in the Cilician plain. Some scholars have identified 'Mukas' as 'Mopsus', which seemed to suggest that the legendary seer was in fact an historical personality. Three other such inscriptions have since been found in the region. The inscriptions are from the eighth century BC, which was to be expected for Neo-Hittite monuments, but the letter, which originally was thought to be from c. 1200 BC, has now been dated to before 1400 BC, which is far too early for the seer Mopsus.

Aspendos is famous for its almost perfectly preserved Roman theatre, which is built up against the acropolis hill. Excavations on the acropolis show that the site was first occupied in the late Bronze Age. According to tradition, Aspendos was founded by men from Argos in the Peloponnesos. Coins minted in Aspendos from the early fifth century BC through the following century give the name of the city as Estwediiya. This has been equated with the name of the Neo-Hittite prince Azitawattas, of the royal 'house of Muksus', leading to the suggestion that Aspendos was founded by the mixed multitudes under Mopsus, as the city claimed.

Strabo, in his description of the coast east of Side says that this is the maritime boundary between Pamphylia and Cilicia. Strabo had in the previous section of the *Geography* explained that the coast of Cilicia below the Taurus Mountains was divided into two parts, one of them Rugged Cilicia, an inhospitable rock-bound shore, and the other, farther to the east, a broad and fertile region called Plain Cilicia, the Turkish Çukurova.

As the coastal highway enters Plain Cilicia it passes the ruins of ancient Soli, which under the Romans was renamed Pompeiopolis. Soli was one of the oldest Greek cities in Cilicia, founded as a Rhodian colony c. 700 BC. Strabo makes note of this, saying that 'it was founded by Achaeans and Rhodians from Lindus'.

It is possible that the Rhodians merely refounded an earlier settlement here, since, according to tradition, Soli was one of the Cilician cities founded by the mixed multitudes after the fall of Troy, for Hesiod writes in the *Melampodia* that 'Amphilochus was killed by Apollo at Soli.'

After Soli, the coastal highway passes in succession the three largest cities on the Cilician coast. First, after ten kilometres, is Mersin; 30 kilometres after that is Tarsus, and then 50 kilometres farther along the highway comes to Adana, all three of them forming part of the same metropolitan area, with a combined population of more than three million, living in what is considered to be one of the most productive agricultural regions in the world, a veritable cradle of civilization. All three have roots dating back to the Neolithic period, and during the Neo-Hittite era they were all part of the kingdom known as Kizzuwatna, whose ruler, as we have seen, claimed to be from the royal house of Mukas, who may be Mopsus.

Twenty-five kilometres to the west of Adana there is a turn-off to the right for the village of Yakapınar, the site of ancient Mopsuestia. Mopsuestia means 'the Hearth of Mopsus', from the tradition that it was founded by Mopsus and the mixed multitudes that followed him here from Troy. Excavations on the acropolis hill of Mopsuestia indicate that it was first settled in the middle of the second millennium BC, when it would have been one of the cities of the Hittite Empire. It remained a place of considerable importance throughout antiquity and up until the early sixteenth century AD, controlling a bridge over the Pyramus on the caravan route to Syria.

South of Mopsuestia, in the delta formed by the rivers Seyhan and Ceyhan, there are the remains of two other ancient cities, Mallus and Magarsa, which, according to Strabo, were founded by the mixed multitudes. According to his biographer Arrian, Alexander the Great made pilgrimages to both of these places just before the battle of Issus in 333 BC.

Beyond the Gulf of Issus, now known as the Gulf of Iskenderun, one comes to the Hatay, the Turkish province that was part of the French mandate in Syria until 1938, when as a result of a plebiscite it was transferred to the Republic of Turkey. The capital of the Hatay is Antakya, ancient Antioch, known in the Hellenistic period as Antiochia on the Orontes, capital of the Seleucid kingdom founded by Seleucus I Nicator (r. 312–281 BC). Strabo says that one of the four quarters of the city was populated by the mixed multitudes led by the descendants of the Corn-God Triptolemus, who were resettled here by Seleucus:

> Nicator also settled here the descendants of Triptolemus … And it is on this account that the Antiocheians worship him [Triptolemus] as a hero and celebrate a festival in his honour on Mt. Cassius in the neighbourhood of Seleucia. It was said that he was sent by the Argives in search of Io, who disappeared first in Tyre, and that he wandered through Cilicia; and that there some of his Argive companions left

him and founded Tarsus, but the others accompanied him into the
next stretch of seaboard, gave up the search in despair, and remained
in the hill country of the Orontes.

The Seleucia mentioned by Strabo is Seleucia ad Pieria, the port
of Antioch, north of the mouth of the Orontes. This is near Turkish
Samandağ, Mt Cassius, known to the Arabs as Jebel Akra, about
50 kilometres south of Antioch, overlooking the border between
Turkey and Syria. The Hittites called it Hazzi and sacrificed to their
mountain gods there, and they erected a temple of Zeus Cassius on
its summit, where the *heroon* of Triptolemus would have stood.

The ancient city of Al Mina was located between Mt Cassius
and Samandağ, at the mouth of the Orontes. The site was excavated
in 1936 by Leonard Wooley, who identified it as a Euboean colony
founded shortly before 800 BC, in direct competition with the
Phoenicians. As we have seen, it was here that the Euboeans acquired
the Phoenician alphabet and brought it back to the Greek world,
where it was used to produce the first written versions of the *Iliad*
and *Odyssey*.

And so, in this remote borderland between Turkey and Syria,
where the mixed multitudes seem to have ended their long wanderings
from Troy, myth and the epic poems of Homer join once again with
history through the archaeologist's spade.

5

Troy After the Fall

After the fall of Troy, around 1200 BC, the site was sparsely inhabited for about five centuries, until it was resettled by Aeolian Greeks, who called it Ilion. Troy and the Troad were then caught up in the tides of history, as recorded by Herodotus of Halicarnassus, who was born around 490–485 BC, shortly after the beginning of the Persian Wars. He states his purpose at the beginning of his *History*:

> I, Herodotus of Halicarnassus, am here setting forth my history, that time may not draw the color from what man has brought into being, nor those great and wonderful deeds, manifested by both Greeks and barbarians, fail of their report, and, together with all of this, the reason why they fought one another.

The Persian king, Cyrus the Great (r. 560/559–530 BC), founder of the Achaemenid dynasty, conquered Sardis, the capital of Lydia, in the upper Maeander, in 546 BC, and then soon afterwards subjugated the Greek colonies on the western coast of Asia Minor, including Troy and the other cities in the Troad. His third successor, Darius I (r. 522–486 BC), began his reign by dividing his vast realm into a score of satrapies, or provinces, each headed by a governor known as a satrap. Most of the Greek cities were in two of these satrapies, namely Lydia, with its capital at Sardis in the upper valley of the River Hermus, and Phrygia, whose capital at Dascylium, about 160 kilometres east of Troy.

During the tenth year of his reign, in 512 BC, Darius went on campaign against the Scythians in what is now southern Russia. He took his army across the Bosphorus on a bridge of boats, which the Greeks of Byzantium dismantled after he left, and so after the campaign he returned to Asia on a bridge of boats across the Narrows of the Hellespont between Sestos and Abydos.

The Ionian cities in Asia Minor revolted against Persian rule in 499 BC, aided by the Athenians, who sent twenty ships, and the Eretrians, who contributed ten. At the beginning of the revolt the Greeks captured Sardis and burned down the city and its temples before retreating to the coast. The Persian fief holders in western Asia Minor came to the rescue and caught up with the Greeks before they re-embarked at Ephesus, inflicting heavy losses on them. The Athenians and Eretrians, then sailed for home, leaving the Ionians to continue the revolt on their own. The war continued until 494 BC, when the Ionian fleet suffered a decisive defeat at the Battle of Lade off Miletus, which was then burned to the ground by the Persians.

Darius vowed to take revenge on the Athenians and Eretrians, and in 492 BC he launched an invasion of Greece under Mardonius, the son of Darius' sister. According to Herodotus,

> Mardonius brought with him a very large land force and a large fleet ... and hastened off to the Hellespont ... Having collected this huge force of army and fleet there, the Persians crossed the Hellespont with the ships and marched by land through Europe, making for Eretria and Athens.

As the Persian fleet rounded the Mt Athos peninsula it was struck by a violent storm which wrecked 300 ships, with more than 20,000 men lost. At the same time the army under Mardonius encountered stiff resistance from the Thracian tribesmen in Macedonia, and so he aborted the campaign and led his battered forces back to Asia, 'having fought very ingloriously'.

The following year Darius sent off another expedition to Greece led by Datis, a Mede. Datis commanded a 'vast and well-equipped army ... with six hundred ships of war' as well as horse-transports for the cavalry. After subjugating the island of Naxos and sacking Eretria they then sailed south to attack Athens, landing on the beach of the Marathon plain, 42 kilometres north of the city. On learning of this the Athenians marched to Marathon, where they totally defeated the Persians, after which Datis sailed his fleet back to Asia.

Darius died in 486 BC and was succeeded by his son Xerxes, who was at the time confronted by a rebellion in Egypt. His cousin Mardonius, who had commanded the expedition into Greece in 492 BC, persuaded him to renew his father's war against Athens after he put down the revolt in Egypt.

According to Herodotus, writing of Xerxes' preparation for the invasion of Greece:

> After the subduing of Egypt, for four full years [484–481 BC] he made ready his host and all that they must have, and at the beginning of the fifth year he started his campaign with a huge force of men. This was the greatest force of any we have heard of.

According to Herodotus, during the years 483–481 BC Xerxes' men had been digging a canal through the narrow isthmus of the Mt Athos peninsula, where the Persian fleet had been destroyed by a storm in 492 BC. At the same time they built a bridge of boats across the River Strymon in Macedonia, as well as storage places for corn and salted meat that the army would need along its line of march. They also constructed a double bridge of boats across the Narrows of the Hellespont, the lower one for the pack animals of the supply train, and the one farther upstream for the cavalry and infantry. At the end of the peninsula on the European side of the Hellespont the Athenian colony of Elaious afforded a calm anchorage just inside the end of the strait, which the Phoenicians and other elements of the Persian navy used as a base for three years before Xerxes' crossing. Shortly after the two bridges across the Hellespont were completed they were destroyed in a great storm. Herodotus says

> On learning this Xerxes was furious and bade his men lay three hundred lashes on the Hellespont and lower into the sea a pair of fetters ... So he commanded the sea be punished, and he ordered the beheading of the supervisors of the building of the bridge.

When all was ready, Xerxes set out with his army in the spring of 481 BC along the Royal Road from Susa to Sardis, where he wintered. The following spring they resumed the march, which took them out to the Aegean coast opposite Lesbos, and then across the Troad to the Hellespont. En route they came to the River Scamander, which the Persian army drank dry, according to Herodotus, who goes on to say that the army camped on the Trojan plain, and Xerxes took the opportunity to make a pilgrimage to the citadel of Troy:

> I say he climbed up to Priam's Pergamus, which he was eager to see. Having observed it and inquired about it all, he sacrificed one thousand cattle to Athena of Ilium and the Magi offered libations to the heroes. After their doing so, the host was seized with panic fear by night, but with dawn they marched away, keeping the city of Rhoetium on the left and also Ophrynium and Dardanus, which borders Abydos.

The two boat-bridges across the Hellespont were both at the Narrows of the strait. The upper one, for the cavalry and the infantry, may have started from the tip of Abydos (Nağara Point) while the lower one, for the baggage-animals and attendants, was probably about five kilometres downstream.

When Xerxes reached Abydos, where a platform of white stone had been erected for him, he reviewed the army and watched the various contingents of his navy race below him on the Hellespont. Then, according to Herodotus:

> When he saw all of the Hellespont covered with ships and all of the shores and plains of Abydos full of men, then Xerxes declared himself a happy man; but after that he burst into tears. Artabanus, his uncle ... noticed the tears and said, 'My lord, how different is what you are doing now compared with a little while since! For then you congratulated yourself, but now you are in tears.' Xerxes answered, 'Yes, for pity stole over me as I made my meditation on the shortness of the life of man; here are all these thousands, and not a one of them will be alive a hundred years from now.'

Herodotus goes on to describe the crossing of the Hellespont, which began the next day at sunrise and went on continuously for seven days:

> When the sun rose, Xerxes, poured the libation from a golden cup into the sea and prayed to the sun that no chance should befall him such that it would check his conquest of Europe until he had come to the furthest limit of that continent. When he had finished his prayer, he threw the cup into the Hellespont and also a golden mixing bowl and a Persian sword.

The Persian army marched southward along the Greek coast, delayed briefly by a Spartan force at Thermopylae, while their navy kept pace by sea, where the allied Greek navy inflicted significant damage on them in the battle of Artemision off Euboea. The Greeks abandoned Athens and their navy made a stand in the strait between the island of Salamis and the mainland, where, with Xerxes looking on from a stone throne, they totally defeated the Persian fleet, which the following day set sail for the Hellespont.

After the battle Xerxes made his way back to Asia with most of his army, leaving 300,000 elite troops under Mardonius to winter in Boeotia. The following year the Greek allies utterly destroyed the Persian army at Plataea, killing Mardonius. At the same time (Herodotus says the same day) the Greeks destroyed the Persian fleet in a battle off Cape Mycale in Asia Minor. The Ionian Greeks, aided by the Athenians, immediately revolted against Persian rule, restoring the freedom of their cities. These battles represent the triumphal beginning of the classical period in Greek history (479–323 BC), when Athens would reach the peak of its glory as the political and intellectual leader of the Greek world.

Athens and the other Greek city-states lost their independence in August 388 BC, when they were defeated by Philip II of Macedon at the battle of Chaeronea. During the following winter Philip summoned the Greek states to send deputies to a congress at Corinth. This created the League of Corinth, also known as the Greek Community, a confederation of the Greek states under the aegis of Macedon. The agreement was ratified by all but one of the Greek states south of Macedon, including many of the islands, the single exception being Sparta. At its first meeting, in the summer of 337 BC, the federation formally entered into an alliance with the Macedonian state, defined as 'Philip and his descendants'. Philip was elected by the community as *hegemon*, or leader, after which they declared war on Persia.

Philip began preparing for the war against Persia, in which he intended to free the Greek cities in Asia Minor. The Achaemenid dynasty had in the meanwhile undergone two violent regime changes. The first occurred in August 338 BC, when Artaxerxes III was assassinated and Artaxerxes IV became king. The second took place in the spring of 336 BC, when Artaxerxes IV was murdered and Darius III succeeded.

Philip launched a preliminary expedition into Asia Minor in the spring of 336 BC, putting 10,000 troops under the command of Parmenio, supported by the Macedonian fleet. But the expedition was aborted that summer, when Philip was assassinated at Pella, the Macedonian capital. His son Alexander, who was then about twenty years of age, was acclaimed by the army as king.

The League of Corinth elected Alexander as *hegemon*, after which they agreed to support him in implementing his father's crusade to liberate the Greeks of Asia Minor from Persian rule. Alexander's campaign began two years later and lasted for the rest of his short life. The story of the campaign is told by the Greek historian Arrian, a Roman citizen, who wrote it in the mid-second century BC, his sources including accounts by many of those who had accompanied Alexander.

Early in the spring of 334 BC, after appointing Antipater to serve as regent in Macedonia, Alexander set out from Pella at the head of his army and headed for the Hellespont. Arrian says the expeditionary force comprised 'not much more than 30,000 infantry, including light troops and archers, and over 5,000 cavalry', but a modern estimate puts it at 43,000 infantry and 6,000 cavalry. The Macedonian fleet, supplied by the League of Corinth, consisted of only 160 ships, a third the size of Phoenicia's navy, which was far more efficient.

According to Arrian, Alexander's army took twenty days to reach Sestos on the European shore of the Hellespont at the Narrows, where his general Parmenio had the cavalry and most of the infantry ferried across to Abydos. Alexander took the rest of the troops down to Elaeus, near the end of the European shore of the Hellespont on the Gallipoli peninsula, where there was a shrine dedicated to Protesilaus, who, according to Homer, in the Catalogue of Ships, was the first of all the Achaeans to die in the siege of Troy.

> Those who hold Phylake and Pyrasos of the flowers,
> the precinct of Demeter, and Iton, mother of sheepflocks,
> Antron by the sea-shore, and Pteleos deep in the meadows,
> of these in turn Protesilaos was leader
> while he lived; but now the black earth had closed him under, whose
> wife, cheeks torn for grief, was left behind in Phylake,
> and a marriage half completed, a Dardanian man had killed him
> as he leapt from his ship, far the first of all the Achaians.

Arrian says that 'Alexander's purpose in performing his ceremony here was to ensure better luck for himself than Protesilaus had.' Alexander then crossed the Hellespont to the Achaean harbour, where Agamemnon had beached his ships during the siege of Troy. According to Arrian:

> It is generally believed that Alexander sailed from Elaeus to the Achaian Harbour, himself at the helm of the admiral's ship, and that halfway over he slaughtered a bull as an offering to Poseidon and poured wine from a golden cup into the sea ... Once ashore he traveled inland to Troy and offered sacrifice to Athena, patron goddess of the city; here he made a gift of his armour to the temple, and took in exchange, from where they hung on the temple walls, some weapons which were still preserved from the Trojan War. These were supposed to have been carried before him by his bodyguard when he went into battle.

Arrian then goes on to tell of how Alexander and his bosom friend Hephaestion made a pilgrimage to the tombs of Achilles and Patroclus, their heroic predecessors: 'One account is that Hephaestion laid a wreath on the tomb of Patroclus; another that

Alexander laid one on the tomb of Achilles, calling him a lucky man, in that he had Homer to proclaim his deeds and preserve his memory.'

Alexander and his troops then rejoined Parmenio and the rest of the army at Arisbe, near Abydos, before marching onward, as Arrian notes: 'From Troy Alexander marched to Arisbe, here his entire force had taken up position after crossing the Hellespont; next day he proceeded to Percote, and the day after passed Lampsacus', which had been captured from the Greeks the year before by the Persian general Memnon. As Alexander approached Lampsacus he was met by a delegation of the Greek townspeople, who persuaded him to spare the town, for Memnon and his troops had retreated to Dascylium, headquarters of Arsites, the Persian satrap of Phrygia. Alexander then headed eastward along the shore of the Marmara toward Dascylium.

Arsites had in the meanwhile sent out an appeal to the two other Persian governors in western Asia Minor: Spithridates, satrap of Ionia and Lydia, and Arsames, satrap of Cilicia, who assembled at Dascylium with their forces, including the Greek mercenaries commanded by Memnon. The Persians set up an entrenched camp on the east bank of the River Granicus, which Alexander would have to cross to attack Dascylium.

Parmenio tried to persuade Alexander not to make a direct assault across the river, given the strength of the Persian position. But Alexander ordered his troops across to charge the Persians arrayed on the east bank. He was in the thick of the battle and killed Mithridates, son-in-law of King Darius, after which he himself was unhorsed and narrowly escaped death twice. The Persians finally fled after suffering heavy loss of life, including Spithridates, who was killed when he was on the point of striking down Alexander. Memnon survived and lived to fight another day. Arrian says that 'Arsites escaped to Phrygia, where he is said to have died by his own hand, because the Persians held him responsible for the defeat.'

Alexander's march of conquest eventually took him as far as Transoxiana and the Indus valley, from where he returned to Persia at the beginning of 324 BC. The end came on the morning of 10 June 323 BC, about a month before Alexander's thirty-third birthday, when he passed away after he had been critically ill for ten days following a night of carousing with his companions.

The Greeks of Asia Minor were now free of Persian rule, more than two centuries after they had been conquered by Cyrus the Great, though it would soon be evident that they had again exchanged one master for another.

The Hellenistic period of Greek history begins with the death of Alexander, by which time Greek culture had spread from the Aegean as far as Afghanistan and the Indus valley. His vast empire was then divided up by his leading generals, the *Diadochi*, or Successors, most notably Antipator, Antigonus Monophthalmus (One-Eyed), Lysimachus, Seleucus and Ptolemy, who fought one another in an interminable series of wars that were continued by their sons, the *Epigoni*.

Ptolemy stole a march on his colleagues by making off with the embalmed remains of Alexander, whom he buried with divine honours at Memphis, while building a grandiose tomb at Alexandria. The *Diadochi* soon went to war with one another expanding their realms, a widespread conflict that went on for more than forty years, during which time the Greek cities in Asia Minor were mere pawns in the struggle for supremacy.

Antipater, who had been named by Alexander as his regent in Macedonia, continued to rule all of Greece except for Thrace, and when he died in 319 BC he was succeeded by his son Cassander. Thrace and north-western Asia Minor, including Troy and the Troad, were under the authority of Lysimachus, Antigonus governed Phrygia and western Asia Minor, Seleucus was satrap of Babylonia, and Ptolemy was satrap in Alexandria.

Ptolemy ruled from 323–283/282 BC, and in 304 BC he proclaimed himself King of Egypt, a title inherited by his son and successor Ptolemy II Philadelphus and all of his successors in the Ptolemaic dynasty down to Cleopatra, who died in 30 BC, by which time Egypt had been conquered by Rome. At its peak the Ptolemaic kingdom expanded beyond Egypt to include Libya, Ethiopia, Arabia Phoenicia, Coele (Southern) Syria, southern Asia Minor, and some of the Aegean islands.

Seleucus declared himself king in 312 BC, with the appellation Nicator (Victorious). Eventually he allied himself with Lysimachus against Antigonus, who was trying to reunify Alexander's empire under his son Demetrius Poliorcetes (Besieger of Cities). The allies defeated Antigonus in 301 BC at the Battle of Ipsus, in Phrygia, destroying his kingdom in Asia Minor, though his son Demetrius later became King of Macedon. Then Seleucus defeated and killed Lysimachus at the battle of Corupedium, near Magnesia ad Maeandrum in Ionia. This gave Seleucus control of Asia Minor, so that his kingdom now stretched from the Aegean to the River Indus.

Later that same year, when Seleucus invaded Thrace, he was assassinated by Ptolemy Keranus (Thunderbolt), a half-brother of Ptolemy II Philadelphus. Seleucus was succeeded by his son

Antiochus I Soter (Saviour), who renounced his father's ambitions in the West and focused his attention on Anatolia and Syria.

Meanwhile Demetrius Poliocetes had been succeeded as King of Macedon by his son, Antigonus II Gonatas. Thus by 281 BC, forty-two years after the death of Alexander, his empire was divided mainly into three parts, two of them ruled by *Epigoni*, sons of the *Diadochi*, the third by a grandson, Antigonus II. Eventually all these realms and those that succeeded them in Anatolia were absorbed by Rome and incorporated into the Roman province of Asia Minor, which came into being in 129 BC.

Meanwhile the ancient city of Troy, which was known as Ilion during the Hellenistic period and then under the Romans as Novum Ilium, continued to be a place of pilgrimage, visited or sent gifts by all of the conquerors who ruled in western Asia Minor from Xerxes, Alexander and the *Diadochi* to the Romans. The Romans considered Homeric Troy as the parent of Rome, which had been founded by Aeneas, leader of the Dardanians, son of Anchises and Aphrodite. The Julian family of the Julio-Claudian imperial dynasty traced their origin to Iulias, son of Aeneas.

Strabo, devotes most of Book 13 of his *Geography* to Troy and the Troad, including an account of the history of the ancient city and the surrounding region.

The site of ancient Troy was identified by most ancient Greek writers with the Hellenistic city of Ilion, on the Trojan plain some five kilometres south of the Hellespont and five kilometres inland from the Aegean. But Strabo held that the Homeric city was about five and a half kilometres farther inland. Strabo was here following Demetrius of Scepsis (fl. *c.* 214 BC), an ancient town in the Troad, who wrote a sixty-book work on the sixteen-line Catalogue of Ships in the *Iliad*. Demetrius says that Troy had been utterly destroyed at the end of the Trojan War and never rebuilt, and that Ilion was not the Homeric city, but a site about five and a half kilometres farther inland which he called 'Village of the Ilians'.

Strabo says that Ilion was restored by Lysimachus, who ruled in north-western Asia Minor after the fall of Antigonus, apparently fulfilling a promise that had been made by Alexander:

> But after his [Alexander's] death Lysimachus devoted special attention to the city, and built a city there and surrounded the city with a wall about forty stadia in circuit, and also incorporated into it the surrounding cities, which are now old and in bad plight. At that time he had already devoted attention to Alexandreia, which had indeed already been founded by Antigonus, and called Antigonia, but changed its name, for it

was thought to be a pious thing for the successors of Alexander to found cities bearing his name before they found cities bearing their own. And indeed the city endured and grew, and at present it not only has received a colony of Romans but is one of the notable cities of the world.

Alexandreia, which soon came to be known as Alexandria Troas, was built on the Aegean shore about halfway between the Hellespont and Cape Lekton, the south-westermost promontory of the Troad. During the Hellenistic era Alexandria Troas became the richest and most populous city in the Troad, for its strategic position near the entrance to the Hellespont made it a convenient port. During the reign of Augustus (r. 27 BC–AD 14) a Roman colony was established here, reaching the height of its prosperity in the time of Hadrian (r. 117–38), as evidenced by the huge gymnasium and baths built during his reign by Herodus Atticus, the principal extant monument in Alexandria Troas.

By the middle of the first century AD a small group of Christians had begun to gather in Alexandria Troas, one of at least a score of such communities known to have formed in Asia Minor at that time. These early Christian communities are mentioned in *Acts of the Apostles*, from which it is known that St Paul visited Alexandria Troas twice during his missionary journeys, probably during the years AD 48 and 53.

Alexandria Troas was still an important town at the beginning of the Byzantine era, when it is recorded as having the status of a bishopric. But eventually it disappeared from the pages of history, like most of the other ancient cities in the Troad. Eventually it fell into ruins, which were so impressive that many early travellers mistook Alexandria Troas for Troy. During the Turkish period the site was callled Eski (Old) Stamboul, the name by which it is still known.

Julius Caesar, who claimed to be a direct descendant of Aeneas, visited Troy in 48 BC and gave the city immunity from taxes. The Latin writer Lucan, in the *Pharsalia*, written in the first century AD, says that Caesar visited the site of Troy, which had been destroyed in 86 BC by the rebel Roman general Fimbria:

> He walked around what had once been Troy, now only a name, and looked for traces of the great wall which the god Apollo had built. But he found the hill clothed with thorny scrub and decaying trees, whose aged roots were embedded in the foundations ... even the ruins had been destroyed.

According to Walter Leaf, Julius Caesar's visit to Troy was 'the beginning of a new era of prosperity for Troy':

> The Romans for many generations fostered the town with privileges fiscal and religious, and made of it what it had never been in all its past city, a really large city. The old city of Hissarlik became merely the acropolis; the city itself spread far over the plateau to the northeast ... Stories were afloat that first Julius and afterwards Augustus had even contemplated making it the capital of the whole Roman Empire ... Nero extended the privileges of the town; Hadrian visited it in [AD] 124 and doubtless left traces in new buildings; Antoninus Pius confirmed its privileges, and Marcus Aurelius appears to have initiated new and splendid religious games. Caracalla in 214 figured as a new Alexander, running around the heroic tumuli and setting up a great bronze statue of Achilles.

After Constantine the Great became sole emperor in 324, he decided to establish his new capital near Troy, on the Sigeum ridge above the Aegean. But he soon changed his mind and chose the city of Byzantium on the Bosphorus, which was rebuilt in 330 as the much larger city of Constantinople. Constantine made Christianity the state religion of his realm, which in time came to be called the Byzantine Empire. Constantine's son and successor Constantius continued the pro-Christian policy of his father, and in 356 he issued an edict closing all pagan temples in the empire and banning all pagan practices.

Constantius' successor, Julian the Apostate (r. 361–4), son of a half-brother of Constantine, openly expressed his paganism as soon as he became emperor. He issued decrees that permitted public observations of all religious ceremonies, pagan as well as Christian and Jewish. When he reorganized the government he excluded Christians in his appointments, influencing many to renounce their fate. But after his death in 364 the state religion once again became Christian, and remained so for the rest of Byzantine history.

Six years before Julian became emperor, when he held the rank of Caesar, he paid a visit to Troy. According to an epistle of Julian, his guide was the Christian Bishop Pegasius, who showed him 'a sanctuary of Hector, where a bronze statue stands in a small chapel. Opposite to him they have put up Achilles in the open air.' Julian was astonished to find that a fire was still burning in Hector's shrine, and when he asked Pegasius about this the bishop answered 'What is there unbecoming if they do homage to a good man, their citizen, just as we do to the martyrs?'

Julian then asked to be taken to the temple of Athena, and
Pegasius took him there and also to the Achilleum, the tomb of
Achilles:

> He also most willingly led the way, opened to me the temple, and, as
> if calling me to witness, he showed me all the statues perfectly well
> preserved ... The same Pegasius followed me also to the Achilleum,
> and showed me the sepulchre unhurt, for I had heard also that he
> had excavated this tomb. But he approached it even with great
> reverence. All this I saw myself. But I have heard from those who are
> now inimically disposed against him, that in secret he prays to and
> worships the sun.

Virtually nothing is known of the further history of Novum
Ilium. The scholarly emperor Constantine VII Porphyryogenitus (r.
911–59), notes in his book on the organization of the Byzantine state
that most cities in the Troad were bishoprics, listing Adramyttene,
Assos, Gargara, Antandros, Alexandria Troas, Ilium, Dardanus, and
Lampsacus, while Parium was the seat of an archbishop.

J. M. Cook, in his book on the Troad (1973), gives a summary of
the coins found on the site of Ilium, which had been thought to have
been abandoned after a devastating earthquake around the year 500:

> One statistic is provided by the catalogue of the Troy excavation
> coins. In this we find nearly 120 coins covering the half century to
> 450, six of the period 457–518, and one of Justinian [r. 527–65]; the
> four and a half centuries that follow are represented only by a single
> coin of the early ninth century – a sufficient evidence that city life
> had come to an end.

And thus the ancient city of Troy disappeared from history, until
it was rediscovered by European travellers and then unearthed by
archaeologists, revealed in successive layers dating back to Homeric
times and beyond, to the earliest occupation of the site in the night
of time.

6

The Rediscovery of Ancient Troy

The general site of Troy was never forgotten, and the accounts of early travellers show that the ruins of Ilium were still pointed out as the site of the Homeric city, though often it was probably the more impressive remains of Alexandria Troas that they saw.

The most remarkable of all the early travellers was the humanist and antiquarian Cyriacus of Ancona (1391–1453/5). He came from a prominent family of Ancona merchants, and embarked on his first voyage at the age of nine in the company of his maternal uncle. He travelled at first on family business, and then to satisfy his own curiosity, his voyages taking him all around the eastern Mediterranean, recording in his journal detailed descriptions of ancient monuments, illustrated by his drawings, along with records of ancient inscriptions in Greek and Latin.

Cyriacus made his first voyage to Constantinople in 1418 and his second in 1425. During the interim he was employed by the Ottoman sultan Murat II in his unsuccessful siege of Constantinople in 1422. He explored the Troad and the Asian coast of the Sea of Marmara in 1431 and 1444. On the latter journey, after having explored the Trojan plain, Cyriacus took a boat to Imbros and saw the summit of Mt Fengari on Samothrace looming above it. This reminded him of the passage in Book 13 of the *Iliad*, where Poseidon observes the fighting on the Trojan plain from the highest summit of Samothrace, which Homer calls Samos in Thrace. Cyriacus noted his observation in his copy of Strabo's *Geography*, now preserved in the Eton College Library, for it was another piece of evidence proving that Homer's epic was based on the actual topography of the Trojan plain and its surroundings.

Cyriacus then went to work for Murat II again, this time as tutor in Latin and Greek for his son Mehmet, who would succeed his father in 1451 as Sultan Mehmet II, when he was nineteen years old. Mehmet besieged and captured Constantinople in 1453, bringing to an end the long history of the Byzantine Empire. Cyriacus was still with Mehmet during the siege and may have remained in the city for a short time after the conquest, when Mehmet began transforming Constantinople into the new Ottoman capital of Istanbul. But Cyriacus then retired to Cremona, where he died within the next two years.

Cyriacus seems to have taught Mehmet to read Homer, which led the sultan to visit both Athens and Troy in the course of his campaigns of conquest. His contemporary Greek biographer Kritoboulos of Imbros describes the sultan's visit to Troy in 1462:

> Sultan Mehmet walked around the periphery of the city, inspected its ruins, saw its topographical advantages, and its favorable position close to the sea and the opposite continent. Then he asked to be shown the tombs of the heroes Achilles, Hector and Ajax, and other great conquerors before him, he made sacrifices at the tomb of Achilles, congratulating him on his great deeds, having found the poet Homer to celebrate them. Then, it is said, he pronounced these words: 'It is to me that Allah has given to avenge this city and its people ... Indeed it was the Greeks who devastated this city, and it is their descendants who after so many years have paid me the debt which their boundless pride had contracted – and then after to us – the people of Asia.'

One of the earliest European travellers to search for the site of ancient Troy was Richard Pococke, who explored the north-western Troad in July 1740. J. M. Cook writes that Pococke 'sought locations inland for both Ilium and the Homeric Troy; and he diffidently recognized the tumuli of Ajax, Achilles and other heroes'.

Modern topographical study of the Troad is said to begin with Jean Baptiste Lechavalier, who in November 1785 first visited the Troad, with the *Iliad* in hand. On this visit Lechavalier convinced himself that the site of Troy was not near the Aegean but up the valley of the Scamander at a place under Ballı Dağ (Honey Mountain) called Bunarbashi, or Pınarbaşı in modern Turkish, meaning 'Source of the Springs'. The eponymous springs are known locally as Kırk Göz, or 'Forty Eyes', which Lechavalier thought to be the hot and cold springs at Troy mentioned by Homer. This is in the dramatic scene in Book 22 of the *Iliad*, where Achilles pursues Hector as he flees around the walls of Troy.

Edward Daniel Clarke, a Fellow of Jesus College, Cambridge, disagreed with Lechavalier's opinion that Bunarbashi was the site of Homeric Troy. He and his pupil John Martin Cripps spent a fortnight touring the Troad in March 1801, travelling inland as far as the site of ancient Scepsis on Kurşunlu Dağ, and then went on to ascend Mt Ida. During the course of this exploration, according to J. M. Cook, 'By an early application of sound archaeological method Clarke and Cripps discovered the site of Ilion.' Clarke wrote of their discovery in volume II of his *Travels in Various Countries of Europe, Asia and Africa* (1812).

The site was known locally as Hisarlık, 'the fortress', because of the ruined walls that covered it, at the western tip of a low ridge some six kilometres from the Aegean across the Trojan plain. When Clarke and Cripps visited the site the local villagers were carrying away the foundation blocks of the ancient walls, which they were using to build their own houses. Clarke concluded that this 'ancient citadel on its elevated spot of ground, surrounded on all sides by a level plain, was evidently the remains of New Ilium'.

The first actual archeological excavation on the Troad was carried out by the antiquarian Johan Georg von Hahn, Austrian consul-general for eastern Greece on the island of Syros. Having been convinced by Lechavalier's arguments that Bunarbashi was the site of Homeric Troy, von Hahn carried out excavations on the summit of Ballı Dağ in the spring of 1864. He unearthed a citadel, but was disappointed to find that it dated from the classical era and not the late Bronze Age. He extended his excavations on the slopes of Ballı Dağ toward Bunarbashi, but he could find no trace of a lower town of Troy, and so he abandoned the project and returned to Syros. J. M. Cook writes that von Hahn was so disillusioned that 'he concluded that there had never been a historical Troy and that the story of the *Iliad* was an old Nordic saga'.

Charles Maclaren, an amateur geologist and founder of *The Scotsman*, the Scottish national newspaper, wrote a thesis in 1822 entitled *A Dissertation on the Topography of the Plain of Troy*, which argued that the site of Homeric Troy must be the same as that of Ilion and Novum Ilium. Maclaren's thesis was soundly based on ancient sources, but he had not been to the Troad and his dissertation did not receive wide attention.

Maclaren first visited the Trojan plain in 1847, and in 1863, at the age of eighty, he finally published the work that gave his views the wide attention they merited: *The Plain of Troy Described*, which, as J. M. Cook remarks, 'advanced the claims of Hisarlık at the same time as von Hahn's excavations depressed those of Lechavalier's site'.

The first excavation on the Hisarlık mound was done by Frank Calvert, of an English family who had been in the Troad since the early nineteenth century. The Calvert family had an estate called Thymbra Farm at Akça Köy, about eight kilometres up the Scamander from Hisarlık. Frank's brother Frederick was British consul in Çanakkale in 1846–62, while his brother James was American consul, a position that he later passed on to Frank. Frank Calvert had originally believed in Lechavalier's theory that Homeric Troy was at Ballı Dağ, and had helped von Hahn in his excavations. But the results of these excavations led Calvert to change his mind in 1864 and he turned his attention to Hisarlık, particularly after he read the dissertation by Charles Maclaren, who undoubtedly met the Calverts when he first visited the Troad in 1847. He had made a trial sounding at Hisarlık that indicated extensive ancient remains on the mound.

Frank Calvert bought a field on the northern half of the Hisarlık mound in 1865, and began to excavate there in the hope of finding Homer's Troy. He dug four trenches, uncovering remains of what he identified as the Temple of Athena and the 'Lysimachian' wall, bringing to light Roman, Hellenistic and prehistoric pottery. He also exposed strata dating from the Bronze Age directly below the Temple of Athena.

Calvert knew that a systematic excavation of the site would require more funds than he had available. He had in 1853 met Charles Newton of the British Museum, who would later excavate the famous Mausoleum at Halicarnassus. At that time Calvert took Newton to both Bunarbashi and Hisarlık as possible sites for Troy. They rejected Bunarbashi because they could find no surface shards of ancient pottery, but at Hisarlık Calvert showed Newton the extensive walls and other remains that were still visible on the mound, and they agreed that this was indeed a possible site of the Homeric city. They corresponded regularly, and after Calvert reported on his first trial excavation at Hisarlık in 1863 to Newton they formulated a plan to have the British Museum support the project, but in the end nothing came of it. Thus the project was left to Heinrich Schliemann, who first visited the Troad in August 1868.

Heinrich Schliemann (1822–90) says in the biographical opening chapter of his *Ilios, City and Country of the Trojans* (1880) that when he was eight years old he first read about Homer and decided that one day he would excavate Troy. He spent his early manhood as a businessman in order to accumulate enough money to enable him to realize his childhood dream.

When Schliemann arrived in the Troad he began by having exploratory trenches dug at Lechavalier's site on Ballı Dağ. The results were unsatisfactory, but then he met Frank Calvert, who convinced him that Hisarlık was the site of Homeric Troy. As Schliemann wrote in his first book, *Ithaque, le Péloponnèse et Troie* (1869): 'After carefully examining the Trojan plain on two occasions, I fully agree with the convictions of this *savant* [Calvert], that the high plateau of Hisarlik is in the position of ancient Troy, and that this hill is the site of its Pergamos.'

Schliemann describes his first inspection of the mound at Hisarlık on 14 August 1868, when he was shown around it by Frank Calvert:

> The site fully agrees with the description Homer gives of Ilium and I will add that, as soon as one sets foot on the Trojan plain, the view of the beautiful hill of Hisarlik grips one with astonishment. That hill seems to be destined by nature to carry a great city ... there is no other place in the whole region to compare with it.

Schliemann was in the US throughout 1869, but he and his Greek wife Sophia returned to the Troad in April 1870 to make a preliminary excavation on the Hisarlık mound. Then in the years 1871–3 he carried out three major excavation campaigns, each about three months long, employing 80 to 160 workmen, all of them Greeks from the local villages, mostly from Yenişehir, Greek Neochorio, both of which mean 'New Town', though it is some 2,000 years old.

Carl Blegen, who excavated the mound at Hisarlık in the years 1932–8, describes Schliemann's first excavations there in 1871–3, beginning with the huge trench that still cuts through the archaeological site:

> The accumulation of debris that formed the mound of Hissarlik before the excavations was soon found by Schliemann to be enormously deep, more than 15 m. Since he started with the assumption, gained from Homer – that the town of Priam was the original establishment on the hill, he thought its ruins must lie at the bottom of the vast deposit. Schliemann therefore resolved to cut a huge trench, some 40 m. wide, straight across the middle of the mound from north to south and to clear away everything in that area that was superposed above the lowest stratum.

During the course of the 1871–3 excavations Schliemann soon became aware of the stratification of the site and he succeeded in identifying four successive strata, which he called 'Cities', below Hellenic Ilion. He claimed that Homeric Troy was the second layer from the bottom, a burnt stratum that he believed was the remains of the city of Priam destroyed by Agamemnon's army.

But there were two principal objections to Schliemann's claim, the first of which was the small extent of the city that he had identified as Homeric Troy, which was only 90 metres in diameter. The second objection was made by Frank Calvert in the Istanbul newspaper the *Levant Herald* on 4 February 1873, in which he noted that

> a most important link is missing between 1800 and 700 BC, a gap of over 1,000 years, including the date of the Trojan War, 1193–1184 BC, no relics of the intervening epoch having yet been discovered between that indicated by the prehistoric stone implements and that of pottery of the Archaic style.

Four months later, near the end of the 1873 excavation campaign, Schliemann made the first of his several discoveries of ancient treasures, known variously as the 'Great Treasure' or the 'Treasure of Priam', which he says he found in the 'House of the City King'.

The 'Great Treasure' contained a collection of jewellery that came to be known as the 'Jewels of Helen', including a magnificent gold diadem, earrings, and necklace, all of which Sophia was shown wearing in a famous photograph taken after Schliemann smuggled the 'Great Treasure' to Athens, which infuriated the Turkish authorities, and when he requested a permit to renew his excavation it was turned down. Only after paying a large bribe in 1876 did he receive permission, and he finally returned to the Troad to carry out two major campaigns in 1878–9.

During these two campaigns Schliemann examined the strata at Hisarlık more closely, and he identified two additional 'Cities'. One of these was in the prehistoric layer, temporarily making the burnt stratum, which he had identified as Homeric Troy, the third from the bottom rather than the second. The other, now the sixth from the bottom, he called the 'Lydian' city which, according to Strabo, had preceded Hellenic Ilion.

After the 1879 campaign he felt that his work at Hisarlık was complete, and he wrote the book that is considered to be his masterpiece: *Ilios, the City and Country of the Trojans* (1881). Schliemann was puzzled by the small size of the ancient city he had uncovered thus far, and in 1882 he resumed his excavations, now assisted by the young German architect and archaeologist Wilhelm Dörpfeld (1853–1940).

Dörpfeld continued to collaborate with him until Schliemann's death in 1890, not only at Troy but also at Mycenae and Tiryns. During that time Schliemann and Dörpfeld discovered two additional

'Cities' in the Hisarlık mound, making nine in all, numbering them upwards from the lowest and presumably the oldest.

Since the lowest layer, Troy I, yielded mostly crude objects of stone and bone, primitive pottery, and very little metal, principally copper, he concluded that he was mistaken in thinking that this was the Homeric city, which he now identified as the thick burned layer which he counted as the third from the bottom. Here he unearthed remains of what appeared to be a much higher culture, finding many objects of gold, silver, and copper or bronze, including one splendid hoard of weapons, vessels and ornaments.

A further revision was made when Dörpfeld pointed out to Schliemann that the 'Burnt City' represented what must have been the final phase of Troy II. Then in 1890 they discovered that yet another modification was necessary; for well outside the fortification wall of Troy II to the south they came upon a large building similar in plan to the throne rooms they had uncovered in the palaces at Mycenae and Tiryns.

Schliemann had first visited Mycenae in 1868, when the young man who took him to the site pointed out the citadel and the so-called Treasury of Atreus, associating both of them with Agamemnon. He returned there to excavate in 1876, when he also dug at Orchomenos and Tiryns.

Schliemann's excavation at Mycenae uncovered five shaft graves in a trench he dug just inside the massive Cyclopean defence wall of the citadel. The graves contained the remains of nineteen men and women and two infants, along with a profusion of gold and silver funerary objects, including bronze swords and daggers with golden hilts, their blades adorned with gold and silver inlay. The faces of the men were covered with gold-leaf death masks formed to show their features, including moustache and beard. One of these came to be known as the mask of Agamemnon, for Schliemann believed that the men were Agamemnon and his companions, as he claimed in his *Mycenae*, published in 1880.

Later studies showed that the shaft graves discovered by Schliemann date from the sixteenth century BC, three or four centuries earlier that the supposed time of Agamemnon. But Schliemann was satisfied that among the precious funerary offerings he had found in these graves there were depictions of weapons and other objects that Homer had described in the *Iliad*.

Schliemann and Dörpfeld paid a visit to Crete in the spring of 1886. They were met in Heraklion, the capital, by a local scholar named Minos Kalokairinos, who had made an excavation at Knossos five years before. Kalokairinos showed them the finds he had made, including a tablet with an inscription in Linear B, the first one known to have been discovered in modern times. He then took them out to Knossos, and what they saw there so excited Schliemann that he immediately wrote, in English, to his friend Max Müller in Oxford, in a letter dated 22 May 1886, in which he speculated on the possibility that the ruins at Knossos might be the remains of a civilization far more ancient than that of the Heroic Age.

Schliemann returned to Crete in the spring of 1889, trying to buy the site that he had seen with Kalokairinos. But he was unable to do so, and the following year he gave up and returned to the Troad, writing that at Knossos 'I hoped to discover the original home of Mycenaean civilization.'

Schliemann's belief that Knossos was the site of an ancient civilization far older than that of the Heroic Age was vindicated by Sir Arthur Evans, who began excavating there on 23 March 1900. During the nine weeks of the 1900 excavation, with a workforce of 50–180 men who dug up two acres, Evans uncovered the main part of the west wing of what he would call the Palace of Minos, which is today one of the major archaeological sites in the Aegean. Evans had discovered a previously unknown civilization, the Minoan, named for the legendary King Minos, who is mentioned in Book 19 of the *Odyssey*.

Evans discovered that the site at Knossos had been inhabited since the Neolithic period, perhaps since the end of the seventh millennium BC. Around 2600 BC there was a great migration of people from western Anatolia to Crete and the Cyclades, who brought with them Bronze Age culture, beginning what came to be known as the Minoan era. A profound change in the structure of Cretan society took place around 2000 BC, when the institution of kingship emerged, along with an hierarchical society and a civil service. This brought about the construction of buildings large enough to be called palaces, the largest of which were erected at Knossos, Phaestos and Mallia. This marks the beginning of the Protopalatial period, 2000–1700 BC, when the great palaces and lesser royal residences elsewhere formed the centre of sizeable towns, with Cretan ships carrying Minoan products to Troy and other places in western Asian Minor and as far abroad as Cyprus, Syria, Egypt, the Greek island of Cythera and the Lipari islands.

The Protopalatial period came to an end about 1700 BC, when all of the Minoan palaces on Crete were destroyed, along with their surrounding towns. This was probably due to a catastrophic earthquake, which is known to have caused widespread disasters throughout the eastern Mediterranean at that time. Soon afterwards new and grander palaces were built on the site of the older ones, beginning the Neopalatial period, 1700–1450 BC. The most majestic of these was the Palace of Minos at Knossos, where Evans discovered extraordinary frescoes depicting scenes of palace life in its golden age.

Around 1450 BC almost all of the Minoan palaces and their surrounding towns were destroyed by fire. Knossos was one of the few places that was not destroyed by fire, although the palace did suffer some damage. This catastrophe is attributed by some scholars to the colossal volcanic explosion that blew out the centre of the Cycladic island of Thera (Santorini), perhaps accompanied by an earthquake and huge tidal waves. Other authorities attribute the destruction to an invasion by the Mycenaean Greeks, who in any event were in control of Knossos by 1450 BC.

Around 1380 BC another widespread catastrophe occurred on Crete, perhaps an earthquake or a war or a combination of both, resulting in the final destruction of the great palace at Knossos. All of the other surviving palaces on Crete seem to have been destroyed at the same time, and none of them were ever rebuilt, bringing to an end the imperial era in Minoan history. When Evans unearthed the debris of this great conflagration at Knossos he discovered some 2,000 clay tablets inscribed in the script that came to be called Linear B, baked by the fire and thus preserved for posterity. Evans himself concluded that there was nothing in the archaeology of Knossos to indicate the arrival of a new people, i.e., the Mycenaean Greeks, since the Linear B script, which had also been found by Carl Blegen in 1939 during his excavation at Pylos, remained a mystery until it was deciphered in 1951–2 by Michael Ventris. As Ventris announced on the BBC Third Programme, reprinted in the *Listener* on 10 July 1952:

> During the last few weeks, I have come to the conclusion that the Knossos and Pylos tablets must, after all, be written in Greek – a difficult and archaic Greek, seeing that it is 500 years older than Homer and written in a rather abbreviated form, but Greek nevertheless.

Most Linear B inscriptions have been found in Knossos and Cydonia (Chania) in Crete, and in mainland Greece at Pylos, Mycenae and Thebes. The oldest of the inscriptions, from the archive in the Room of the Chariot Tablets at Knossos, has been dated by its associated pottery to 1425–1390 BC. The thousands of tablets seem to have been written in a relatively small number of 'hands', indicating that the script was used only by a guild of professional scribes who served in the bureaucracies of the kings in the great Mycenaean palaces. Once the palaces were destroyed, the Linear B script disappeared, and through the four or so centuries of the Dark

Ages the Greeks were illiterate until the emergence of the ancient Greek alphabetic language in the latter half of the eighth century BC. Meanwhile in 1888 Schliemann went to the south-western Peloponnesos looking for King Nestor's palace at 'sandy Pylos'. But although he discovered Mycenaean sherds there he found no royal graves nor did he find a trace of Nestor's palace.

Schliemann died in Naples on Christmas Day 1890, while Dörpfeld was at work completing his part of their joint work in the recent discoveries they had made. Dörpfeld returned to Hisarlık in the spring of 1893 and took charge of the renewed excavations, which were financed by Sophia Schliemann and Kaiser Wilhelm II. During the years 1893–4 he unearthed the massive fortifications of what is now known as Troy VII, dramatic evidence that this was in fact the city that Homer had described in the *Iliad*. Dörpfeld concluded his excavations at Hisarlık in the summer of 1894, convinced that he and Schliemann had discovered the Homeric city there.

After Dörpfeld's last excavation at Hisarlık in the summer of 1894, the site was untouched until 1932, when a team of American archaeologists from the University of Cincinnati began excavating under the direction of Carl Blegen. Blegen's team continued excavating at Hisarlık until 1938, but the outbreak of World War II the following year ended the project and delayed the publication of their findings until 1950.

Blegen summarized the results of the University of Cincinnati expedition, as well as earlier excavations dating back to 1870, in his *Troy and the Trojans*, first published in 1963. He and his colleagues were able to differentiate a total of forty-six substrata among the nine major layers. He noted:

> In broader terms ... it has now become clear that the layers and periods from Troy I to and including Troy V belong to an era that corresponds to the Early Aegean Bronze Age, while the beginning of Troy VI marks the sharp turn to the Middle Bronze Age ... With Troy VIIb2 ... we come to an abrupt change, apparently signaling the arrival of a new people. Exactly how long this régime survived is not yet known, but the site seems ultimately to have been abandoned and left deserted for some centuries and reoccupied about 700 BC by Hellenic colonists. The corresponding layer is called Troy VIII; and Troy IX designates the period and ruins of the Hellenistic and Roman city of Ilion.

Blegen's chronological table for the main strata from Troy I to the beginning of Troy VIII is: Troy I (3000–2500 BC); Troy II (2500–2200 BC); Troy III (2200–2050 BC); Troy IV (2050–1900 BC); Troy

V (1900–1800 BC); Troy VI (1800–1300 BC); Troy VIIa (1300–1260 BC); Troy VIIb1 (1260–1190 BC); Troy VIIb2 (1190–700 BC); Troy VIII (700 BC–).

Blegen concluded that the uppermost sub-layer of Troy VII, which he called Troy VIIa, represented the city that had been destroyed in the Trojan War, *c.* 1260 BC:

> Whatever the precise date, the destruction was undoubtedly the work of human agency, and it was accompanied by violence and by fire. A great mass of stones and crude brick, along with other burned and blackened debris, was heaped up over the ruined houses as well as in the streets, and once again the ground level rose appreciably. Amid the wreckage in House 700 – the first on the right inside the South Gate – were found fragments of a human skull; other bits, collected in the street outside the house, may have belonged to the same individual.

Blegen goes on to say that the shattered remains of other individuals were found in the ruins of other houses in this stratum, where

> the cumulative evidence seems to me to demonstrate that fighting and killing must have accompanied the destruction of Troy VIIa ... The fire-blackened wreckage and ruins of the settlement offer a vivid picture of the harsh fate ... meted out to a town besieged, captured and looted by implacable enemies.

A new excavation project was begun in 1982 by a team of German archaeologists from the University of Tübingen directed by Professor Manfred Korfmann (1942–2005), who in annual campaigns, over the next five years excavated sites around Beşik Tepe, a huge tumulus on the Aegean at the northern edge of Beşik Bay seven kilometres south-west of Hisarlık. The tumulus had been excavated in 1879 by Schliemann and again in 1924 by Dörpfeld, who had shown that an earlier prehistoric mound had been transformed into its present form, a conical tumulus, at some time in the late Bronze Age.

Korfmann's team found that Beşik Bay was the main harbour of Bronze Age Troy rather than the so-called Achaean Harbour on the Hellespont at the mouth of the Scamander. They also concluded that the tumulus is almost certainly the one that in the classical period was thought to be the tomb of Achilles, rather than the so-called Tumulus of Achilles below the northern end of the Sigeum ridge, some 9 km to the north of Beşik Bay.

Korfmann was able to determine the original seashore in the late Bronze Age, when Beşik Bay was more deeply indented and the tumulus stood on a promontory that projected nearly one and a half kilometres into the Aegean.

Korfmann's team found that the prehistoric levels of Beşik Tepe dated from the early Bronze Age (third millennium BC) and the Neolithic period (fifth millennium BC). They also unearthed a cemetery of the thirteenth century BC, as well as the settlement of Achilleion, dating from the seventh to sixth century BC. The cemetery, which was close to the ancient seashore, contained over fifty cremations and burials, with Mycenaean pottery and funerary offerings, including a sword, and five seal stones from mainland Greece. The question arose as to whether this was the burial ground of Agamemnon's army, or perhaps the cemetery of a Mycenaean mercantile colony, which was more likely since the remains included those of women and children.

Korfmann found that in the late Bronze Age the sea came some 500 metres farther into Beşik Bay than it does today. Behind the beach there was a freshwater lagoon 800 metres long and some 350 metres across, now silted up. Thus Beşik Bay was an ideal port, with a deeply indented harbour and a constant supply of fresh water. Ships harboured there while they waited for a favourable wind to sail up the Hellespont, as they did up until the early years of the twentieth century, or else they unloaded their goods for trans-shipment by land on the old track from Beşik Bay to Troy, as did Schliemann for his supplies and equipment.

Korfmann's studies have shown that the site at Beşik Bay was inhabited continuously from the third millennium BC to the medieval Byzantine era. It was almost certainly the site of Agamemnon's camp when the Achaeans were besieging Troy.

Then in 1988 the Turkish government gave Korfmann an exclusive licence to excavate the mound at Hisarlık, which had remained fallow for fifty years after the end of Blegens's dig. He organized an international team of archaeologists, mainly German, American and Turkish, which he continued directing until his death in 2005. The excavations continue annually in the summer months. The ancient structures that had been unearthed in previous excavations were restored, the lower town of Troy was explored and mapped, and a comprehensive geomorphological survey was made of the mound and the Trojan plain.

The excavations have led to a more detailed identification and dating of the 'Nine Cities' studied by Schliemann, Dörpfeld and Blegen, as well as widening the scope of the investigation. The dating of the various strata is somewhat different than those given by

Blegen, additional substrata have been identified, and Troy VIII and IX, the Greek and Roman cities, respectively, have been studied in more detail and dated more precisely. The dates now assigned to the main layers are: Troy I (3000–2500 BC); Troy II (2500–2300 BC); Troy III. IV. V (2300–1700 BC); Troy VI (1700–1250 BC); Troy VIIa (1250–1180 BC); Troy VIIb (1180–1000 BC); Troy VIII (1000–85 BC); Troy IX (85 BC–AD 400 or 600).

Troy I was a mere village, with a diameter of about ninety metres, surrounded by a roughly-built stone wall two and a half metres thick which was periodically rebuilt and strengthened, with its main gateway on the south side, which was only two metres wide, flanked by massive towers. The scanty remains of the defence wall, founded on bedrock, were first uncovered by Schliemann when he dug his great North-South Trench. During all phases of Troy I the interior of the citadel was occupied by free-standing houses of various shapes and sizes, almost all of which had a single room with a doorway. None of the houses appear to have had windows; they had flat roofs of clay and thatch. They seem to have been arranged in a regular system of alignment, but there is no evidence of streets, nor of roads leading in from the gateways.

Korfmann and his colleagues reached much the same conclusions about the inhabitants of Troy I as had Blegen and his group: 'The people of Troy I were engaged in farming, animal husbandry and fishing, and they had cultural connections with the coastal regions of the northern Aegean and the Sea of Marmara that extended far into southern Europe and Anatolia.'

Troy II began, as Blegen notes, 'with a complete reconstruction of the citadel after the disaster that had brought the First Settlement to its end. There is no evidence of a break or of any appreciable chronological gap; on the contrary the culture of Troy I seems to pass with uninterrupted continuity into that of Troy II.'

Troy II was surrounded by a defence wall with a circumference of some 330 metres, only slightly larger than Troy I. The wall was more massive than that of Troy I, with which it was in large part incorporated on its northern side. The two surviving gateways, on the south-east and south-west, are described by Korfmann and Mannsperger:

> The southeast and southwest gates have typical entrance chambers, and leading up to the southwest gate is a steep, paved ramp with a parapet. The interior is separated off by a further gateway, Propylon IIC, and a roofed colonnade. Within lie large long-houses – the 'megaron' style of building, thought to be the antecedent of the Greek 'temple in antis'.

Opposite the propylon, or inner gateway, is the largest of the megara within the citadel, measuring *c.* 30 metres by 14 metres. The great megaron, which faced south-east, was preceded by a large portico, approximately square in plan, which led into a large hall of state, which may have had one or two wooden columns to support the roof. This is believed to have been the throne room of the king. On either side there were structures of almost identical plan, but built on a much more modest scale. These two buildings probably provided living and sleeping quarters for the royal family. The other megara in the citadel were probably also used by the king.

Korfmann and Mannsperger, who refer to the ancient city as Troia, conclude from their excavations that the citadel of Troy II was probably reserved for the ruler and the aristocracy, while the rest of the populace dwelt in the areas lower down outside the walls.

Both Blegen and Korfmann agreed that Troy VI represents a complete and striking break with the past. According to Korfmann and Mannsperger:

> A completely new princely or royal citadel was built covering an area of 20,000 sq. m. In size, and probably in importance, it surpassed the citadel previously known at Hisarlık and all others so far investigated in western Asia Minor ... The fortifications are in a new style 552 metres long and technically superior, with gently sloping walls of ashlar masonry with offsets and massive towers. The walls are four to five metres thick and more than six metres high ... the principal gate lying to the South, flanked by a tower ... Behind the citadel wall, buildings in the interior were placed on concentric terraces rising up towards the centre of the citadel. There were large free-standing buildings (including megara), sometimes with two storeys; but these are only preserved around the edge of the acropolis.

Blegen writes of what was undoubtedly the most significant novelty found in the excavation of Troy VI:

> That was the horse, whose bones were not found by the Cincinnati Expedition in any of the earlier layers. In the stratum representing the first phase of the Sixth Settlement horse bones came to light, and henceforth they continued to occur more or less frequently in all subsequent strata. The newcomers who at the start of the Middle Bronze Age assumed domination over the site must have brought along the horse, an advantage that must have given them superiority over the Trojans of the Early Bronze Age.

Korfmann's excavation at Hisarlık began with a search for the lower town of Troy VI below the citadel.

> Its existence has long since been demonstrated, and it is now known that it is bordered by a defensive installation *c.* 400 m. to the South of the citadel. Impressive wooden structures have been discovered. With a settlement covering an area of nearly 200,000 sq. m., Troia is now ten times larger than previously supposed. The population has been estimated at *c.* 7000. These findings place Troia among the leading trading and palatial cities of Asia Minor and the Near East in this period. Troia is linked into this trading network at several levels.

Both Blegen and Korfmann concluded that Troy VI was destroyed in a catastrophic earthquake, and that the city was immediately rebuilt to create the settlement known as Troy VIIa. As Korfmann and Mannsperger write of the transition from Troy VI to Troy VIIa, which they date to the period 1250–1180 BC:

> The remains of houses of Troia VI, together with parts of the citadel walls, were repaired and reused. There is no cultural break between Troia VI and Troia VIIa, but the buildings have a clear arrangement and are noticeably smaller and more cramped. There is an increase in the population, and in the number of storage vessels, both inside the settlement and probably also in the settlement around. Mycenaean pottery continued to be used. The American excavators [the Cincinnati Expedition] equate the Troia VIIa settlement, which was destroyed by fire, with the 'Troia' or 'Ilios' of the Iliad. The interpretation is not undisputed.

The new Greek city of Ilion, Troy VIII, was dated by Korfmann and his collaborators to the period 1000–85 BC. According to Korfmann and Mannsperger, 'the mostly abandoned site was resettled by Greeks from Asia Minor':

> Remains of the Troia VI/VII monuments were incorporated in the newly erected fortification walls and houses. At first it was a modest settlement, but later, and especially from the beginning of the Third Century BC, there was deliberate veneration of the 'Holy City of Ilion,' with the building of a sanctuary of Cybele outside to the Southwest, and of a temple to Athena inside the citadel ... When the temple was built, if not before, the central and most elevated buildings of Troia VII and Troia VI were cut away. To the South a lower town of regular design extended over and among the ruins

of the lower town of Troia VI/VII. In 85 BC the site was suddenly destroyed by the Romans.

The Roman city of Novum Ilium, Troy IX, was dated by Korfmann's team to the period 85 BC–AD 400 or 600, when it seems to have been destroyed in a powerful earthquake. The temple of Athena was rebuilt, probably by the emperor Augustus, who venerated Troy as the home of his supposed ancestor Aeneas, the progenitor of the Julio-Claudian line. Korfmann and Mannsperger describe the remains of the temple and other extant remnants of the Roman city:

> Of this monument there survive only long sections of the massive foundations supporting the porticoes and surrounding wall of the 9500 sq. m. rectangular sacred precinct; on the southern slope of the ruins of 'sacred Ilios,' altars and an assembly-hall, also a small covered theatre (the Odeion) from the period of Augustus but rebuilt under Hadrian; not far from these a possible sports-and-baths complex with mosaic floors (no longer preserved); and a large theatre set in a natural hollow to the Northeast of the temple mount. Ilium received generous patronage from Rome until the Third Century AD. The lower town was rebuilt and several times enlarged following the traditional insula-system, and was enclosed by a city wall 3.5 km long.

Such is the story of the rediscovery of ancient Troy, at least thus far. As Michael Wood writes at the end of the second edition of *In Search of the Trojan War* (1996): 'It is of course premature to suggest that the long search for the historicity of Troy and the Trojan War may be nearing a climax; but we may now be reaching the point where the intersection of history and myth can be firmly delineated.'

7

Troy and the Troad

I first visited the site of ancient Troy in April 1961, on my spring vacation at Robert College in Istanbul, where I had started teaching the previous September. My wife Toots (Dolores) and I and our three small children, Maureen, Eileen and Brendan, set out from Istanbul aboard a ship of the Turkish Maritime Lines, which brought us to the port of Çanakkale on the Asian shore of the Dardanelles, the Greek Hellespont. We were accompanied by my student Andreas Dimitriades, an ethnic Greek with Turkish citizenship, who had decided to join us at the last moment, when he learned that we were going to visit Troy and go on from there to look at other Greek archaeological sites along the Aegean coast of Asia Minor.

Tourism had not yet begun in Turkey, and so we had the site of Troy all to ourselves, except for a Turkish gendarme who was guarding the ruins. I had reread the *Iliad* in preparation for our visit, as well as the works of the archaeologists who had studied the site up to that time.

It was a beautiful spring day, and after we explored the ruins we had a picnic under a valonia oak on the peak of the Hisarlık mound, which was still deeply scarred by Schliemann's excavation trenches. The mound commanded a sweeping view to the north-west, the noonday sun glinting on what Homer called the 'lovely waters' of the Skamandros as it meandered through the 'blossoming meadow' of the Trojan plain, on its way to join the 'swift flowing' Hellespont just above the Asian promontory at Kum Kale, where the strait joins the Aegean.

A short way to the south of Kum Kale we could see two conical mounds standing close by one another near the Aegean shore. I realized that these were the tumuli that Schliemann had identified as the tombs of Achilles and Patroclus. Andreas and I decided that we would hike out across the plain to Kum Kale to have a close look at the tumuli, while Toots watched the children as they played among the ruins on the mound. I estimated from my map that Kum Kale was about six kilometres distant, which shouldn't take us much more than an hour. But it took at least twice as long because our way was blocked by the Scamander, which we finally managed to cross near Kum Kale on a primitive Tarzan-like bridge made from two cables, one to tightrope walk on and the other to grasp hand over hand.

We found the tumuli about a kilometre south of Kum Kale, and we stopped to rest at the one that Schliemann had identified as the tomb of Achilles, which was surrounded by the turbaned tombstones of an old Turkish graveyard.

While we were examining the tumulus we were startled to hear the sound of approaching hoof-beats, and then we saw half-a-dozen horsemen approaching us from the ridge that parallels the Aegean shore between Kum Kale and the Sigeum promontory, one of the landmarks in the topography of Homeric Troy.

We walked out to the road to meet the horsemen, who bade us welcome and asked us who we were and what we were doing. Andreas told them that I was an American professor and that he was my student, explaining that we were exploring the surroundings of ancient Troy. The oldest of the horsemen, who appeared to be in his mid-seventies, knew that Troy was an ancient Anatolian city which had been conquered by the Greeks, or so he had been told at school. He said that he and his companions were from the village of Yenişehir, and that in his youth at least half of his neighbours had been Greeks. He told us that he had always gotten along well with his Greek neighbours and had often been invited to join them at *paniyeria*, their religious festivals. But they had all left in 1923, during the population exchange that followed the Turkish War of Independence, in which he himself had fought, as he told us proudly. Pointing toward the Hisarlık mound, he said that 'The Greeks conquered Troy long ago but we drove them away, and now Anatolia is ours.'

The old man then said that they had work to do and would be off, and he wished us well on our way home. After he and his companions left, Andreas and I rested for a while beside the mound before we started back to Hisarlık, reflecting on our encounter.

I recalled Schliemann noting that he hired 100 Greek workmen from Yenişehir and two other nearby villages to excavate the mound at Hisarlık in 1871, noting that 'Turkish workmen were not to be had, for they were at present occupied with field work.' He complained that the work was often interrupted 'owing to the various Greek festivals, for even the poorest Greek of this district would not work on a festival even if he could earn 1000 francs in an hour'. Elsewhere he remarked on his amazement that the Greeks, after three centuries of Turkish domination, still preserved their national language intact. But now, less than a century later, the Greeks were all gone, though they were still remembered in Yenişehir. Thus at the tomb of Achilles I felt that I was in touch with the beginning and ending of the Greek presence in Asia Minor, spanning more than three millennia, during which much of Anatolia was Hellenized before the tide of history turned with the Turkish conquest.

The next day we hired a little fishing boat in Çanakkale, so that we could travel down the European side of the Dardanelles to the Aegean and then back along the Asian shore. We crossed from Çanakkale, Greek Abydos, to Kilitbahir 'Lock of the Sea', the picturesque fortress built by Mehmet II just before his conquest of Constantinople in 1452, one of the Inner Fortresses with which he closed off the Hellespont before his siege of the city. From there we travelled along the shore of the Gallipoli peninsula, passing the towering Turkish war memorial to their soldiers who fell in the Gallipoli campaign in 1915. We went as far as Seddülbhir, 'Barrier of the Sea', built in 1659 as one of the two Outer Fortresses to close off the entrance to the Dardanelles, the other fort being Kum Kale, 'Sand Castle', on the Asian shore, both of which had been badly damaged during the Gallipoli campaign.

We crossed to Kum Kale, where since antiquity there has been a lighthouse to mark the entrance to the Hellespont, the other being at Cape Helles at the tip of the Gallipoli peninsula. Aeschylus, in his tragedy *Agamemnon*, describes how Clytemestra received news of the fall of Troy through a series of fire signals flashed all the way from the Hellespont to Mycenae.

We then started up the Asian shore of the strait, passing a marshy estuary just to the east of Kum Kale where the Scamander and then the Simoeis flow into the Hellespont. Strabo writes of the estuary in his description of the first stretch of the Asian coast of the Hellespont, from Kum Kale to Rhoeteium, some eight kilometres from the Aegean, noting that we pass

> the Harbour of the Achaeans and the Achaean Camp and Stomalimne [Mouth of the marsh], as it is called, and the mouths of the Scamander; for after the Simoeis and the Scamander meet in the plain, they carry down great quantities of alluvium, silt up the coast, and form a blind mouth, lagoons, and marshes.

This is where the Achaeans are supposed to have landed and set up their camp when they began the siege of Troy, although Korfmann and his colleagues claim that the landing-place and campsite were at Beşik Bay on the Aegean.

This stretch of the Dardanelles is where most early travellers had their first view of the Trojan plain. Strabo writes that 'This is called the Trojan Plain in the special sense of the term; and here it is that we see pointed out the places named by the poet.'

Beyond the estuary we passed a tumulus known locally as In Tepe. Early travellers tended to identify this with the tomb of Telamonian Aias. The supposed tomb of Aias was dedicated as a *heroon*, the shrine of a hero who has taken his place with the gods. Strabo says that near Rhoetium, there is

> a low-lying shore on which are a tomb and statue of Aias, and also a statue of him, which was taken up by Antony and carried off to Egypt; but Augustus Caesar gave it back again to the Rhoeteians, just as he gave back other statues to their owners. For Antony took away the finest dedications from the most famous temples, to gratify the Egyptian woman [Cleopatra], but Augustus gave them back to the gods.

The emperor Hadrian made a pilgrimage to the shrine of Aias during his tour of Asia Minor in AD 124. He found that the waters of the Hellespont had worn away part of the tumulus, exposing the whitened bones of a gigantic man, which he kissed reverentially and had reburied under a new tumulus on higher ground, the one standing there today. The tumulus was excavated in 1879 by Schliemann, who dated it to the Hadrianic era (AD 117–138), but he also found evidence that the mound was probably erected on the site of an earlier *heroon*. Close to the tumulus Schliemann discovered 'a mutilated statue of a warrior, draped and of a colossal size'. This was probably the cult statue of Ajax that had been removed by Antony and returned by Augustus. The sculpture has since disappeared, probably used by locals for building material or burned to make lime, the fate of so many statues of the Graeco-Roman world.

Five kilometres farther up the strait we passed a promontory called Baba Kale. This has been identified as the site of Rhoeteium, which in the classical period was one of the richest towns on the Hellespont, as evidenced by the large tribute it was assessed by the Delian Confederacy in 425 BC. Strabo says of Ilium that 'When the city was wiped out, its territory was divided up between the inhabitants of Sigeum and Rhoeteium and several other neighbouring peoples, but the territory was given back when the place was refounded. Archaeological excavations have revealed that the site of Rhoeteium was inhabited from *c.* 700 BC up until the beginning of the Roman era, but there is virtually nothing to be seen there today.

Another three kilometres up the coast brought us to a small cape which is near the site of ancient Ophrynium, whose few scattered remnants are in an old Turkish graveyard overlooking the Dardanelles. Strabo mentions it briefly, writing that 'Near by [to Rhoeteium] is Ophrynium, near which, in a conspicuous place, is the sacred precinct of Hector.'

An archaeological exploration of the site has revealed foundations of ancient structures, along with potsherds and other objects dating back as far as *c.* 600 BC, as well as bronzes of the early Byzantine era. But there is no trace whatsoever of a shrine of Hector, whose supposed tumulus here was still pointed out to travellers as late as the seventeenth century AD.

Five kilometres farther along we passed a promontory that has been identified as the site of ancient Dardania. The city was named for Dardanos, son of Zeus and Electra, who was the founder of the Trojan royal family. According to ancient tradition, it was the first city built in the Troad, giving its name to the surrounding region of Dardania and ultimately to the Dardanelles. Dardanos is mentioned in Book 20 of the *Iliad*, where Aeneas addresses Achilles before they do battle, telling him of his ancestry: 'First of all Zeus who gathers the clouds had a son, Dardanos/who founded Dardania, since there was no sacred Ilion/made a city on the plain to be a centre of peoples,/but they lived yet in the underhills of Ida with all her waters.'

Pottery sherds found on the site range in date from the early Bronze Age to the Roman period. Otherwise virtually nothing remains of the ancient city other than a burial mound known as the Dardanus Tumulus. Funerary objects found in the tomb range in date from the fourth to second century BC.

We then rounded the point known as Kephez Burnu, formerly called Cape Dardanus, bringing us into the broad bay just to the south of Çanakkale. There the Inner Castles at Kilitbahir and Çanakkale came into view at the Narrows, framing the stupendous spectacle of the Hellespont surging past Cape Nagara between the converging continents of Europe and Asia.

The following day all three of our children became quite ill and a local doctor examined them and said they had come down with scarlet fever, and so Toots had to stay with them in an isolation ward in the Çanakkale hospital for several days. After we took them to the hospital Andreas and I hired a jeep for the following day to explore the Troad.

We set out very early the next day and made our first stop at Ezine, the main town in the interior of the Troad, on the Akçin Çay, the principal tributary of the Scamander, whose sources are on the northern and western slopes of Mt Ida. Here we were in the heart of Homeric Dardania, the region listed in the Catalogue of Trojans as being ruled by Aeneas, who in Virgil's *Aeneid* became the founder of Rome.

As we crossed the bridge over the river we saw a crowd gathered on the bank and so we went over to join them. They had just pulled from the river a huge ancient relief, showing a group of Roman soldiers being reviewed by their commander. The townspeople at first thought that we were archaeologists from the museum in Çanakkale, but Andreas told them who we were and said that I thought the relief dated from the Roman period. The relief is now in the Istanbul Archaeological Museum, and is identified as a work of the imperial Roman era.

We then continued our journey, leaving the main road and taking a dirt track to the village of Behramkale on the southern coast of the Troad. This is the site of ancient Assos, first excavated in 1881–3 by an American expedition sponsored by the antiquarian Society of Boston, with J. T. Clarke and F. H. Bacon directing the excavations. Most of the antiquities found by the American expedition have been on exhibit for more than a century at the Boston Museum of Fine Art, as well as a few at the Louvre and the Istanbul Archaeological Museum. As a result, Assos was well-known in the West, though seldom visited until the beginning of tourism in Turkey, and it is now one of the most popular sites on the Aegean coast. When Andreas and I signed the visitor's book we found the names to be few and far between, and ours were the first in several years.

The site of ancient Assos has been restudied extensively since our first visit, with a Turkish team working on the acropolis and French archaeologists excavating in the lower city, which is on the seaward slope below the sheer north face of the great rock on which the city was founded.

The American expedition unearthed objects on the acropolis indicating that the site was first occupied in the early Bronze Age. Clark identified this Bronze Age settlement with the city of Pedasos mentioned by both Homer and Strabo. Homer mentions this city in Book 6 of the *Iliad*, where he says that 'the lord of men, Agamemnon, brought death to Elatos,/whose home had been on the shores of Satnioesis' lovely waters,/sheer Pedasos'.

He also refers to Pedasos in Book 21, where he speaks of Altes, king of the Leleges, allies of the Trojans, whose daughter Laothoë was one of Priam's wives: 'Altes, lord of the Leleges, whose delight is in battle,/and holds headlong Pedasos on the river Satnioeis./His daughter was given to Priam, who had many wives beside her.'

Archaeological evidence indicates that the city of Assos whose ruins we see today was founded in the seventh century BC. According to Strabo, who quotes earlier Greek historians, Assos was founded by Aeolians from Methymna, a city on the northern tip of Lesbos, which can be seen just across the strait, the present Greek town of Molivos.

The most illustrious period in the history of Assos came in the years 347–344 BC, when Aristotle directed a school of philosophy here under the aegis of the eunuch Hermeias, a benevolent despot known as the Tyrant of Atarnaeus, who had studied in Athens under Plato.

The defence walls of Assos are among the most impressive in Asia Minor, dating mostly from the mid-fourth century BC. They were originally about five kilometres in circumference, of which about half the circuit remains standing. At the peak of the acropolis is the temple of Athena, dating from 530 BC, one of the earliest in Asia Minor. The acropolis is 236 metres above the sea below. It commands a magnificent view that on one side ranges across the southern Troad to Mt Ida, while on the other it looks across the Adrymettene Gulf to Lesbos and the Aeolian coast.

After leaving Assos we drove westward on a rough track along the coast to Lekton (Lectum), known in Turkish as Baba Burnu, the cape that forms the south-western corner of the Troad. When we reached Baba Burnu the people in the tiny hamlet there crowded around us, and we were told that outsiders rarely came to their village. A young man offered to sell me a terracotta doll which appeared to be Roman, but I turned him down because Turkey had very strict laws concerning antiquities, even the most minor.

Strabo refers to Cape Lectum several times, since it is a pivotal point in the topography of the Troad. One of his references also concerns an otherwise unknown Homeric monument. He says that 'On Lectum is to be seen an altar of the twelve gods, said to have been founded by Agamemnon', but no trace of this has ever been found.

After seeing Cape Lectum Andreas and I retraced our route back to Çanakkale. Two days later Toots and the children were allowed to leave the hospital, and we all returned to Istanbul on a ship of the Turkish Maritime Lines, ending our first exploration of Troy and the Troad.

Toots and I returned frequently in the years that followed, sometimes accompanying friends in their car, and then later by ourselves in our own car, a third-hand Opel that we called Opeless, because it was always breaking down. Toots drove (I have never learned to drive) while I navigated, using modern road-maps and atlases of ancient sites, stopping frequently to ask directions when we became hopelessly lost on the uncharted back roads of the Troad and other regions of Anatolia.

On one of our trips Toots and I explored the central Troad between Ezine and Odunluk Iskelesi, a tiny hamlet on the Aegean where there is a ferry service across to Tenedos.

A few kilometres west of Ezine we turned left on a rough track signposted for ancient Neandria. The site is on the bare summit of Çığrı Dağı, 520 metres above sea level, a granite mountain forming a conspicuous ridge five kilometres long, the northernmost spur of Mt Ida. The impressive defence walls of Neandria, dating from *c.* 400 BC, are three metres thick and enclose an area measuring 1,400 by 450 metres, with the well-preserved main gate on the south side.

The site was excavated in 1899 by the German archaeologist Robert Koldewey. Pottery finds indicate that Neandria was founded in the late eighth century BC by Aeolian settlers from Lesbos. The city lasted until the last decade of the fourth century BC, when Antigonus I Monophthalmus transferred its inhabitants to the new city of Antigonia (later to be known as Alexandria Troas), that he had built on the coast. The site has been abandoned since then, used by local herders to graze their cattle, as we saw when we visited the site. It is interesting to note that coins of Neandria have on their reverse the figure of a grazing horse.

The acropolis is on a hilltop near the eastern corner of the city, once surrounded by a polygonal wall of the sixth century BC, part of which is still standing. The only extant monument of Neandria is marked by a single wind-bent tree some 200 metres north-west of the main gate. This is the platform of an Aeolic temple of Apollo dating from *c.* 600 BC, its handsome Aeolic capitals now preserved in the Istanbul Archaeological Museum.

We then returned to the main road from Ezine to Odunluk Iskelesi, and soon afterwards we began passing through the extensive ruins of Alexandria Troas, whose circumference was estimated by Schliemann to be five kilometres. The site has been used as a quarry, so, with one notable exception, there is little definite to be seen other than the scattered ruins of unidentified buildings and a number of sarcophagi along the roadway. The only structure still standing is the enormous ruined edifice known locally as Bal Saray, the 'Honey Palace'. This was part of a Roman gymnasium and baths complex erected in AD 135 by Herodus Atticus, who lived in Alexandria Troas when he was chief administrator of the province of Asia under his close friend, the emperor Hadrian.

According to Strabo, the original settlement on this site was an ancient Greek colony called Sigeia. A new and much larger city was founded on the site c. 310 BC by Antigonus I, who called it Antigonia in his own honour. After Antigonus was defeated and killed at the Battle of Ipsus in 301 BC by Lysimachus, the name of the city was changed to Alexandria. But travellers, even in antiquity, were led by the proximity of Troy to call the city Alexandria Troas.

A rough track to the left took us down to the sea at Dalyan, a tiny hamlet clustering around a crescent-shaped cove with a sandy beach, all that remains of the silted-up harbour of Alexandria Troas. The cove presented an extraordinary sight, for along its beach lay a number of huge granite monoliths, all of them broken in the middle. I later learned that they had been made in a quarry up in the northern spur of Mt Ida during the Ottoman era, intended for one of the imperial mosques in Istanbul, and had been brought here for shipment to the capital but had broken and been abandoned.

While at Dalyan we were shown a larger than life-sized marble statue of a Nike, similar to the famous Winged Victory in the Louvre. It had been discovered that morning by a local farmer while digging in his field, and he had smashed it apart while looking for the treasure he thought to be hidden within, a common belief among the villagers who inhabit the ancient Graeco-Roman ruins in Asia Minor. The farmer offered to sell me the broken-off right hand of the Nike for five Turkish liras, a little more than half a dollar, but I politely declined.

We then continued up the coast on a rough track to Odunluk Iskelesi, where a caique was just about to set off for Tenedos, just six kilometres across the strait, all of the dozen or so passengers speaking Greek. Tenedos and Imbros were awarded to Turkey by the Treaty of Lausanne in 1923, after the Graeco-Turkish War of 1919–22. The population of the two islands was predominately Greek, but settlers from Turkey are now in the majority.

At the beginning of the great Hellenic migration to the Aegean coast of Asia Minor, an Aeolian expedition established a colony on Tenedos, probably at the present site of Kale, the largest town on the island. Later Aeolians from Tenedos founded settlements on the Aegean coast of the Troad, gaining control of the territory known as the Tenedaean Peraea. The Aeolian islanders retained possession of this coastal strip until the close of the fourth century BC, when it was given over to the new city of Alexandria Troas.

Tenedos played an important part in Agamemnon's capture of Troy, when the Achaean fleet hid behind the island, when their companions in the wooden horse gained entrance to the citadel and opened the gates for them. This episode is not in the *Iliad*, but it is told in the *Little Iliad*, one of the tales in the Epic Cycle.

The tale was known to Virgil, and he relates it in Book 2 of the *Aeneid*, where Aeneas tells of how the Achaeans gained entrance to the city: 'Offshore there's a long island Tenedos,/famous and rich while Priam's kingdom lasted,/a treacherous anchorage now, and nothing more./They crossed to this and hid their ships behind it/on the bare shore beyond. We thought they'd gone.'

On a later visit, after the back roads in the Troad had been improved and new roads built, Toots and I drove along the coastal route all the way from Çanakkale to Edremit, ancient Adramyttene, stopping at places we had not seen before, using Homer and Strabo as our guides.

Leaving Çanakkale, we drove along the Izmir highway as far as the turn-off for the new road to Kum Kale. Then at Kum Kale we followed the coast road as it headed south passing the tumuli of Achilles and Patroclus. We made our first stop at Beşik Tepe, where Korfmann and his team would later excavate the remains of a settlement contemporary with Troy I. This was also the site of the archaic city of Achilleion, dating from the seventh to sixth century BC.

One of the few references to Achilleion is by Herodotus, in a brief account of the so-called Lelantine War. This was a conflict between Achilleion and the Athenian colony of Sigeum in the early sixth century BC. Among those who fought in this war was the lyric poet Alcaeus of Lesbos, a contemporary of Sappho, who served with the forces of Achilleion. Alcaeus fled from the battle to save his life, leaving his shield behind to be taken as a trophy by the victors. Alcaeus wrote of this incident in a poem addressed to his friend Melanippus of Mytilene, concluding with these lines: 'now is the moment, now,/to take what happiness the gods allow'.

We continued south along the coast, passing Odunluk Iskelesi and Dalyan, the silted-up port of Alexandria Troas, making our next stop at Gülpınar, a village some five kilometres north of Cape Lectum. This is the site of ancient Chryse, where Achilles had captured Chryseis, daughter of Chryses, priest of Apollo Smintheus. Chryse is the scene of one of the most lyrical episodes in the *Iliad*, where Odysseus returns Chryseis to her father, who prayed to Apollo to lift the plague he had inflicted on the Achaeans, 'and Phoibos Apollo heard him'.

After the Achaeans returned Chryseis they celebrated in a day-long feast in thanksgiving to Apollo, before returning to their camp the following morning: 'All day long they propitiated the god with singing,/chanting a splendid hymn to Apollo, these young

Achaians,/singing to the one who works from afar, who listened in gladness.'

We visited Gülpınar again in the mid-1990s, after Turkish archaeologists had excavated and restored a temple of Apollo Smintheus dating from the latter half of the third century BC. It is an Ionic temple with a peripteral colonnade of eight by fourteen columns, standing on a stylobate, or platform, measuring 24 metres by 43 metres. A small museum in the village contains architectural members from the temple, along with interesting fragments of the reliefs with which it was decorated.

We drove on down the coast, passing Cape Lectum and stopping briefly at Assos, before continuing along the coast road as it traversed the Gulf of Edremit. The scenery along the north side of the gulf is surpassingly beautiful, as the highway runs along the shore past olive groves, beaches of white sand, and pine-clad promontories. Above us to the left loomed the majestic peak of Mt Ida, its summit rising to 1,724 metres above sea-level, dominating all prospects in the Troad.

At Küçükkuyu a turn-off on the left is signposted for the so-called Altar of Zeus. This leads up to the village of Adatepe, near which there is a huge flat rock that Schliemann called the Altar of Idaean Zeus. Although there is virtually no archeological evidence to support this identification, Schliemann was convinced that this was Homeric Gargaros, the Idaean peak from which Zeus watched the ebb and flow of the fighting on the Trojan plain.

Returning to the coastal highway, we continued driving eastward along the northern shore of the gulf. Near the head of the gulf, almost directly under the summit of Mt Ida, we came to the village of Devren, identified as the site of ancient Antandros.

Both Herodotus and the poet Alcaeus write that Antandros was inhabited before the Aeolians first settled on the northern Aegean coast of Asia Minor. By the fifth century BC the city was inhabited by Aeolian Greeks from Lesbos, for the name Antandros appears at that time on tribute lists as a colony of Mytilene. Herodotus writes that the Idaean peak directly above Antandros was called Alexandreia, after Alexandros, better known as Paris, son of Priam and Hecuba. According to mythology, Paris spent his youth tending sheep on Mt Ida directly above Antandros, and it was there that he judged the famous Contest of Beauty between Hera, Athena and Aphrodite that led to the Trojan War.

The first reference to Mt Ida in the *Iliad* is in Book 2, in the Catalogue of Trojans, where the poet describes the contingent led by Aeneas, son of Anchises, second cousin of King Priam. According to Greek myth, when Anchises was a youth he was tending his sheep on Ida, where Aphrodite fell in love with him and bore him Aeneas.

According to Virgil, after the fall of Troy, Aeneas embarked on his voyage of exile from Antandros, as he tells the story in Book 2 of the *Aeneid*:

> Lordly Ilium had fallen and all of Neptune's Troy lay a smoking ruin on the ground. We the exiled were forced by divine command to search the world for a home in some uninhabited land. So we started to build ships below Antandrus, the city by the foothills of the Phrygian Ida, with no idea where destiny would take us or where we would be allowed to settle ... In tears I left my homeland's coast, its havens and the place where Troy had stood. I fared out alone on the high seas, an exile with my comrades and my son, with the little Gods of our home and the Great Gods of our race.

When we first visited Antandros all that remained of the ancient city were some scattered architectural fragments built into the terrace walls of seaside olive groves. But when we revisited it in the mid-1990s we saw that Turkish archaeologists had unearthed extensive remains on both sides of the highway, including buildings with mosaic floors that appeared to be from the Roman era.

On all of our tours of the Troad we stopped at Troy, which up until the beginning of Korfmann's excavations remained the same as when we had first seen it in 1961. But when we revisited it in the mid-1990s, after an interval of two decades, the site was transformed, with new excavations and signs identifying the various strata of Troy and their principal monuments, along with a museum and a model of the Trojan Horse, not to mention the Casino Helen and Paris, where tourists are served 'Trojan Wine', which is at least from Tenedos.

Much of the site is now roped off because of the excavations, and so visitors are limited to a fixed itinerary. This took us on a circuitous route through the excavations, which we approached from the south-east, turning right on a path that led us up past the eastern arc of the defence walls. These extremely well-built walls were part of the fortifications of Troy VI and Troy VIIa, described by Blegen as 'a masterpiece of military engineering of the Late Bronze Age'.

We passed through the circuit of fortifications of the East Gate, part of Troy VIIa, noticing the lighter-coloured stones in the Roman walls of Troy IX. Inside the gate we saw the foundations of a number of houses of Troy VI and Troy VIIa, built after the city had expanded beyond its bounds of the early Bronze Age.

Then in the north-eastern sector of the mound we came to the site of the Graeco-Roman temple of Athena, restored or rebuilt

by Augustus, its extant remains and architectural fragments dating
from the Hellenistic and Roman periods. The temple, whose base
measured 16 metres by 36 metres, had a peripteral Doric colonnade
with six columns at the ends and thirteen on the sides, counting
corner columns twice, with two columns *in antis* in its front and
rear porches. The colonnade supported a coffered ceiling, of
which two panels lie among the ruins along with fragments of the
sculptural decoration. The entablature above the front porch had
metopes with reliefs, the most famous of which, now in the Berlin
Archaeological Museum, shows the sun-god Apollo/Helios, with a
nimbus of rays radiating from his head as he drives a quadiga, a
four-horse chariot. The temple was near the north-west corner of
a huge temenos, or sacred enclosure, a rectangular area of some
9,500 square metres, whose main entrance was in the middle of the
south side of the precinct wall.

Down the north-east slope of the mound we could see the large
Graeco-Roman theatre, which was still under excavation. The
theatre, whose seating capacity is estimated to have been six to eight
thousand, was also restored or rebuilt by Augustus.

We then passed into the citadel of Troy I, whose primitive
fortification wall has been traced over a length of 15 metres, the
most prominent feature being the east tower of the main gate
on the south. At the centre of the acropolis we came upon the
foundations of a palatial megaron and other houses of the same
type, the first of the megara perched on the brink of Schliemann's
great north-south trench.

A gateway in the south-western corner of the walls of Troy II
led to a paved ramp that brought us down within the confines of
Troy VI. We turned left to walk within the walls of Troy VI, passing
a number of large megara, the most impressive of which were the
Pillar House and the House with Columns. It has been suggested
that the Pillar House, which stands just inside and to the left of the
south gate of Troy VI, occupies the site of the 'wonderfully built
palace of Priam'.

The southern gate of Troy VI would seem to be the Homeric
Scaean Gates, for this was the principal entryway to the city from the
plain below, with the Great Tower of Ilion just beside it to the west.

After passing through the south gate of Troy VI we saw several
structures of Troy VIII and Troy IX, the Greek and Roman cities. Just
to the right of the gate is the bouleuterion, or council chamber, part
of which is built over the citadel walls of Troy VI. Like the temple
of Athena and the theatre on top of the mound, the bouleuterion
was restored or rebuilt by Augustus, probably after he visited Troy
in 20 BC.

On the other side of the gate is the Roman odeion, a little semicircular theatre built by Augustus for musical performances. The upper arc of the odeion is built over the walls of Troy VI and almost touches the Pillar House, one of whose pillars can be seen just behind it. Only eight rows of seats in the odeion have survived, the marble seat in the centre of the uppermost being reserved for the emperor. The structure that forms the front of the orchestra is all that remains of the skene, or stage building, in which there was a larger than life-sized statue of the emperor Hadrian, who restored or rebuilt the odeion.

Continuing past the odeion, we saw on our right the partially excavated Roman baths and gymnasium. The baths, the odeion and the bouleuterion were at the edge of the agora, the marketplace of the Graeco-Roman city and the focus of its public life.

Further on in the same direction, we came to a sanctuary built up against the walls of Troy VI just beside its south-west gate. The sanctuary is believed to date back as far as the eighth century BC, when it was dug into the lower town of Troy VI and VII. It remained in use up until the late Roman imperial era, although frequently rebuilt and altered. The sanctuary consists of several altars and sacrificial pits, as well as the stepped foundations of what was probably a tiered stand for viewing religious ceremonies. Numerous cult-statuettes of Cybele and Demeter found at Troy suggest that the sanctuary may have been dedicated to them. Perhaps it was originally a sanctuary of Cybele, since she was the Phrygian fertility goddess, the 'mother of beasts', a later form of the Great Anatolian Earth Mother, and then in the Hellenic era it was dedicated to the Greek fertility goddess Demeter.

On our most recent visit to Troy, early in the new millennium, the view from the acropolis was much the same as it had been on that warm and pellucidly-clear day in April 1961: the ancient mound brooding above the windy Trojan plain, whose greening farmland was bright with myriads of poppies undulating in the breeze that ruffled the olive groves and clusters of valonia oaks in the surrounding hills. The Scamander sparkled here and there as it meandered out to the Hellespont, whose swirling waters flowed into the spray-flecked Aegean between the floating isles of Imbros and Tenedos. Far off to the south the cloud-plumed summit of Ida loomed majestically over the highlands of the Troad, a landscape that Homer would have recognized.

8

The Heroes Return

When Odysseus departed from Ithaca to join Agamemnon's expedition to Troy, he left behind his wife Penelope and his infant son, Telemachus. A few years before his return, the young bachelors of Odysseus' kingdom began courting Penelope, presuming that her husband was dead. But she still hoped that he would return and held off her suitors, who came as uninvited guests in Odysseus' palace, feasting on his sheep and cattle.

Homer begins the *Odyssey* with an invocation to Calliope, Muse of epic poetry, calling on her to tell of the homeward voyage of Odysseus after the end of the Trojan War:

> Tell me, Muse, of the man of many ways, who was driven
> far journeys, after he had sacked Troy's sacred citadel.
> Many were they whose cities he saw, whose minds he learned of,
> many the pains he suffered in his spirit on the wide sea,
> struggling for his own life and the homecomings of his companions
> ...
> Then all the others, as many as fled sheer destruction,
> were at home now, having escaped the sea and the fighting.
> This one alone, longing for his wife and his homecoming,
> was detained by the queenly nymph Kalypso, bright among goddesses.

Like the *Iliad*, which begins in the tenth year of the Trojan War, the *Odyssey* starts in the tenth year of the homeward journey of Odysseus, with the story nearing its climax. After his invocation of the Muse, Homer sets the time, place and circumstances at the beginning of the story, with Odysseus detained on the islet of Ogygia by the nymph Calypso, prevented from completing his journey by Poseidon, who had convinced the other gods to delay his return to Ithaca.

Poseidon was angry with Odysseus for having blinded the Cyclops Polyphemus, his son. All of the other immortals pitied Odysseus, particularly Athena, and so when Poseidon went off to visit the Ethiopians, she took the opportunity to plead his case to Zeus at an assembly of the gods on Mt Olympos.

Athena complained to Zeus that he had forgotten 'wise Odysseus/unhappy man', who was being detained on Calypso's island, 'straining to get sight of the very sight of the smoke uprising/ from his own country, longs to die'. Zeus answered Athena, saying he had not forgotten 'Odysseus the godlike', and that 'It is the Earth Encircler Poseidon who, ever relentless, nurses a grudge because of the Cyclops, whose eye he blinded.'

Zeus goes on to say 'But come, let all of us who are here work out his homecoming/and see to it that he returns.' Athena then answered Zeus, suggesting that they send Hermes to tell Calypso to release Odysseus, while she herself went to Ithaca, where she would stir up Telemachus 'and put some confidence in him'.

Athena flew to see Telemachus in Ithaca, where she disguised herself as Mentes, ruler of 'the oar-loving Taphians'. She told Telemachus that his father was still alive 'on a sea-washed island', his homeward voyage impeded by the will of the gods. She urged him to go and see Nestor and Menelaus, two of the heroes who have returned home, to learn if they knew whether Odysseus was alive and if he was still on his way to Ithaca.

Telemachus sailed from Ithaca to Pylos, on the south-western shore of the Peloponnesos, where he met Nestor and asked about his father. Nestor said that during the siege of Troy he and Odysseus were constantly together, 'forever one in mind and in thoughtful/ planning', but that on their homeward voyages they were scattered by the will of the gods:

> But after we had sacked the sheer citadel of Priam,
> and were going away in our ships, and the god scattered the Achaians,
> then Zeus in his mind devised a sorry homecoming
> for the Argives, since we were considered not righteous;
> therefore many of them found a bad way home, because of
> the ruinous anger of the Gray-Eyed One [Athena], whose father is
>   mighty.
> It was she who had made a quarrel between the sons of Atreus.

Athena was angered because Locrian Aias, the Lesser Ajax, had raped Cassandra, daughter of Priam, who had taken refuge in the temple of Athena when Troy was being sacked by the Achaeans. Afterwards Cassandra was captured by Agamemnon, who made her his mistress and brought her back to Mycenae, where both of them were killed by his wife Clytemestra and her lover Aegisthus.

Nestor told of the quarrel between Menelaus and Agamemnon, which took place after the sack of Troy. Menelaus urged all the Achaeans to think about going home, but Agamemnon wanted to remain long enough to offer hecatombs 'so as to soften Athene's deadly anger, poor fool/who had no thought in his mind that she would not listen to him'.

Nestor says that half of the Achaeans remained with Agamemnon, while the other half, including he himself and his followers, went off with Menelaus, stopping at Tenedos to make 'sacrifice to the immortals'. But there another quarrel broke out, with some following Odysseus as he 'went back, bringing comfort to Atreus' son, Agamemnon'.

Nestor also related how he and his followers, along with those of Menelaus and Diomedes, continued on their homeward voyages:

> It was on the fourth day when the companions of Diomedes
> breaker of horses, Tydes' son made fast their balanced
> ships at Argos. I held on for Pylos. Never once
> did the wind fail, once the god had set it to blowing.
> So, dear child, I came back, without news, and I know nothing
> of those other Achaians, which had survived, which ones had perished.

Nestor went on to tell Telemachus of what he had learned 'by hearsay, sitting here in my palace'. He said that he had heard of the safe return of Achilles' son Neoptolemus, and also those of Philoktetes and Idomeneus, though Agamemnon on his return had been murdered by Aegisthus, his wife's lover.

Four of these Achaean heroes – Diomedes, Neoptolemus, Idomeneus, and Philoktetes – had adventurous travels after they returned from Troy, and, in some versions of their myths, each one of them died far from his original home. Their stories are part of the *Nostoi*, the post-Homeric stories of the Achaean heroes returning from Troy.

During the siege of Troy, Diomedes had wounded Aphrodite when he was fighting her son Aeneas, whom she had come to protect. Aphrodite had taken her revenge by having Diomedes' wife Aegiale commit adultery in his absence, and on his return to Argos he barely escaped the traps she had set for him. He and his companions took refuge in the temple of Hera, from which they fled under the cover of night.

Diomedes then moved on to Aetolia, and from there to Daunia (Apulia) in Italy, where he was welcomed by King Daunus. Daunus begged Diomedes for help in fighting the Messapians, offering him part of his kingdom and the hand of his daughter Euippe. When Diomedes was victorious he married Euippe and fathered two sons, sharing his part of the kingdom with his companions. He went on to found at least ten cities in Italy, including Brundusium (Brindisi). He is said to have lived to a great age and was buried in southern Italy, where he was worshipped as a deified hero.

Neoptolemus had been advised by the Trojan seer Helenus, son of Priam and Hecuba and twin brother of Cassandra, who told him to remain at Troy for a few days after the other Achaeans left in their ships, and to return by land rather than by sea, and so he escaped the fate of many of his comrades.

Neoptolemus had taken Hector's widow Andromache as his captive mistress, bringing her and Hector's brother Helenus, along with him. On the advice of Helenus, who had prophetic powers, he settled in Epiros rather than Phthiotis, his father's kingdom. There he married Hermione, daughter of Menelaus and Helen, but their marriage was barren, whereas he fathered three sons with Andromache. This aroused the jealousy of Hermione and she summoned Orestes, her former fiancé. Orestes then killed Neoptolemus, after which he married Hermione.

Idomeneus returned to Crete to find that his adopted son Leucus had usurped his throne. While Idomeneus was away at Troy, Leucus had seduced the king's wife Meda, and then later he had killed her and her daughter Clisithera. He tried to regain his throne, but Leucus drove him from Crete. Idomeneus then went to southern Italy, where he settled in Salentium and built a temple dedicated to Athena.

Philoktetes returned to his kingdom at Magnesia in Thessaly, but he was deposed and moved on to Campania, near Naples. He is said to have founded several cities around the area of Croton in southern Italy, particularly Macalla, where he dedicated a temple to Apollo. He died in battle aiding colonists from Rhodes, who were being attacked by the local inhabitants. A number of the cities founded by Philoktetes claimed to be his burial place.

Thus tradition places the final journey of a number of Achaean heroes to southern Italy, which is surely due to the founding of the first Greek colonies in Magna Graecia in the eighth century BC, the period when the stories in the *Nostoi* began to take form.

Telemachus then asked about Menelaus, and Nestor says that he and Menelaus had sailed back together as far as 'holy Sounion, the cape of Athens/there Phoibos Apollo, with a visitation of his painless arrows killed the steersman of Menelaos'. He went on to say that Menelaus paused to bury the steersman and then continued

on his voyage, but at Cape Maleia in the Peloponnesos, where a
storm divided the fleet into two parts, one of which was wrecked off
Crete and the other was blown all the way to Egypt, where Menelaus
gathered considerable wealth before he returned home.

Nestor advised Telemachus to visit Menelaus, 'for he is newly
come from abroad', and 'You yourself must entreat him to speak
the whole truth to you./He will not tell you any falsehood; he is too
thoughtful.'

The following day Telemachus, leaving his ship and men in the
harbour at Pylos, set off in a chariot together with Nestor's son
Peisistratus. Two days later 'They came into the cavernous hollow of
Lakedaimon/and made their way to the house of glorious Menelaos.'
Menelaus had his servants stable their horses and then his maids
bathed the guests, anointed them with oil, put fresh clothes on them,
and sat them beside Menelaus at a table loaded with platters of meat
and golden goblets for wine.

> Then in greeting fair-haired Menelaos said to them:
> 'Help yourself to the food and welcome, and then afterward,
> when you have tasted dinner, we shall ask you who
> among men you are, for the stock of your parents can be no lost one,
> but you are of the race of men who are kings, whom Zeus sustains,
> who bear scepters; no mean men could have sons such as you are.'

While they were eating, Telemachus whispered to Peisistratus,
'The court of Zeus on Olympos must be like this on the inside,/such
abundance of everything. Wonder takes me as I look on it.' Menelaus
overheard him, 'and now he spoke to both of them and addressed
them in winged words':

> Dear children there is no mortal who could rival Zeus, seeing
> that his mansions are immortal and his possession. There may be
> some man who could rival me for property, or there may be
> none. Much did I suffer and wandered much before bringing
> all this home in my ships when I came back in the eighth year.
> I wandered to Cyprus and Phoenicia, to the Egyptians,
> I reached the Aethiopians, Eremboi, Sidonians,
> and Libya where the rams grow their horns quickly.

He went on to say that while he was wandering and gathering
these riches, his brother Agamemnon was murdered by his unfaithful
wife and her lover, and 'So it is with no pleasure I am lord of all these
possessions.' Then he said that most of all he grieved for Odysseus:

since no one of the Achaians labored as much
as Odysseus labored and achieved, and for him the end was
grief for him, and for me a sorrow that is never forgotten
for his sake, how he is gone so long, and we knew nothing of whether
he is alive or dead. The aged Laertes
and temperate Penelope must surely be grieving for him,
with Telemachos, whom he left behind in his house, a young child.

When Telemachus heard this he began to weep, holding his
purple cloak before his eyes so that the others would not notice. But
Menelaus had perceived it:

and now he pondered two ways within, in mind and spirit
whether he would leave it to him to name his father,
or whether he should speak first and ask and inquire about everything.
While he was pondering these things in his heart and his spirit,
Helen came out of her fragrant high-roofed bedchamber,
looking like Artemis of the golden distaff.

Helen seated herself on a chair, and 'At once she spoke to her
husband and questioned him about everything':

Do we know, Menelaos beloved of Zeus, who these men
announce themselves as being, who have come into our house now?
Shall I be wrong, for I think I never saw such a likeness, neither
in man nor woman, and wonder takes me as I look on him,
as this man has a likeness to the son of great-hearted Odysseus,
Telemachos, who was left in his house, a young child
by that man when, for the sake of shameless me, the Achaians
went beneath Troy, their hearts intent upon reckless warfare.

Menelaus then answered her, saying that he too had been struck
by their young guest's resemblance to Odysseus:

'I also see it thus, my wife, the way you compare them,
for Odysseus' feet were like this man's, his hands were like this,
and the glances of his eyes and his head and the hair growing.
Now I too was remembering things about Odysseus
of him, what misery he had in his hard work
for me', and he let fall a heavy tear from under his eyelids,
holding before his eyes the robe that was stained with purple.

Peisistratus now spoke up and addressed Menelaus, saying that
his companion was indeed Telemachus. Menelaus responded by

telling of his love for Odysseus, saying that if Zeus had permitted both of them to return home he would have brought him and his family from Ithaca to Argos, and 'both here, we would have seen much of each other; nothing/would then have separated us two in our friendship and pleasure,/until the darkening cloud of death had shrouded us over.'

This set all of them weeping, including Peisistratus, who then 'addressed them in winged words', speaking of his older brother Antilochus, who had been killed at Troy: 'I myself had a brother who died, he was not the meanest/of the Argives, and you would have known him. But I for my part/never met or saw him. They say he surpassed all others:/Antilochos: surprisingly swift of foot, and a fighter.'

Menelaus, realizing that Peisistratus was the son of Nestor answered him in turn:

> Dear friend, since you have said all that a man who is thoughtful
> could say or do, even one that is older than you are –
> why, this is the way your father is, so you too speak thoughtfully
> ...
> Now we shall let the weeping be, that came to us just now,
> and let us think again about dinner, let someone pour us
> water for our hands, and there will be time for words tomorrow
> at dawn, for Telemachos and me, to talk with each other.

When they had washed their hands and began to eat and drink, Helen told them about an exploit of Odysseus, his spying expedition into the citadel of Troy, disguised as a beggar. She said that she recognized Odysseus but swore a great oath not to give him away, whereupon he told her of his intention to strike down many of the Trojans and return with much information.

> The rest of the Trojan women cried out shrill, but my heart
> was happy, my heart had changed by now and was for going back
> home again, and I grieved for the madness that Aphrodite
> bestowed when she led me there away from my own dear country,
> forsaking my own daughter, my bedchamber, and my husband,
> a man who lacked no endowment either of brains or beauty.

Menelaus then spoke up in answer to Helen, telling the story of the Trojan Horse, a stratagem of Odysseus. Menelaus was in the wooden horse, along with Odysseus and other Achaean leaders, when the curious Trojans pulled it inside the citadel walls and began to examine it, led by Helen herself, as Menelaus describes the scene:

Three times you walked around the hollow ambush, feeling it,
and you called out, naming them by name, to the best of the Danaans,
and made your voice sound like the voice of the wife of each of the
     Argives.
Now I myself and the son of Tydeus and great Odysseus
were sitting there in the middle of them and we heard you crying
aloud, and Diomedes and I started up, both minded
to go outside, or else to answer your voice from inside,
but Odysseus pulled us back and held us, for all our eagerness.

Soon afterwards they all took to their beds, and then in the
morning Menelaus rose and sought out Telemachus, saying to him:
'What is the need that has brought you here, O hero Telemachos,/to
shining Lakedaimon over the sea's wide ridges?/A public or private
matter? Tell me this truly.' Then Telemachus said to him in answer:

Great Menelaos son of Atreus, leader of the people.
I have come to see if you could tell me some news of my father,
for my house is being eaten away, the rich fields are ruined,
and the house is full of hateful men, who now forever
slaughter my crowding sheep and lumbering horn-curved cattle,
these suitors of my mother, overbearing in their rapacity.
That is why I have come to your knees now, in case you might wish
to tell me of his utter destruction, whether you saw it
perhaps with your own eyes, or heard the tale from another.

Menelaus expressed his anger at the behaviour of the suitors,
and then told Telemachus what he knew of Odysseus. All of this he
had learned on the island of Pharos off Egypt from the seer Proteus,
the Old Man of the Sea, who told Menelaus that he was being held
there by the will of the Olympians, saying 'you should have made
grand sacrifices to Zeus and the other/immortal gods, and so gone
on board, so most quickly/to reach your own country, sailing over
the wine-blue water.'
     Menelaus told Proteus that he would do as he advised, and return
to Egypt to offer holy hecatombs 'in honor of all the immortal gods
who hold wide heaven'. Then he asked Proteus about the fate of
the Achaeans whom he and Nestor had left behind at Troy: 'Did all
those Achaians Nestor and I left behind when we went/sailing from
Troy come back in their ships, without injury,/or did any of them die
by dismal death on shipboard/or in the arms of his friends after he
had wound up the fighting?'
     Proteus answered him, warning him that he will not be 'free of
tears for long, once you have heard the whole story':

There were many of these men who were lost and many left over,
but two of those who were leaders of the bronze-armored Achaians
died on the way home. You yourself were there at the fighting.
And there is one who is being held alive on the wide sea
somewhere. Aias was lost, and his long-oared vessels with him.

Proteus recounted the destruction of the fleet of Aias and his
death off the Cycladic isle of Gyrai, now known as Giaros, where
Poseidon had driven him against the great rocks after he shouted his
defiance of the gods.

Proteus then outlined for Menelaus the homeward voyage of his
brother Agamemnon, who survived the storm that had killed Aias:

Your brother somehow got away and escaped the death spirits
with his hollow ships. It was the lady Hera who saved him.
But now as he had come close to the point of making the sheer peak
Maleia, then the stormwinds caught him away and carried him,
groaning heavily, out on the open seas where the fish swarm
...
Agamemnon stepped rejoicing on the soil of his country
and stroked the ground with his hand and kissed it, and his thronging
hot tears streamed down, so dear to him was the sight of his country.

Proteus went on, explaining to Menelaus how his brother was
killed by Aegisthus, who had hired a watchman to tell him when
Agamemnon returned, and then set an ambush for him:

Choosing out the twenty best fighting men in the district,
he set an ambush, and beside it had them arrange a festival,
and went down to welcome Agamemnon, shepherd of the people,
with horses and chariots, and with shameful thoughts in his mind,
    then
led him in all unsuspicious of death, and feasted him
and killed him feasting, as one strikes down an ox at his manger.
Not one of Agamemnon's men who followed him was left
alive, nor one of Aigisthos' men. All were killed in the palace.

Menelaus tells Telemachus that when he heard the story of
Agamemnon's death 'he sat down on the sand and cried, nor did
the heart in me/wish to go on living any longer nor to look on the
sunlight'. Proteus however, told him not to waste his time mourning,
but to return with all speed to his homeland to take his revenge,
though Agamemnon's son Orestes might have already killed
Aegisthus, 'but you might be there for the burying'.

Menelaus regained his composure and addressed Proteus 'in winged words', asking him about the other hero who had not yet returned home. Proteus answered him:

> 'That was Odysseus son of Laertes, who makes his home in
> Ithaka, whom I saw on an island, weeping big tears
> in the palace of the nymph Kalypso, and she detains him
> by constraint, and he cannot make his way to his country,
> for he has not any ships by him, nor any companions
> who can convey him back along the sea's wide ridges.
> ...
> But for you, Menelaos, O fostered of Zeus, it is not the gods' will
> that you shall die and go to your end in your horse-pasturing Argos,
> but the immortals will convey you to the Elysian
> Field, and the limits of the earth, where the fair-haired Radamanthys
> is, and where there is made the easiest life for mortals,
> for there is no snow, nor much winter there, nor is there ever
> rain, but always the stream of the Ocean sends up breezes
> of the West Wind blowing briskly for the refreshment of mortals.
> This, because Helen is yours and you are son-in-law therefore
> to Zeus.' He spoke and dived back into the tossing deep water.

When Menelaus finished his story he invited Telemachus to stay on for a while in his palace. But Telemachus said that he must leave, for his companions in Pylos were waiting for him to return with them to Ithaca. And so Menelaus presented Telemachus with a silver bowl edged in gold, and held a farewell banquet for his guests the evening before their departure.

The suitors at Odysseus' palace on Ithaca had by now realized that Telemachus was gone, and they sent a ship to intercept his vessel on the way home and kill him. Penelope learned of this and was distraught, but Athena appeared to her in a dream and told her that Telemachus would return safely.

Athena then flew to Menelaus' palace and appeared to Telemachus in a dream, warning him that the suitors had sent a ship to ambush him on his return voyage. She advised him to keep his ship well clear of the shore and sail by night:

> But when you make land, at the first promontory on Ithaka,
> Then speed your ship and all your companions along to the city
> but you yourself go first to the swineherd, that man
> who is in charge of the pigs, and whose thoughts toward you are
>   kindly.
> There spend the night, but speed the man along to the city

To take your message to circumspect Penelope, saying
That you are alive and safe, and you have come home to Pylos.

The next morning Telemachus bade farewell to Menelaus and
Helen, who gave him rich gifts to take home. As he and Peisistratus
departed, Menelaus poured a libation as he stood before their
chariot and pledged them: 'Farewell, young men, give my greeting to
the shepherd of the people,/Nestor, for he was always kind to me like
a father,/when we sons of the Achaians were fighting in Troy land.'

When they reached Pylos, Telemachus asked to be dropped off at
his waiting ship, where he bid farewell to Peisistratus, saying that it
was imperative that he return home at once. Telemachus then told
his companions to 'Put all running gear in order, friends, on the black
ship,/and let ourselves go aboard, so we can get on with the journey.'

They then set off, as 'Athene sent them a favoring stern wind',
and by dawn the next day they reached Ithaca, having eluded the
ship that the suitors had sent to ambush them. They beached the
ship on a strand out of view of the city, and Telemachus told his
companions to drop him there so that he could check on his estate
and his herdsmen. He said that he would meet them that evening in
the city, where 'I will set a good feast before you, meats and sweet-
tasting wine, to be my thanks for sharing the journey with me.' He
started walking to the house of the faithful swineherd Eumaeus,
unaware that his father Odysseus was waiting there in disguise.

9

Leaving Calypso's Isle

When the gods again convened on Olympos, Athena reminded Zeus and the other gods that Odysseus was still detained by the nymph Calypso on her island, unable to return to his homeland, where the suitors were plotting to kill his son Telemachus.

Zeus spoke to his beloved son Hermes, also called Agreïphontes telling him that he should inform the nymph Calypso that she should release Odysseus so that he can resume his homeward journey.

Hermes immediately put on his sandals and took up his staff, winging his way across land and sea till he came to Calypso's isle. He walked to the great cave where she dwelt and found that she was inside.

There was …
a great fire blazing on the hearth, and the smell of cedar
split in billets, and sweetwood burning, spread all over
the island. She was singing inside the cave with a sweet voice
as she went up and down the loom and wove with a golden shuttle.

Hermes went into the cave, where Calypso recognized him immediately. 'But Hermes did not find great-hearted Odysseus indoors,/for he was sitting out on the beach, crying, as before now/ he had done, breaking his heart in tears, lamentation, and sorrow,/ as weeping tears he looked out over the barren water.'

After Calypso greeted and entertained Hermes she asked why he had come to see her, and he told her that Zeus wanted her to let Odysseus continue his homeward voyage. Calypso shuddered when she heard these words. 'You are hard-hearted you gods, and jealous beyond all creatures/beside, when you are resentful toward the goddesses for sleeping/openly with such men as each has made her true husband.'

Hermes answers Calypso's complaint, saying 'Then send him accordingly on his way, and beware of the anger/of Zeus, lest he hold a grudge hereafter and rage against you.'

After Hermes departed, Calypso set out in search of Odysseus and found him sitting on the seashore, weeping.

> Poor man, no longer mourn here beside me nor let your lifetime
> fade away, since now I will send you on, with a good will.
> So come, cut long timbers with a bronze ax and join them
> to make a wide raft, and fashion decks that will be on the upper
> side, to carry you over the misty face of the water.

She continued, telling him what she would do to help him survive his homeward voyage on the raft, the gods willing:

> Then I will stow aboard her bread and water and ruddy
> wine, strength-giving goods that will keep the hunger from you,
> and put clothing on you, and send a following wind after,
> so that all without harm you can come back to your home country,
> if only the gods consent. It is they who hold wide heaven.

She then led Odysseus back to her cave, where 'her serving maids set nectar and ambrosia before her'. When they finished their feast, Calypso spoke to Odysseus, asking him if he was still eager to go home, assuring him that she would do everything she could to help him.

> but if you only knew in your own heart how many hardships
> you were fated to undergo before getting back to our country,
> you would stay here with me and be the lord of this household
> and be an immortal, for all your longings once more to look on
> that wife for whom you are pining all your days here. And yet
> I think I can claim that I am not her inferior
> either in build or stature, since it is not likely that mortal
> women can challenge the goddesses for build and beauty.

Odysseus spoke in turn and answered the goddess who had confined him to her island for seven years as her prisoner of love:

> Goddess and queen, do not be angry with me. I myself know
> that all you say is true and that circumspect Penelope
> can never match the impression you make for beauty and stature.

She is mortal after all, and you are immortal and ageless.
But even so, what I want and all my days pine for
is to go back to my house and see my day of homecoming.
And if some god batters me far out on the wine-blue water,
I will endure it, keeping a stubborn spirit inside me,
on the waves and in the fighting. And so, let this adventure follow.

After Odysseus finished speaking to Calypso the two of them, 'withdrawn in the inner recess of the hallowed cavern enjoyed themselves in love and stayed all night by each other'.

But when the young Dawn showed again with her rosy fingers,
Odysseus wrapped himself in an outer cloak and a tunic,
while she, the nymph, mantled herself in a gleaming white robe
fine-woven and delightful, and around her waist she fastened
a handsome belt of gold, and on her head was a wimple.
She set about planning the journey for great-hearted Odysseus.

Calypso provided Odysseus with a double-bladed bronze axe and an adze, leading him to woods at the far end of the island, where he cut down twelve tall trees. He 'trimmed them well with his bronze ax,/and planed them expertly, and trued them straight to a chalkline'. The nymph brought him an auger 'and he bored through them all, and pinned them together with dowels, and then with his cords lashed he lashed his raft together.'

After that he went to work 'setting up the deck boards and fitting them to close uprights/he worked them on, and closed in the ends with sweeping gunwales'. He 'fashioned the mast, with an upper deck fitted to it,/and made in addition a steering oar by which to direct her,/and fenced her in down the whole length with wattles of osier/to keep the water out, and expended much timber upon this'.

Calypso then 'brought out the sail cloth/to make the sails with, and he carefully worked these also,/and attached the straps and halyards and sheets all in place aboard her,/and then with levers worked her down to the bright salt water'. The raft was finished on the fourth day, and on

the fifth day shining Kalypso saw him off from the island
when she had bathed him and put fragrant clothing upon him,
and the goddess put two skins aboard, one filled with dark wine
and the other, the big one, filled with water, and put on provisions
in a bag, and stored there many good things to keep a man's strength up,
and sent a following wind to carry him, warm and easy.

Odysseus sailed before the wind, navigating at night by the stars, following the instructions given to him by Calypso:

> For so Kalypso, bright among goddesses, had told him
> to make his way over the sea, keeping the Bear on his left hand.
> Seventeen days he sailed, making his way over the water,
> and on the eighteenth day there showed the shadowy mountains
> of the Phaiakian land where it stood out nearest to him,
> and it looked like a shield lying on the misty face of the water.

Most writers, both ancient as well as modern, have identified Scheria, the land of the Phaeaceans, as Corfu, Greek Kerkyra, northernmost of the Ionian Islands, lying off the Greek coast and extending south from the present boundary between Albania and Greece. The island is long and narrow, extending for some 70 kilometres north-west to south-east, tapering from a width of 30 kilometres in the north to only four kilometres in the south. The northern part of the island is dominated by Mt Pantocrator, 906 metres high, which, to someone approaching the island from the west, does indeed look like 'a shield lying on the misty face of the water'.

Meanwhile Poseidon, on his way back from the land of the Ethiopians, looked out from the mountains of the Solymoi in Lycia and saw Odysseus sailing over the sea. Poseidon was all the more angered with him, for he realized that the other gods had changed their intentions

> about Odysseus while I was away in the Aethiopians'
> land, and he nears the Phaiakian's country where it is appointed
> that he shall escape this great trial of misery that is now his.
> But I think I can still give him a great full portion of trouble.
> ...
> He spoke, and pulled the clouds together, in both hands gripping
> the trident, and staggered the sea, and let loose the stormblasts
> of all the winds together, and huddled under the cloud scuds
> land alike and the great water. Night sprang from heaven.
> East Wind and South Wind clashed together, and the bitter blown
>   West Wind
> and the North Wind born in the bright air rolled up a heavy sea.

The storm terrified Odysseus, and a great wave spun the raft in a circle, knocking him into the sea, snapping off the mast and blowing the sail along with the upper deck. He was able to swim back to what remained of the raft and 'laid hold of it,/and huddled down in the middle of it, avoiding death's end'.

The sea-goddess Ino, also called Leukothea, took pity on Odysseus as he drifted helplessly in the storm, and 'likening herself to a winged gannet she came up/out of the water and perched on the raft and spoke a word to him'. She told him to 'Take off these clothes and leave the raft to drift at the winds' will,/and then strike out with your hands and make for a landfall/on the Phaiakian country, where your escape is destined.'

Then, before the goddess 'slipped back into the heaving sea', she said to him:

> And here, take this veil, it is immortal, and fasten it under
> Your chest, and there is no need for you to die, nor to suffer.
> But when with both your hands you have taken hold of the mainland,
> untie this veil and throw it out into the wine-blue water
> far from the land; and turn your face away as you do so.

The goddess handed him the veil and then slipped back into the sea. Odysseus was undecided about what to do, and he said to himself 'Ah me, which of the immortals is weaving deception/against me, and tells me to put off from the raft?' He decided that he would stay on the raft as long as it remained intact, but at that moment a huge wave smashed it to pieces, leaving him 'astride one beam, like a man riding on horseback'.

> Then he was driven two nights and two days on the heavy
> seas, and many times his heart foresaw destruction,
> but when Dawn with the lovely hair had brought the third morning,
> then at last the gale went down and windless weather
> came on, and now he saw the land lying very close to him
> as took a sharp look, lifted high on the top of a great wave.

But as he approached land he could hear the surf pounding on one of the rocky promontories. A great wave smashed him up against a cliff, which he clung to until the backward swell carried him away. He got clear of the surf and swam along until he came to the mouth of a river, clear of rocks and sheltered from the wind. Odysseus prayed to the spirit of the river-god, who 'stayed his current, stopped the waves breaking,/and made all quiet in front of him and let him get safely/into the outlet of the river'. When Odysseus got his breath back and regained his spirit, he at last took off Ino's veil, which drifted with the current until the goddess 'took it back into her hands'.

'Odysseus staggered from the river/and lay down again in the rushes and kissed the grain-giving soil.' Considering where he would spend the night, he went up the slope to a pair of closely-intertwined bushes at the edge of a wood. There 'Odysseus buried himself in the leaves, and Athene/shed a sleep on his eyes so as most quickly to quit him,/by veiling his eyes, from the exhaustion of his hard labors.'

The place where Odysseus swam ashore has been identified with a number of sites on the western coast of Corfu, the leading candidates, from north to south, being Afionas, Palaeokastritsa and Ermones, all of which have a sandy cove with a river of sorts running into the sea. Having looked at all three coves, I would agree with Ernle Bradford that Odysseus landed in the bay of Ermones.

Meanwhile Athena had made her way to the city and palace of Alkinoös, King of the Phaeaceans, which most authorities put at the present town of Corfu, capital of the island, 13 kilometres east of Ermones across the narrow waist of the island. There the goddess went into the bedchamber of Nausicaa, daughter of Alkinoös, putting into her mind that she should go with her attendants the following day to do the palace laundry in the river that flows into Ermonos Bay.

Early in the morning Nausicaa spoke to her father about this and he arranged for the mule wagon to be brought out and made ready for her, while her mother Arete put into a hamper food and wine for the expedition. After the palace laundry was put on the wagon, Nausicaa took the reins and whipped the mules and the wagon went forward, with her maid-servants walking behind.

When they reached Ermones, they unyoked the mules to graze along the bank of the river, while 'they lifted the wash in their hands and carried it to the black water,/and stamped on it in the basins, making a game and a race of it'. When they finished doing the laundry they spread it out on 'the big pebbles up on the dry shore'.

> Then they themselves, after bathing and anointing themselves with
>   olive oil,
> ate their dinner all along by the banks of the river
> and waited for the laundry to dry out in the sunshine.
> But when she and her maids had taken their pleasure in eating,
> they all threw off their veils for a game of ball, and among them
> it was Nausikaa of the white arms who led in the dancing.

Nausicaa threw the ball toward one of her maids, but it missed and went off into the swirling water, whereupon all of them cried out in dismay. This awakened Odysseus, who emerged 'and from the dense foliage with his heavy hand he broke off/a leafy branch to cover his body and hide the male parts,/and went in the confidence of his strength, like some hill-kept lion'.

All of the maids were terrified and ran away, but Nausicaa stood her ground and faced Odysseus, and 'blandishingly and full of craft he began to address her':

> I am at your knees, O queen. But are you mortal or goddess?
> If indeed you are one of the gods who hold wide heaven,
> then I must find in you the nearest likeness to Artemis
> the great daughter of Zeus, for beauty, figure and stature
> ...
> I have never with these eyes seen anything like you
> neither man nor woman. Wonder takes me as I look at you.

He then told Nausicaa that for twenty days the winds and current had swept him 'along from the island Ogygia, and my fate has landed me/here; here too I must have evil to suffer; I do not think it will stop; before then the gods have much to give me'.

Odysseus asked Nausicaa to have pity on him: 'Show me the way to the town and give me some rag to wrap me/in; if you had any kind of cloth when you came here.' Nausicaa answered him, saying that it was Zeus who determined a man's fortune, 'and since he must have given you yours you must even endure it'.

She told him that as an unfortunate suppliant he would lack for nothing in her country, the land of the Phaeaceans, which was ruled by her father Alkinoös. She then called out to her attendants:

> Stand fast, girls. Where are you flying, just because you have
>   looked on
> a man? ...
> But, since this is some poor wanderer who has come to us,
> we must now take care of him, since all strangers and wanderers
> are sacred in the sight of Zeus, and the gift is a light and a dear
>   one.
> So, my attendants, give some food and drink to the stranger,
> and bathe him, where there is shelter from the wind, in the river.

The maidservants did as they were told, 'and laid out for him to wear a mantle and tunic,/and gave him limpid olive oil in a golden oil flask,/and told him he could bathe himself in the stream of the river'. Odysseus told them to stand off, saying that he would bathe himself, for he felt embarrassed 'in the presence of lovely-haired girls to appear all naked'.

When Odysseus had bathed and anointed himself with oil, he dressed himself in the clothing that Nausicaa had given him, after which 'he went a little aside and sat by himself on the seashore.

The young princess looked at him admiringly and spoke to her attendants':

> A while ago he seemed an unpromising man to me. Now
> he even resembles one of the gods, who hold high heaven.
> If only the man to be called my husband could be like this one,
> a man living here, if only this one were pleased to stay here.
> But come, my attendants, give some food and drink to the stranger.

After Odysseus finished eating, and the laundry had been folded and placed in the wagon, Nausicaa called out to her guest: 'Rise up now, stranger, to go to the city, so I can see you/to the house of my own prudent father, where I am confident/you will be made known to all the highest Phaiakians.'

She told him that he should follow along behind her with the maids, but when they reached the outskirts of the city he should stop when they reached a grove of poplars sacred to Apollo, where he should remain until she and her maids had time to reach the palace, for his presence with her would provoke gossip. She said that the palace was known to everyone, and any child could guide him there. When he arrived at the palace, he should go straight across the hall to embrace her mother, Queen Arete, for 'if she has thoughts in her mind that are friendly to you,/then there is hope that you can see your own people, and come back/to your strong-founded house, and to the land of your fathers'.

When they reached the grove of Apollo, Odysseus remained behind while Nausicaa and her maids went on. When he thought that sufficient time had passed Odysseus set out for the city, and as he approached it he met Athena, disguised as a little girl, who agreed to guide him to the palace. Athena put a magical mist about Odysseus, so that he was not noticed by those they passed. When they reached the palace Athena left Odysseus to enter on his own, giving him the same instructions as had Nausicaa, that he should go straight to Arete, and embrace her, for if she looked upon him favourably he would finally make his way back to his homeland.

After admiring the fabulous palace for a while, Odysseus went in and headed for the throne room, unnoticed since he was still shrouded by Athena's magical cloud of mist, which lifted when

> he came to Arete and to the king, Alkinoös.
> Odysseus clasped Arete's knees in his arms, and at that time
> the magical and surrounding mist was drifted from him,
> and all fell silent through the house when they saw the man there,
> and they wondered looking on him, and Odysseus made his entreaty:

'Arete, daughter of godlike Rhexenor, after much hardship
I have come to your house as a suppliant, and to your husband
and to these feasters, on whom may the gods bestow prosperity
...
But for me, urge that conveyance be given quickly
to my country, since long now far from my people I suffer hardships'.

Having made his plea, Odysseus 'sat down beside the hearth in
the ashes/near the fire, while all of them stayed stricken in silence'.
The first to speak was the hero Echeneus, oldest of all the Phaeaceans,
who said to Alkinoös that the stranger should be seated among them
and given supper, because of the sacred rights of suppliants.
Alkinoös then took Odysseus to the table and set him in a chair,
displacing Laodamas, his favourite son. A maidservant brought
water and poured it into a silver basin for him to wash, and a
housekeeper served him supper, after which Alkinoös told his herald
to serve everyone wine. When they had drunk their fill, Alkinoös
stood up and made a speech, telling them that they should all come
at dawn to the place of assembly, bringing along the elders,

... and after that we shall think of
conveyance, and how our guest without annoyance or hardship
may come again, conveyed by us, to his own country,
in happiness and speed, even though it lies very far off,
and on the way between suffer no pain nor evil
until he sets foot on his own country.

Odysseus stayed on with Alkinoös and Arete after the others
left, sitting by them while the servants cleaned up. Arete was
the first to speak, for she recognized the mantle and tunic that
Odysseus wore, 'splendid/clothes which she herself had made, with
her serving women'. 'Stranger and friend, I myself first have a
question to ask you./What man are you and hence? And who was
it who gave you this clothing?/Did you not say you came here
ranging over the water?'
Then Odysseus spoke in turn and answered her: 'It is a hard
thing, O queen, to tell you without intermission,/all my troubles,
since the gods of the sky have given me many./But this now I will tell
you in answer to the question you asked me.'
He then proceeded to tell of his trials, beginning with the sinking
of his ship with the loss of all his companions, and of how he was
washed ashore on Ogygia, where he stayed with Calypso for seven
years before she released him to continue his homeward journey.
He concluded by telling of how, after Poseidon had blown up a

tremendous storm that destroyed his raft, he swam ashore and spent the night sleeping under the bushes, until he was awakened the next morning by the voices of women nearby:

> Then I was aware of your daughter's attendant women playing
> on the beach, and she, looking like the goddesses, went there among
>   them.
> I supplicated her, nor did she fail of the right decision;
> …
> she gave me food in plenty to eat, she gave me gleaming
> wine, and a bath in the river. She also gave me this clothing.
> Sorrowful as I am, all this is true I have told you.

Alkinoös said that Nausicaa should have brought him directly to the palace, but Odysseus explained how she feared that this might cause embarrassment and anger her father. The king responded by stating: 'being the man you are and thinking the way that I do,/you could have my daughter and be called my son-in-law, staying/here with me. I would dower you with a house and properties,/if you stayed by your own good will.'

Alkinoös then assured Odysseus that on the following day, after his guest had rested, he would arrange for conveyance back to his home country, while Arete ordered her maids to make up a bed for him in the porch of the palace, whereupon they all retired.

The following morning Alkinoös escorted Odysseus to the place of assembly, where the Phaeaceans now gathered to be addressed by their king, who told them that the stranger had petitioned to be conveyed back to his home country. He went on to say that they would outfit a new ship, manned by fifty-two of the finest young men of the district, which he would provision. He then invited everyone to join him in a feast at the palace, after which he sent a herald to summon the fifty-two youths who would crew the vessel, inviting them to the feast along with the bard Demodokus.

When they had eaten their fill at the feast, the Muse inspired Demodokus to sing of a famous incident during the Trojan War, where Odysseus quarrels with Achilles. Hearing this, Odysseus was moved to tears, drawing the purple mantle across his face to hide his weeping. 'Alkinoös alone understood what he did and noticed,/since he was sitting next to him and heard him groaning heavily.'

Alkinoös then spoke to the Phaeaceans, saying 'Now let us all go outside and make our endeavor/in all contests, so that our stranger can tell his friends, after/he reaches his home, by how much we surpass all others/in boxing, wrestling, leaping and speed of our feet for running.'

The first contest was a foot race, which was won by Clytoneus, after which Euryalus surpassed all others in wrestling, Amphialus outdid his competitors in the jump, and Elatreus threw the discus farthest. Euryalus then spoke, addressing Odysseus: 'Come now you also, father stranger, and try these contests/if you have skill in any.'

Stung by this mockery, and with his mantle still on, Odysseus sprang up and took hold of a discus heavier than the one used by the other competitors. He spun and let it fly, and the Phaeaceans 'shrank down against the ground, ducking/under the flight of the stone which, speeding from his hand lightly,/overflew the marks of all others'.

Odysseus then challenged the young Phaeaceans to best him in the discus or in any other sport:

> Now reach me that mark, young men, and I will make another
> throw, as great as this, I think, or one even better.
> Let any of the rest, whose heart and spirit are urgent for it,
> come up and try me, since you have irritated me so, either
> at boxing or wrestling or in a foot race.

Alkinoös placated Odysseus and then, to lighten the atmosphere, he called upon the best dancers among the Phaeaceans to perform for their guest:

> do your dance, so that our guest, after he comes home
> to his own people, can tell them, how far we surpass all others
> in our seamanship and the speed of our foot and dancing and singing.
> Let someone go quickly and bring Demodokos his clear-voiced
> lyre, which must have been set down somewhere in our palace.

The herald fetched the lyre 'for Demodokos, who moved into the middle, and about him stood forth/young men in the first of their youth, well trained in dancing/and beat the wonderful dancing floor with their feet./Odysseus gazed on the twinkling of their feet, his heart full of wonder.'

Demodokus then struck his lyre and began singing the story about the love of Ares and Aphrodite, after which Alkinoös had his sons Halis and Laodamas perform an acrobatic dance in which they leaped in turn into the air while passing between them a beautiful red ball, while the rest of the young men 'stamped out the time and a great sound rose up'.

Odysseus spoke to Alkinoös, complimenting him on the dancing of the Phaeaceans, saying 'Wonder takes me as I look on them'. This pleased Alkinoös, who addressed the Phaeacean nobles, bidding twelve of them to join him in sending their herald to fetch a rich present for the stranger, saying also that 'Euryalos shall make amends to him with a spoken/word and a gift, for having spoken out of due measure.'

Each of the nobles sent his herald to bring back the gifts, while Euryalus presented Odysseus with his precious sword, saying to him:

Farewell, father and stranger, and if any word was let slip
that was improper, may the stormwinds catch it away and carry it
off, and the gods give you safe homecoming to your own country
and wife; since here, far from your own people, you must be suffering.

Then Odysseus spoke in turn and answered him: 'Farewell also to you, dear friend, and may the gods grant you/prosperity; may you never miss this sword you have given/me now, as a gift, and made amends to me with words spoken.'

When the feast ended Alkinoös and Arete brought out the farewell presents for their guest, after which the housekeeper prepared him a bath. The maids bathed him and anointed him with oil, and then they dressed him in a tunic and mantle. As he stepped from the bath he encountered Nausicaa, who 'gazed upon Odysseus with all her eyes and admired him,/and spoke to him aloud and addressed him in winged words, saying:/"Goodbye, stranger, and think of me sometimes when you are/back at home, and how I was the first you owed your life to."'

Then resourceful Odysseus spoke in turn and addressed her:

Nausikaa, daughter of great-hearted Alkinoös,
even so may Zeus, high-thundering husband of Hera,
grant me to reach my house and see my day of homecoming.
So even when I am there I will pray to you, as to a goddess,
all the days of my life. For, maiden, my life was your gift.

Odysseus went to sit by Alkinoös just as the herald passed, escorting the bard Demodokus to a chair 'in the middle of the feasters, propping it against a tall column'. Odysseus cut a piece of pig and sent the herald to give it to Demodokus, 'who received it happily'. When they had finished eating Odysseus spoke to Demodokus, asking him to sing to them the story of the wooden horse, 'the stratagem great Odysseus filled once with men and brought it/to the upper city, and it was these men who sacked Ilion'.

When the bard had finished his song, Alkinoös addressed the Phaeaceans, saying that 'Ever since we ate our supper and the divine singer/began, our guest has never ceased since then his sorry/lament.

Great sorrow must have come on his heart, surely.' He then turned to Odysseus, speaking to him directly:

> So do not longer keep hiding now with crafty purposes
> the truth of what I ask you. It is better to speak out.
> Tell me the name by which your mother and father called you
> …
> Tell me your land, your neighborhood and your city,
> So that our ships … can carry you there.

Odysseus spoke in turn and answered Alkinoös, telling him his name and his origin:

> I am Odysseus son of Laertes, known before all men
> for the study of crafty designs, and my fame goes up to the heavens.
> I am at home in sunny Ithaka. There is a mountain
> there that stands tall, leaf-trembling Neritos, and there are islands
> settled around it, lying very close to one another.
> There is Doulichion and Same, wooded Zakynthos,
> but my island lies low and away, last of all on the water
> toward the dark, with the rest below facing east and sunshine,
> a rugged place, but a good nurse of men; for my part
> I cannot think of any place sweeter on earth to look at.

He concluded by saying, 'But come, I will tell you of my voyage home with its many troubles, which Zeus inflicted on me as I came home from Troy land.' And with that Odysseus began telling them the long story of the epic journey that had brought him from Troy to the land of the Phaeaceans.

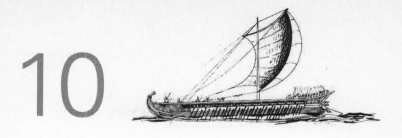

10

Across the Wine-dark Aegean

Odysseus begins by telling Alkinoös and his court about the first stage of his homeward journey, which brought him and his men from Troy to the city of Ismaros in Thrace, home of the Ciconians, who had fought as allies of Priam in the Trojan War.

The Ciconians disappeared from history, along with their place names, but Ismaros was undoubtedly near Doriskos, a Persian fortress built by Darius and used by Xerxes. According to Herodotus, Doriskos was on the west bank of the River Hebrus, and the Ciconians ruled the territory extending westward from there to the River Nestus. The Hebrus is now the border between Turkey and Greece, and the site of ancient Doriskos is a village of that name on the Greek side of the border, near the town of Ferai some 20 kilometres east of Alexandropolis, which we have passed through many times when driving between Istanbul and Athens.

Odysseus would not have sailed directly from Troy to Ismaros, because the strong southward current south of the Hellespont would have led him to cross the strait between the Trojan plain and Tenedos, where he would have waited for a favourable wind. The prevailing wind in the Aegean is from the north, the Etesian winds, known to Greeks today as the *meltemi*. Odysseus would have waited for a southerly wind to take him north, passing east of Imbros and Samothrace to the Thracian coast, where he attacked Ismaros.

From Ilion the wind took me and drove me ashore at Ismaros
by the Kikonians. I sacked their city and killed their people,
and out of their city taking their wives and many possessions
we shared them out, so no one might be cheated of his proper
portion. There I was for the light foot and escaping,
and urged it, but they were greatly foolish and would not listen.

Then they drank a great deal of wine and slaughtered sheep and
cattle on the beach,

> But meanwhile the Kikonians went and summoned the other
> Kikonians, who were their neighbors living in the inland country,
> more numerous and better men, well skilled in fighting
> ...
> Both sides stood and fought their battle by the running
> ships, and with bronze-headed spears they cast at each other,
> ...
> then at last the Kikonians turned the Achaians back and beat them,
> and out of each ship six of my strong-greaved companions
> were killed, but the rest of us fled away from death and destruction.

Later, Odysseus tells of how he spared the priest of Apollo at
Ismaros, Maron, along with his wife and child. Maron showed his
gratitude to Odysseus by giving him rich presents, including twelve
jars of wine.

> He gave me seven talents of well-wrought gold, and he gave me
> a mixing bowl made all of silver, and gave along with it
> wine, drawing it off in storing jars, twelve in all. This was
> a sweet wine unmixed, a divine drink ...
> From there we sailed further along, glad to have escaped death,
> but grieving still at heart for the loss of our dear companions ...
> [Zeus] drove the North Wind against our vessels
> in a supernatural storm ...
> The ships were swept along yawing down the current; the violence
> of the wind ripped our sails into three or four pieces. These then,
> in fear of destruction, we took down and stowed in the ships' hulls,
> and rowed them on ourselves until we made the mainland.
> There for two nights and two days together we lay up,
> for pain and weariness together eating our hearts out.

Odysseus and his men would have spent those two days at Aenus,
a Greek city some 16 kilometres from Doricus, on the east side of the
mouth of the Hebrus.

> But when the fair-haired Dawn in her round brought on the third
>　　day,
> We, setting the masts upright, and hoisting the white sails on them,
> sat still, and let the wind and the steersman hold them steady.
> And now I would have come home unscathed to the land of my
>　　fathers,

1   Bellerophon

2 The Oracle of Apollo at Claros

3   The tomb of Achilles on the Trojan plain

4   Yenişehir village above the Trojan plain

5   The walls of Troy VI and the South Gate

6   Roman odeum at Troy

7   Baths of Herodus Atticus at Alexandria Troas

8   Temple of Athena at Assos

9   Odysseus receives wine from Maron, priest of Apollo at Ismaros

11   Odysseus and his companions resist the lure of the Sirens

12   Odysseus slays the suitors

but as we turned the hook of Maleia, the sea and current
beat me off course, and drove me on past Kythera.

Odysseus gives no indication about the course of his voyage
through the Aegean until he reaches Cape Maleia, the south-
easternmost of the three peninsulas of the Peloponnesos, and the
nearby island of Kythera. One can only guess the route of the voyage,
but the possibilities are few in number, based on a couple of clues in
the *Odyssey*, as well as a knowledge of the winds and weather in the
Aegean.

One clue is furnished by Nestor's account of his own homeward
voyage, where he describes his route after he parted company with
Odysseus, who sailed back from Tenedos to rejoin Agamemnon
at Troy. Nestor told Telemachus that he 'cut across the middle
main sea for Euboia', where they passed Geraistos (Karistos), the
southern cape of the island. They then passed Cape Poseidon, the
promontory of the Attica peninsula, from where they continued
south to round Cape Maleia and then make their way around the
coast of the Peloponnesos to Pylos. This was the route Odysseus
would have followed after leaving Ismaros, had it not been for the
great storms that he encountered, first in the Aegean and then off
Cape Maleia.

But Odysseus makes no mention of the places described by
Nestor, other than Cape Maleia, and so his ships must have been
swept southward through the Cyclades, 'the encircling isles' that
surround the sacred centre of Delos, the birthplace of Apollo. The
Cyclades spread across the central Aegean from the southern tip of
Euboea and Cape Sounion to the westernmost of the islands that lie
off the coast of Asia Minor, so that anyone sailing south from the
Thracian coast is bound to pass through them, and if they continue
southward they will come to Crete.

Odysseus mentions Delos in his first conversation with Nausicaa,
where he compares her to a young palm tree he had seen on Delos:
'Yet in Delos once I saw such a thing, by Apollo's altar./I saw the
stalk of a young palm tree shooting up. I had gone there/once, and
with a following of a great many people,/on that journey which was
to mean hard suffering for me.'

The Homeric *Hymn to Delian Apollo*, which describes the god's
birth on Delos, mentions the palm tree as being close to the spot
where he was born to Leto. When we first visited Delos in the early
1960s we found that a palm tree had been planted on the spot where
the myth places the birthplace of Apollo.

The wind-blown voyage of Odysseus and his companions from
Ismaros probably carried them south though the Cyclades as far as

Crete, where they would have waited for a favourable wind to take them north-westward toward Kythera and Cape Maleia.

Odysseus gives a clue in one of the 'lying stories' he tells when he is a tramp pretending to be a dispossessed noble. This is the tale that he tells to Penelope, pretending that he was the younger brother of Idomeneus and had met Odysseus at Amnisos on Crete when the latter was on his way to Troy. He said that Odysseus had been blown off course at Cape Maleia and had landed at Amnisos before going on to Troy, thus reversing the actual course of the voyage to hide his true identity:

> It was there that I knew Odysseus and entertained him,
> for the force of the wind had caught him, as he was making for Ilion,
> and brought him to Crete, driving him off course past Maleia.
> He stopped at Amnisos, where there is a cave of Eileithyia,
> in difficult harbors and barely he had escaped from the stormwind.

He then goes on to tell Penelope of how he entertained Odysseus and his companions while they were storm-bound in Amnisos, waiting for a favourable wind to take them to Troy:

> He went up to the town at once, and asked for Idomeneus,
> for he said he was his hereditary friend, and respected;
> but it was now the tenth or eleventh day since Idomeneus
> had gone away along with his curved ships for Ilion.
> But I took him back to my own house, and well entertained him.

When we were on Crete in the 1980s we visited the archaeological site at Amnisos, which in the Minoan period was the port of Knossos. The cave of Eileithyia, known locally as Neraidaspilios, or the Cavern of the Nymphs, is about two kilometres inland from Amnisos. This is one of the most ancient and important shrines on Crete, dating back to the Neolithic period, and votive offerings found within the cave indicate that it was dedicated to Eileithyia, who was worshipped here from as early as 3000 BC through the Graeco-Roman period and on into the early Christian era as the protectress of women in childbirth, an attribute of the ancient fertility goddess. Eileithyia is renowed in Greek mythology for having assisted Leto when she gave birth to Apollo beside the palm tree on Delos, the divine midwife having been summoned there by her mother Hera.

So here again the palm tree on Delos appears, and thus, in his 'lying story' to King Alkinoös, Odysseus reveals the true course of the first stage of his great wanderings, which took him from Troy to Ismaros, then south through the Cyclades to Crete.

From Crete, Odysseus would have headed north-west to pass Cape Maleia and Kythera and round the Peloponnesos to sail up through the Ionian Islands to Ithaca.

Kythera is only nominally one of the Ionian Islands, the Eptanissia, or Seven Isles, for it is far, far away from the Ionian Sea off the south-easternmost promontory of the Peloponnesos – Cape Maleia – with Cape Matapan, the ancient Taenarian promontory, off to its west. Its companion isle – Antikythera – is more remote, lying halfway between Kythera and the north-western capes of Crete. Strabo considered that Kythera and Antikythera marked part of the maritime boundary between the Cretan and Sicilian Seas, forming stepping-stones as they do between Crete and the Peloponnesos.

Kythera is historically linked with the other six isles of the Eptanissia because of an administrative decision made by Venice in 1669, and it remained part of the Ionian Islands until Queen Victoria presented them to the Kingdom of Greece in 1864. When it became part of Greece, Kythera was still known by its Latin name – Cerigo – while Antikythera was called Cerigotto, and only in the past century have they reacquired their classical names.

The earliest references to Kythera are in the *Odyssey* and the *Iliad*. In both epics Homer refers to the island as 'sacred Kythera' because of its famous shrine of Aphrodite Kytheria, the 'sweet garlanded' goddess of love.

As Odysseus tells the story of his wanderings to King Alkinoös, when he reached Cape Maleia the wind drove him off course past Kythera into unknown seas. But he does not describe the island of Kythera or Cape Maleia. The strait between Kythera and Cape Maleia has been feared by Greek mariners since antiquity, for until the opening of the Corinth Canal in 1893 ships sailing between the Ionian and Aegean Seas had to pass this way to round the Peloponnesos, many of them never to return. An old Greek proverb, first quoted by Strabo, says 'But when you double Cape Maleia, forget your home.'

The strait between Kythera and the mainland is just over five nautical miles wide off Elefonissi, an islet off the promontory just west of Cape Maleia. Anciently this was known as Onugnatos, or Donkey's Jaw, and originally it must have been connected to the mainland, for Strabo describes it as 'a low-lying peninsula'. The main port on the mainland for Kythera is Gythion, at the head of the Lakonian Gulf between capes Maleia and Matapan, where ferries cross to Ayia Pelagia and Diakofti, the northernmost of the three ports on the island. The other island port is on the south coast at Kapsali, the harbour of Chora, Kythera's capital, two kilometres inland. Ayia Pelagia is four kilometres south-east of

Akri Spathi, the Kytherean cape known in antiquity as Platania, the Plane Trees. Pausanias writes that in his day the crossing was made

> from the cape on the mainland known as the Donkey's Jaw to the cape on the island called the Plane Trees, a distance of five miles sailing. The people of Kythera have the port of Skandeia on the coast, but the city of Kythera itself is about a mile and a quarter inland from Skandeia. The sanctuary of the Heavenly goddess [Aphrodite] is most sacred and the most ancient of all the sanctuaries in Greece.

Thucydides, in describing the fighting during the seventh year of the Peloponnesian War, 425/424 BC, writes of the Athenian amphibious landing on Spartan Kythera, noting that the port, then called Skandeia, was used by 'merchant ships from Egypt and Libya and also served as a protection to Laconia from attack by pirates from the sea'.

These passages from Thucydides and Pausanias have led most authorities to identify Kastri as the site of Skandeia and Palaeopolis as that of the ancient city of Kythera, capital of the island in classical times.

Hesiod gives an account of Aphrodite's birth in the *Theogony*. There he describes how Uranus, god of the heavens, was castrated by his son Chronus, who threw his father's severed genitals into the sea, giving birth to Aphrodite:

> And as soon as he had cut off the members with flint and cast them from the land into the surging sea, they were swept away over the main a long time: and a white foam spread around them from the immortal flesh, and in it there grew a maiden. First she drew near holy Cythera, and from there, afterwards, she came to sea-girt Cyprus, and came forth an awful and lovely goddess, and grass grew up beneath her shapely feet. Her gods and men call Aphrodite, and the foam-born goddess and rich-crowned Cytherea, because she grew amid the foam, and Cytherea, because she reached Cythera, and Cyprogenes because she was born in billowy Cyprus.

Herodotus writes that the earliest sanctuary of the goddess was at Askalon in Syria, where she was worshipped as Aphrodite Urania, the Heavenly One, with her cult brought from there to Cyprus and Kythera by the Phoenicians. She was worshipped in Mesopotamia in earlier times as the fertility goddess and celestial deity Ishtar, whose name is perpetuated in the Indo-European languages as the word for 'star', including the Greek 'astir', as well as by the Greek name of the planet Venus, 'Aphrodite'.

Pausanias says that 'the Assyrians were the first of the human race to worship the Heavenly One; then the people of Paphos in Cyprus and of Phoenician Askolon in Palestine, and the people of Kythera, who learnt her worship from the Phoenicians'.

According to Aristotle, in prehistoric times the island was known as Porphyrousa, for it was a source of murex (*purpura haemastoma*), the mollusk shell that was much sought after in antiquity for making purple dye. Extensive beds of murex have been found on the southeast coast of Kythera at Avlemonas; the Phoenicians may have had a trading colony there, for Xenophon writes that the port was originally called Phoenicus.

Archaeological excavations in Kythera have unearthed Mycenaean remains, indicating that here, as in Crete, the Achaeans from the Peloponnesos seized power from the Minoans in the late Bronze Age. The island is not included in the Homeric Catalogue of Ships, but elsewhere in the *Iliad* Homer mentions two warriors from Kythera – Amphidamas and Lykophron – who served in Agamemnon's army at Troy.

Schliemann was the first to undertake an archaeological exploration of the island, and in 1888 he thought that he had discovered the famous temple of Aphrodite at Palaeopolis, inland from Kastri, in the bay of Avlemonas on the south-east coast, facing toward Crete. Sylvia Benton of the British School of Archeology in Athens began excavating at Kastri in 1932, unearthing the remains of a Minoan trading post dating from *c*. 2000–1450 BC. Subsequent researches by Benton and other archaeologists of the British School showed that the Minoan colony at Kastri traded with places as far away as Pylos, Troy and Egypt. They also confirmed that ancient Skandeia was in this general area. Palaeocastro, farther inland, is believed to be the site of ancient Kythera, the capital of the island. Here the fourteenth century church of Ayios Kosmas incorporates Doric capitals and other architectural fragments believed to be from the famous temple of Aphrodite. As Peter Levi notes, in a footnote in his translation of Pausanias: 'In July 1437 Cyriaco of Ancona drew the temple ruins *in summa civitatis arca*, and his drawing has survived.' Thus it would seem that Schliemann was once again correct.

The first European traveller known to have visited Cerigo was Cyriacus of Ancona, who in 1437 explored Palaeopolis. By that time a legend had developed that Helen of Troy had been living in Cerigo with Menelaus when she was raped by Paris and taken to

Troy. The English traveller Sir Richard Guylforde repeats this tale in his garbled account of the island and its mythology, published in 1511.

> Upon tewsdaye ayenst nyght we passed by the yle called Cerigo
> whiche yle was sometyme called Citheria where Helena the Grekysshe
>   Queene was borne
> but she was ravysshed by Paris in ye next yle by
> called Cicerigo Doynge sacryfyce in the Temple
> for the whiche Rape followed the distruccion of Troye
> as ye famouse Storye thereof sheweth
> known in every tonge...
> And the sayde yle Cerigo is directly ayenst the poynt of Capo Maleo
>   in Morea
> and in the same eyle was Venus borne.

The ruins of the temple were last seen in 1551 by Nicholas Daulphinios, the French Court Chamberlain and geographer. Daulphinios reported that while in Cerigo he saw the ruins of Aphrodite's temple 'on a high mountain'; two Ionic columns were still standing along with a great portal surmounted by 'a statue of a woman of monstrous size clothed in Greek fashion', presumably Aphrodite. Below the temple an islander showed him the supposed ruins of the 'Castle of Menelaos', though he failed to see the 'Baths of Helen' pointed out to later travellers. George Wheler and his party visited the island in 1675, by which time the Baths of Helen were on the itinerary for foreign sightseers; as he writes:

> Cerigo hath the Morea North of it; and was anciently called Cithera; famous for being the native country of Venus and Helena. So that we are to frame an Idea of this place from the fame of these Beauties, we might imagine it as one of the most charming places of the World. But, on the contrary, the greatest part of it is a barren, rocky and Mountainous Soil, ill peopled, and can brag of no plenty, neither Corn, Wine or Oyl; which undoubtedly made Venus change her own country for Cyprus; and Helena so willing to be stollen and carried into the pleasant plains of the continent. What beauties it now produceth, I am ignorant of; for I remember not that I saw a woman there.

Wheler's ship then entered Avlemonas Bay to take on fresh water at Agios Nikolaos, the cove known to the Venetians as Porto San Nikola, where a local guided them to the ruins.

We found ancient ruins near this place, which we took to be the ruins of Menelaus his City, in old times the King of this Isle. They are almost level with the ground. Among the ruins are some Grottos cut out of the Rock, which one of the Island pretending to be an Antiquary, assured us was anciently the Baths of Helena, affirming that her Palace was not three or four miles thence in the Hills. We took this Antiquary for our guide, and we went to see what we could find of it. But all we discovered were two Pillars standing upright, but without Chapitars [capitals], and the Bases so deep in the ground, that we could not judge what order they were ... I rather believe it to have been some ancient Temple than a Palace. They now call this place Paleo-Castro, or Old Castle.

The French writer Fenelon used the *Odyssey* as the model for his *Telemaque*, published in 1699, which chronicles the wanderings of Telemachus in search of his lost father, describing his stay in Kythera as a pastoral idyll. Fenelon set the scene for romantic paintings of this remote and supposedly enchanted isle, the most famous being Watteau's *Voyage to Cythera*. But some who travelled there were soon disappointed, as was Francis Pouqueville, whose *Travels in the Morea* was published in 1813.

Cerigo is well known to be the ancient Cythera. Here, by a strange caprice of imagination, altars were built to the gay laughter-loving goddess in the midst of a most wild and desolate country. The view from the rocks, though some cultivated fields are to be seen here, is sufficient to disenchant the ideas of poets and lovers who visit the island to indulge in the recollections of antiquity. Instead of Celadons they will see rough peasants; instead of Venus and the Graces, half wild Greek women; and instead of beautiful lawns enamelled with flowers, naked and rugged rocks or valleys overgrown with brushwood.

Travellers approaching the island by sea from Athens usually land at Kapsali, from which a winding road leads up to Chora, the capital of Kythera. The tiered white houses of Chora give it the appearance of a Cycladic village rather than one on the Ionian isles.

The road north into the interior of the island comes to a crossroads at Livadi, where a turn-off to the left leads out to the Myrtidia Monastery on the west coast of the island. Local tradition dates the founding of this monastery to the thirteenth century, though the present structure dates only to 1841. The monastery was built to house an icon of the Virgin that a shepherd boy found on the branches of a myrtle tree on the west shore of the island, and thus it was originally called Myrtidiotissa, Our Lady of the Myrtles, known locally as Myrtidia. The *paneyeri* of the Myrtidia is celebrated on 7 October, when the sacred icon is carried in a procession led by the Bishop of Kythera. This has been the most important festival of Kythera since late Byzantine times, and William Miller, in *The Latins in the Levant*, suggests that the Myrtidiotissa is a survival of the ancient cult of Aphrodite Kytheria, for on that day all of the islanders flock here to celebrate 'the festival of their patron saint, Our Lady of the Myrtle Bough, whose image borne by the waves to the island and found in a myrtle tree represents the Christian version of Aphrodite rising from the sea'.

Those coming out to Kythera via the ferry from Gythion will have come down on the road from Sparti, ancient Sparta, the home of Menelaus. Just outside the harbour at Gythion there is an islet called Marathonisi, ancient Kranae, which is mentioned by Homer in Book 3 of the *Iliad*. According to Homer, this is where Paris and Helen first made love after they fled from the palace of Menelaus on their way to Troy. Paris mentions Kranea when he returns to the citadel after being bested in fighting with Menelaus and is reproved by Helen for risking his life:

> Lady, censure my heart no more in bitter reprovals.
> This time Menelaos with Athene's help has beaten me;
> another time I shall beat him. We have gods on our side also.
> Come, then, rather let us go to bed and turn to love-making.
> Never before as now has passion enmeshed my senses,
> not when I took you the first time from Lakedaimon the lovely
> and caught you up and carried you away in sea-faring vessels
> and lay with you in the bed of love on the island Kranae,
> not even then, as now, did I love you and sweet desire seize me.

Antikythera, the Latin Cerigotto, is one of the loneliest and most remote of the Greek isles, lying in the seldom-travelled seas between Kythera and the north-western capes of Crete. During the summer months there is a twice-weekly ferry service to Kythera, Crete and the Piraeus, but in the winter service is less frequent and during bad weather the island is often cut off from the rest of the world for days on end.

Potamos, the island's only village, nestles in its deeply-indented bay at the northern end of the island. Most of the island's population of some 120 souls lives there, although a few have farm dwellings and summer houses elsewhere on the island. Potamos is near the site of Aigilia, the principal city of ancient Antikythera, whose fragmentary defence-walls can be seen on the Palaeokastro headland, about one and a half kilometres north-east of the town. Palaeokastro was also the site of the medieval town, which throughout the Venetian period was ruled by the Viari, a noble family from Venice who took possession of Cerigotto soon after the Latin conquest of Constantinople in 1204.

Remote as it is, Antikythera must have been a stopping-point for ancient mariners sailing between Crete and the Peloponnesos or those passing between the Aegean and Sicilian Seas. Dramatic evidence of this was discovered in 1900, when a sponge-boat from Symi anchored in Potamos Bay to escape from a storm. A diver from the boat went down to look for sponges and found a wrecked ship of the Roman period on the sea-bottom, its cargo including a consignment of statuary, including an almost perfectly preserved bronze figure of a young man, since placed in the National Archaeological Museum in Athens. Now known as the Ephebe of Antikythera, the statue represents a nude and well-muscled youth, his right arm raised with the fingers curled around as if holding a spherical object, now lost. It has been suggested that the youth is Paris, son of King Priam of Troy, and that he is offering the apple of Eros to Aphrodite in the contest of beauty that was held on Mt Ida in the Troad, judging her the winner over Hera and Athena, whose jealousy provoked the Trojan War. If so, this would be the famous statue of Paris done by the renowned sculptor and painter Euphranor, who worked in Athens in the mid-fourth century BC. The ship on which it was found has been dated to the first or second century BC, perhaps a merchant vessel taking works of art from Athens to Rome, wrecked here on this most remote of the Ionian Isles.

Odysseus and his companions would have seen Antikythera as the wind swept their ships from the Aegean into the western Mediterranean, bringing them from the *oecumenos*, the 'inhabited world', into a world of wonders.

A World of Wonders

Odysseus, telling King Alkinoös and the Phaeacean court of his homeward voyage from Troy, says that the north wind drove him off course past Kythera, and for nine days he was swept along before reaching an unknown land on the tenth day. Thus in rounding Cape Maleia, Odysseus left the known world of the Aegean and entered a world of wonders, through which he wandered for nine years until he finally returned home after many fantastic adventures.

This element of fantasy has led many writers from antiquity till the present to take widely differing attitudes toward the wanderings of Odysseus, ranging from credulity to disbelief. Eratosthenes (*c*. 276–194 BC), head of the famous Library at Alexandria and editor of Homer's epics, believed that the geography of the *Odyssey* was largely imaginary and fabulous, and he wrote that 'you will find the scene of the wanderings of Odysseus when you find the cobbler who sewed up the bag of the winds'. But, as Strabo writes:

> 'And when some skillful man overlays gold upon silver,' just so was Homer wont to add a mythical element to actual occurrences, thus giving flavor and adornment to his style; but he has the same end in view as the historian who narrates facts. So, for instance, he took the Trojan war, an historical fact, and decked it out with his myths; and he did the same in the case of the wanderings of Odysseus; but to hang an empty story of marvels on something wholly untrue is not Homer's way of doing things.

The prevailing wind in the eastern Mediterranean is known in Greek as the *meltemi*, which blows steadily out of the north-east for five or more days at a time. Thus when Odysseus passed Kythera he would have been swept down across the Libyan Sea to the coast of

North Africa, a distance of almost 1,000 kilometres, and would have landed somewhere on the shore of what is now the border between Libya and Tunisia.

I first sailed through the Mediterranean in October 1945, aboard a US Navy troopship, which at the end of World War II was bringing us back from Calcutta to New York via the Suez Canal. I had read the *Odyssey* two years earlier, before dropping out of high school to join the Navy and see the world, and when we passed through the canal and headed westward through the Mediterranean I knew that I would soon cross the wake of Odysseus.

After going through the canal early in the morning, just before dawn the next day, looking out to starboard from the flying bridge, I caught sight of the rockbound promontory of Cape Trypiti on the Greek island of Gavros south of Crete, marking the southernmost point of Europe. Shortly after sunrise, now looking out on the port side, I could see that we were passing the northernmost cape of Libya, known to Strabo as Cape Phycus, just west of the ancient Greek city of Cyrene, capital of Cyrenaica, founded *c.* 630 BC. Then we started across the immense gulf that Strabo called Syrtis Major, stretching from Bengazi to Tripoli, which we passed during the night. At dawn the next day we began turning north-westward to go through the Sicilian Strait, with the coast of Tunisia visible on the port side, passing the deeply indented Gulf of Gabes, Strabo's Syrtis Minor. By sunset we emerged from the strait as we passed Cape Bone to port, turning westward as we passed within sight of Tunis, the site of ancient Carthage. I didn't know it at the time, but that day I had crossed the path of Odysseus twice, the routes he took to and from the coast of North Africa.

Homer, in Book 9 of the Odyssey, describes the first landing-place of Odysseus and his companions after their storm-swept voyage past Cape Maleia and Kythera:

> Nine days then I was swept along by the force of the hostile
> winds on the fishy sea, but on the tenth day we landed
> in the country of the Lotus-Eaters, who live on a flowering
> food, and there we set foot on the mainland, and fetched water,
> and my companions took their supper there by the fast ships.

Strabo, in his description of this part of the North African coast along the Sicilian Strait, writes:

> Near the beginning of the Syrtis [the northern horn of Syrtis Minor]
> lies a long island, Cercinnis [Chergui], which is rather large and

contains a city of the same name; and there is another smaller island, Cercinnitis [Gharbi].

Continuous with these is the Little Syrtis, which is also called the Syrtis of the Lotus-Eaters. The circuit of this gulf is 1,600 stadia [about 200 miles], and the breadth of the mouth 600; and at the breadth of the mouth are islands close to the mainland – the Cercinna above-mentioned and Meninx [Djerba], which are about equal in size. Meninx is regarded as the land of the Lotus-Eaters mentioned by Homer; and certain tokens of this are pointed out – both an altar of Odysseus and the fruit itself; for the tree which is called the lotus abounds on the island and its fruit is delightful.

Odysseus, in Book 9 of the *Odyssey*, tells of what happened to three of his companions when they met the Lotus-Eaters and partook of the lotus:

> But any of them who ate the honey-sweet fruit of lotus
> was unwilling to take any message back, or to go
> away, but they wanted to stay there with the lotus-eating
> people, feeding on lotus, and forget the way home. I myself
> took these men back weeping, by force, to where the ships were,
> and put them aboard the rowing-benches and tied them
> fast, then gave the orders to the rest of my eager
> companions to embark on the ships in haste, for fear
> someone else might taste of the lotus and forget the way home.

Then 'the men quickly went aboard and sat to the oarlocks,/and sitting well in order dashed the oars in the gray sea'.

The Lotus-Eaters, *Lotophagi* in Greek, are also mentioned by Herodotus, who places them in the same area that Strabo does, although his knowledge of the coast here is sketchy:

> There is a cape that projects into the sea from the land of the Gindanes, and there dwell the Lotophagi, who live solely from the enjoyment of the lotus fruit. The fruit of the lotus is about as big as a mastic berry and in sweetness is like the fruit of the palm tree. The Lotophagi also make wine of this fruit.

How and Wells, in their *Commentary on Herodotus* (1912), give some interesting information about this fruit:

> H. [Herodotus] is precise in describing the lotus, because of its legendary fame in Homer as causing forgetfulness of home and family; Polybius describes it even more fully. It is a species of thorn

tree, the jujube (*zizyphus vulgaris*) of the genus Rhamnescea, to which the English buckthorn belongs, with a fruit like a plum in size and shape, which is eaten, especially when dried. The Egyptian lotus is quite distinct ... A sort of wine is still made from the fruit.

Djerba has been populated since prehistoric times by Berbers, the indigenous people of North Africa west of the Nile Valley. They are continuously distributed from the Atlantic coast to the Siwa oasis, on the present border between Libya and Egypt, and from the Mediterranean to the River Niger. Historically they spoke varieties of the Berber language, which together form a branch of the Afro-European family of languages. The modern Berbers are descended from the proto-Berbers, the tribespeople mentioned in the records of ancient Egypt. The proto-Libyan tribes formed during Homeric times, the late Bronze to early Iron Age.

The traditional beliefs of the North African Berbers have been influenced successively by contact with ancient Egypt, Phoenicia, Judaism, Hellenistic Greece, early Christianity, and then medieval Islam. Djerba is a centre of the Islamic sect Al-Ibadhiya, and also had an ancient Jewish community, members of the Cohanim sect, who still worship in the El Ghriba synagogue, one of the oldest in the world, dating to *c.* 500 BC.

Djerba, the largest island of North Africa, with a population of 140,000, is one of the few places in Tunisia where Berber is still spoken. Its beautiful beaches, one of which would have been where Odysseus and his companions landed, have made it a popular tourist destination. Djerba Ajim, the island's third largest town, situated on the narrow channel separating Djerba from the mainland, was in 1977 headquarters for the crew doing the first *Star Wars* film, probably chosen because of the other-worldly atmosphere of the Land of the Lotus-Eaters.

After Odysseus took aboard those of his companions who had partaken of the lotus, they set off on the next stage of their journey, which took them to the Land of the Cyclopes. The voyage may have been a short one, since Odysseus describes it in just two sentences, albeit rather long ones:

> From there, grieving still at heart, we sailed on further
> along, and reached the country of the lawless outrageous
> Cyclopes who, putting all their trust in the immortal
> gods, neither plow with their hands or plant anything,
> but all grows for them without seed planting, without cultivation,
> wheat and barley and also the grapevines, which yield for them
> wine of strength, and it is Zeus' rain that waters it for them.

These people have no institutions, no meetings for counsels;
rather they make their habitations in caverns hollowed
among the peaks of the high mountains, and each one is the law
for his own wives and children, and cares nothing about all the
    others.

Plato suggested (*Laws* 3.680) that Homer's portrayal of the life
of the Cyclopes presents an example of the first stage of civilization,
before mankind engaged in communal and inter-communal activities
and formulated laws. According to Greek mythology, the Cyclopes
were the sons of Uranus, god of the Underworld, and Gaia, Mother
Earth. Hesiod describes them in writing about the children of Gaia:

> And again she bare the Cyclopes, overbearing in spirit, Brontes
> [the Thunderer], Steropes [the Lightener], and stubborn-hearted
> Arges [the Vivid One], who gave Zeus the thunder and made the
> thunderbolt; in all they were like the god, but only one eye was set
> in the midst of their foreheads. Strength and might and craft were in
> their works.

Polyphemus, son of Poseidon, is the most famous of all the
Cyclopes. He is described by Homer in Book 1 of the *Odyssey*, where
Zeus tells Athena that Poseidon is angry at Odysseus because he
blinded his son: 'for Polyphemos like a god, whose power is greatest/
over all the Cyclopes. Thoösa, a nymph, was his mother,/and she was
the daughter of Phorkys, lord of the barren salt water./She in the
hollows of the caves had lain with Poseidon.'
    The first landfall made by Odysseus and his companions in the
land of the Cyclopes was an uninhabited isle that came to be called
the Island of Goats: 'There is a wooded island that spreads away
from the harbor,/neither close in to the land of the Cyclopes nor
far out/from it: forested; wild goats beyond number breed there,/for
there is no coming or going of human kind to disturb them.'
    Odysseus continues, developing the theme that the Cyclopes are
beings who had not gone beyond the first stage of civilization, for
otherwise they would be living on the Island of Goats and would
have built ships to engage in commerce, and would be practicing
agriculture and viniculture, as did the Hellenes:

> For the Cyclopes have no ships with cheeks of vermillion,
> nor have they builders of ships among them, who could have made
>   them
> strong-benched vessels, and these if made could have sailings
> to all the various cities of men, in the way that people

cross the sea by means of ships and visit each other,
and they could have made this island a strong settlement for them.

They sailed to the head of the harbour 'through the gloom of
night, nothing to look at,/for there was a deep mist about the ships,
nor was there any moon/showing in the sky, but she was under
the clouds and hidden'. They then beached the ships, took down
the sails, 'and we ourselves stepped out onto the breach of the sea
beach,/and there we fell asleep and waited for the divine dawn'.

They rose at dawn and 'made a tour about the island admiring
everything'. Seeing all the 'hill-roving goats', they took out their
bows and javelins and killed 109 of them, nine for each of the twelve
ships and one extra for Odysseus. 'So for the whole length of the day
until the sun's setting,/we sat there feasting on unlimited meat and
sweet wine.'

They looked across at the land of the Cyclopes and 'saw their
smoke and heard sheep and goats bleating'. At sunset they lay down
to sleep on the beach, and the next morning Odysseus held an
assembly, saying that he and his crew would cross over to the land
of the Cyclopes, while the rest of the ships should wait where they
were.

> But when we had arrived at that place, which was nearby, there
> at the edge of the land we saw the cave, close to the water,
> high, and overgrown with laurels, and in it were stabled
> great flocks, sheep and goats alike, and there was a fenced yard
> built around it with a high wall of grubbed-out boulders
> and tall pines and oaks with lofty foliage. Inside
> there lodged a monster of a man, who now was herding
> the flocks at a distance away, alone, for he did not range with
> others, but stayed away by himself, his mind was lawless,
> and in truth he was a monstrous wonder to behold, not
> like a man, an eater of bread, but more like a wooded
> peak of the high mountains seen standing away from the others.

Odysseus chose the twelve best men of his companions and went
on with them, telling the rest of his men to remain by the ship. He
filled a wineskin with the sweet red wine that had been given to him
by the priest of Apollo in Ismaros, and took that and a bagful of
provisions along with him.

Polyphemus was off herding his flocks, and so Odysseus and
his companions made their way into the cave, admiring everything
inside it.

Baskets were there, heavy with cheeses, and the pens crowded
with lambs and kids. They had all been divided into separate
groups, the nestlings in one place, and then the middle ones,
the babies again by themselves. And all his vessels, milk pails
and pans, that he used for milking into, were running over
with whey.

Odysseus says that his companions begged him 'to take some of
the cheeses, come back again, and the next time/to drive the lambs
and kids from their pens and get back quickly/to the ships again, and
go sailing off across the salt water'. But Odysseus 'would not listen
to them ... because he was curious to see Polyphemos and try to get
a guest present from him'.

Meanwhile, Odysseus and his companions built a fire and
sacrificed to the gods, helping themselves to the cheeses, waiting for
Polyphemus 'inside, until he came home from his herding. He carried
a heavy/load of dried-out wood, to make a fire for his dinner,/and
threw it down inside the cave, making a terrible/crash, so in fear we
scuttled away into the cave's corners.'

They watched as Polyphemus drove into the cave all the 'fat
flocks that he would milk; leaving the other animals outside in the
yard'. Next 'he heaved up and put in position the huge door stop',
after which he milked his sheep and goats, drawing off half and
putting it in wickerwork baskets to make cheeses, letting the rest
stand in milk pails from which he would drink when he had supper.

But after he had briskly done all his chores and finished,
at last he lit the fire, and saw us, and asked us a question:
'Strangers, who are you? From where do you come sailing over the
        watery
ways? Is it on some business, or are you recklessly roving
as pirates do, when they sail on the salt sea and venture
their lives as they wander, bringing evil to alien people?'
So he spoke, and the inward heart in us was broken
in terror of the deep voice and for seeing him so monstrous;
but even so I had words for an answer.

Odysseus told Polyphemus that they were Achaeans from the
army of Agamemnon returning home after sacking Troy. They had
been blown off course and had come to him as suppliants, hoping
that he might give them

a guest present or otherwise
some gift of grace, for such is the right of strangers. Therefore

respect the gods, O best of men. We are your suppliants,
and Zeus the guest god, who stands behind all strangers with honors
due them, avenges any wrong toward strangers and suppliants.
So I spoke but he answered me in pitiless spirit:
'Stranger, you are a simple fool, or come from far off,
when you tell me to avoid the wrath of the gods or fear them.
The Cyclopes do not concern themselves over Zeus of the aegis,
nor any of the rest of the blessed gods, since we are far better
than they, and for fear of the hate of Zeus I would not spare
you or your companions either, if the fancy took me
otherwise. But tell me, so I may know: where did you
put your well-made ship when you came? Nearby or far off?'

Odysseus says he understood that Polyphemus was just trying
him out, 'but I knew too much and was not/deceived, but answered
him in turn, and my words were crafty'. He told him that

Poseidon, Shaker of the Earth, has shattered my vessel.
He drove it against the rock on the outer coast of your country,
cracked on a cliff, it is gone, the wind on the sea took it;
but I, with those you see, got away from sudden destruction.
...
So I spoke, but he in pitiless spirit answered
nothing, but sprang up and reached for my companions,
caught up two together and slapped them, like killing puppies,
against the ground, and the brains ran all over the floor, soaking
the ground. Then he cut them limb by limb and got supper ready,
and like a lion reared in the hills, without leaving anything,
ate them, entrails, flesh, and the marrowy bones alike. We
cried out aloud and held up our hands to Zeus, seeing
the cruelty of what he did, but our hearts were helpless.

Odysseus waited until Polyphemus fell asleep after eating,
thinking to kill him with his sword, but then he realized that if he
did so they would be trapped in the cave for they would not be able
to remove the great boulder that blocked the entrance.
The next morning Polyphemus milked his flocks:

after he had briskly done all his chores and finished,
again he snatched up two men, and prepared them for dinner,
and when he had dined, drove his fat flocks out of the cavern,
easily lifting off the great doorstone, but then he put it
back again, like a man closing a lid on a quiver.

Odysseus then began thinking about how they might escape, and when he formulated his plan he got his companions to work with him in preparation for carrying it out.

Polyphemus had left lying in the cave 'a great bludgeon of olive wood, still green', which he had cut so that when dried he could use as a cudgel. Odysseus cut off a six-foot length of it and had his companions shave it smooth, while he carved one end to a sharp point, 'then put it over the blaze of the fire to harden'. He then hid the stake away, after which he had his companions draw lots to determine 'which of them must endure with me to take up the great beam/and spin it into Cyclop's eye when sweet sleep had come over him'.

When Polyphemus returned he drove his flocks into the cave and 'set in place the huge door stop', after which he milked his sheep and goats.

> But after he had briskly done all his chores and finished,
> again he snatched two men and prepared them for dinner.
> Then at last I, holding in my hands an ivy bowl
> full of the black wine, stood close up to the Cyclops and spoke out:
> 'Here, Cyclops, have a drink of wine, now you have fed on
> human flesh, and see what kind of wine our ship carried
> inside her. I brought it for you, and it would have been your libation
> had you taken pity and sent me home, but I cannot suffer
> your rages. Cruel, how can any man come and visit
> you ever again, now you have done what has no sanction.'

'So I spoke, and he took it and drank it off, and was terribly/pleased with the wine he drank and questioned me again, saying:/"Give me still more, freely, and tell me your name, straightway./Now, so I can give you a guest present to make you happy."'

Polyphemus drank the wine down and kept calling for more, and when it seemed to be getting to him Odysseus identified himself:

> 'Cyclops, you ask me for my famous name. I will tell you
> then, but you must give me a guest gift as you have promised.
> Nobody is my name. My father and mother call me
> Nobody, as do all the other who are my companion.'
> So I spoke, and he answered me in pitiless spirit:
> 'Then I will eat Nobody after his friends, and the others
> I will eat first, and that shall be my guest present to you.'

Polyphemus collapsed and fell on his back in a drunken stupor, whereupon Odysseus shoved the tip of the sharpened olive beam

into a bed of glowing cinders, heating it until it was on the point
of igniting. He then had his companions position the beam above
Polyphemus, prepared to blind him:

> They seized the beam of olive, sharp at the end, and leaned on it
> into the eye, while I from above putting my weight on it
> twirled it, like a man with a brace and bit who bores into
> a ship timber, and his men from underneath, grasping
> the strap on either side whirl it, and it bites resolutely deeper.
> So seizing the fire-point-hardened timber we twirled it
> in his eye, and the blood boiled around the hot point, so that
> the blast and scorch of the burning ball singed all his eyebrows
> and eyelids, and the fire made the roots of his eye crackle.

Polyphemus screamed in agony, while Odysseus and his
companions 'scuttled away in fear'. Then, after he pulled the beam
out from his eye and threw it away, he cried out to the other Cyclopes
who dwelt in the surrounding caves. They heard him and came
swarming up around the cave and asked him what was his trouble:

> 'Why, Polyphemos, what do you want with all this outcry
> through the immortal night and have made us all sleepless?
> Surely no mortal against your will can be driving your sheep off?
> Surely none can be killing you by force or treachery?'
> Then from inside the cave Polyphemos answered:
> 'Good friends, Nobody is killing me by force or treachery.'

So then the others answered him:

> 'If alone as you are none uses violence on you,
> why there is no avoiding the sickness sent by great Zeus;
> so you had better pray to your father, the lord Poseidon.'
> So they spoke as they went away, and the heart within me
> laughed over how my name and my perfect planning had fooled him.

Polyphemus, groaning in agony, felt his way to the mouth of
the cave and removed the great boulder, 'spreading his arms wide/
to catch anyone who tried to get out with the sheep, hoping/that I
would be so guileless in my heart to try this'.

Odysseus thought for a while until he came up with a plan of
escape. Working silently through the night, he rounded up the rams
in the cave, lashing them together in groups of three each with pliant
willow withes from the bed of Polyphemus:

'I had them in threes, and the one in the middle carried
a man, while the other two went on each side, so guarding
my friends. Three rams carried each man, but as for myself,
there was one ram, far the finest of all the flock. This one
I clasped around the back, snuggled under the wool of the belly,
and stayed there still, and with a firm twist of the hands and enduring
spirit clung fast to the glory of this fleece, unrelenting.
So we grieved for the time and waited for the divine Dawn.

At the break of dawn the rams

hastened out of the cave, toward pasture,
but the ewes were bleating all through the pens unmilked, their
   udders
ready to burst ...
Meanwhile their master, suffering and in
bitter pain, felt all over the backs of his sheep, standing
up as they were, but in his guilelessness did not notice
how my men were fastened under the breasts of his fleecy
sheep. Last of all the flock the ram went out of the doorway
loaded with his own fleece, and with me, and my close counsels.

When they were some distance from the cave, Odysseus got
himself loose from his ram and then freed his companions, whereupon
they drove the sheep down to their ship. He cautioned his waiting
companions to be silent, as they all loaded the 'sheep on board our
vessel and set sail out on the salt water'. When they were almost out
of earshot Odysseus shouted back to Polyphemus, taunting him:

Cyclops, in the end it was no weak man's companions
you were to eat by violence and force in your hollow
cave, and your evil deeds were to catch up with you, and be
too strong for you, hard one, who dared to eat your own guests
to your house, so Zeus and the rest of the gods have punished you.

Polyphemus was so angered that

He broke away the peak of a great mountain and let it
fly, and threw it in front of the dark-prowed ship by only
a little, it just failed to graze the steering-oar's edge,
but the sea washed up in the splash as the stone went under, the tidal
wave it made swept us suddenly back from the open
sea to the mainland again, and forced us back on shore.

Odysseus pushed the ship off from the shore and they rowed hard to escape. When they had gone twice the previous distance he again called out to Polyphemus: 'Cyclops, if any mortal man ever asks you who it was/that inflicted upon you this shameful blinding,/ tell him that you were blinded by Odysseus, sacker of cities./Laertes is his father, and he makes his home in Ithaka.'

Polyphemus groaned aloud and answered, saying that a prophet had once told him that he would lose the sight of his eye at the hands of someone named Odysseus, but now he would call on his father Poseidon to heal him. Odysseus again answered him, saying: 'I only wish it were certain I could make you bereft of spirit/and life, and send you to the land of Hades, as it is certain/that not even the Shaker of the Earth will ever heal your eye for you.'

Polyphemus then called out to Poseidon in prayer, saying if truly '"I am your son, and you acknowledge yourself as my father,/grant that Odysseus, sacker of cities, son of Laertes,/who makes his home in Ithaka, may never reach that home ..."/So he spoke in prayer, and the dark-haired god heard him.'

Polyphemus then lifted a far greater stone than he had before and hurled it at the ship, just missing it. The tidal wave it caused washed the ship up on to the island where the other ships were waiting, and there they shared out the flocks of Polyphemus. Odysseus and his companions spent the rest of the day 'feasting on unlimited meat and sweet wine' until sunset, after which they 'lay down to sleep among the break of the seashore'. At dawn the next day they went aboard their ships, cast off the stern cables, 'and sitting well in order dashed their oars in the gray sea./From there we sailed on further along, glad to have escaped death,/but grieving still for the loss of our dear companions.'

Most writers, both ancient and modern, put the Island of Goats and the Land of the Cyclopes at the eastern tip of Sicily. An interesting minority opinion, which I agree with, is that of the brothers Armin and Hans-Helmut Wolf in their *Die wirkliche Reises des Odysseus. Zur Reconstruction des Homerischen Weltbildes* (The Real Journey of Odysseus ...) (1990). They identify the Island of Goats as Chergui, ancient Cercinna, one of the Kerkennah Islands, off the town of Sfax the northern horn of Syrtis Minor (the Gulf of Gabes).

If the voyage of Odysseus from the Land of the Lotus-Eaters to their next landfall was indeed a short one, say a day and part of the following night, some seventeen hours, at a speed of four knots they would have travelled sixty-five nautical miles, which, according to Strabo, is the distance across the Gulf of Gabes from Mininx (Djerba) to the Kerkennah Islands. The little archipelago was used as a naval base by both the Phoenicians and Romans, both of whom have left ruins on the islands, with Roman mosaics still visible under the drifting sands. Chergui has dense groves of date palms under which goats and sheep still graze, and thus the brothers Wolf identified it as the Island of Goats.

According to the Wolf brothers, the Land of the Cyclopes was on the mainland around the Gulf of Gabes, the northern horn of which, at Sfaz, is 20 kilometres from the nearest point of Chergui, and in my opinion their identification is correct. In antiquity this region was pockmarked with the troglodyte dwellings of the local Berber tribespeople, who, according to tradition, would go underground during invasions and emerge under the cover of night to kill the invaders. This gave rise to the legend that the caves were inhabited by monsters, such as the Cyclopes, who preyed upon strangers.

It has been suggested that the Greek legend of the Cyclopes came from the Libyan myth of the giant Antaeus, son of Poseidon and Gaia, Mother Earth. Polyphemus and Antaeus were both sons of Poseidon, and the Greeks may have absorbed the Libyan legend after they began founding colonies in North Africa during the latter half of the seventh century, following the routes of Mycenaean traders in the late Bronze Age.

According to both Greek and Berber mythology, Antaeus (known to the Berbers as Anti) was a giant in the interior desert of Libya who challenged all passersby to wrestle with him, and when he killed them he collected their bones so that he could use them to construct a temple dedicated to his father Poseidon. One day Heracles visited Antaeus on the way to the Garden of the Hesperides and was challenged to wrestle with him. Heracles found that he was overmatched by his opponent as long as Antaeus was in contact with the earth, his mother, who was his source of strength. But once he lost contact with the ground he lost much of his power, so Heracles finally managed to lift up Antaeus and then crushed him to death in a bear-hug. The Roman poet Ovid writes of this in his *Metamorphoses*, where Heracles says: 'I uprooted Antaeus from his mother's nourishment.'

When the Greeks first colonized Libya in the mid-seventh century BC, they heard tales of this giant Libyan hero, which they soon amalgamated with their travelling hero Heracles. Perhaps Homer, a century earlier, had heard a Mycenaean version of the same legend, which he adapted to have his travelling hero Odysseus defeat the Libyan giant Polyphemus.

The best preserved of the Berber troglodyte dwellings are around Marmata, a village near the southern horn of the Gulf of Gabes, accessible by road from the town of Gabes, the administrative capital of the region. These underground settlements remained unknown to the outside world for centuries, for they were in a very hostile region inhabited mostly by nomadic tribespople.

Then in 1967 the region was deluged by intensive rain that lasted for twenty-two days, inundating the troglodyte homes and causing many of them to collapse. A delegation of the inhabitants went to Gabes, where the authorities provided help in building new houses above ground. But most of the locals eventually rebuilt their troglodyte homes and continue to live in them, as did their ancestors in the night of time.

Marmata was the location for the outdoor scenes in the first *Star Wars* film in 1977, and since then it has been a popular tourist attraction. The Hotel Sidi Driss, a traditional troglodyte dwelling in Marmata, served in the film as the home of Luke Skywalker on the planet Tatooine, and some of the remaining set pieces have been incorporated in its walls.

This was the stretch of North African coast that I passed one day in October 1945, wondering when I would cross the wake of Odysseus.

12

The Witch's Palace

Most ancient and modern writers agree that when Odysseus left the North African coast he sailed north-eastward, and that his next adventures were in and around Sicily and southern Italy. This region was known to the Greeks as Magna Graecia, 'Great Greece', where, beginning early in the eighth century BC, city-states in Greece, most notably Chalcis in Euboea, established more than a score of colonies and emporia, or trading stations.

The earliest of the emporia, founded by the Euboeans not later than 775/770 BC, was on Pithecusae, Italian Ischia, an offshore island 11 kilometres from the northern extremity of the Gulf of Cumae, now the Bay of Naples. Greek pottery dating from the late Bronze (Mycenaean) Age (*c.* 1400 BC) has been unearthed on the island.

Around 750 BC Greek traders moved over from Pithecusae to Cumae on the Italian mainland and established an emporium, which within a quarter-century became an independent *polis*, or city-state. Then, *c.* 730–720 BC they founded Rhegium (Reggio Calabria) on the toe of the Italian peninsula, and across the strait in Sicily they established Zancle (Messina). Subsequently they founded a number of other colonies around the coast of Sicily, including Himera, Catana, and Naxos, the latter in collaboration with the Cycladic island of Naxos. Excavations in Messina have revealed evidence of human occupation as early as the Bronze Age, indicating that here, as elsewhere, the Greeks were resettling on what had been Mycenaean emporia.

And so it was that most of the places in the 'world of wonders' that Odysseus describes in his travels are set in the new Greek world of Magna Graecia, in and around southern Italy.

Homer gives no indication of how long or in what direction Odysseus and his companions sailed after leaving the North African coast. He says only that their next landfall after leaving the land of the Cyclopes was the 'floating island' of Aeolus, mythical ruler of the winds. Aeolus and his wife lived there with their twelve children:

> six of them daughters and six sons in the pride of their youth, so
> he bestowed his daughters on his sons, to be their consorts.
> And evermore, beside their dear father and gracious mother,
> these feast, and good things beside number are set before them;
> and all their days the house fragrant with food echoes
> in the courtyard, but their nights they sleep each one by his modest
> wife, under coverlets, and on bedsteads corded for bedding.

Strabo and most other writers, both ancient and modern, identifies the home of Aeolus as Lipari or one of the other Aeolian Islands north of Sicily. Ernle Bradford differs slightly, putting it at Ustica, an island about 160 kilometres west of Lipari, and I can only agree, given his knowledge of the winds and currents of these seas.

Odysseus narrates:

> We came to the city of these men and their handsome houses,
> and for a whole month he entertained me and asked me everything
> of Ilion, and the ships of the Argives and of the Achaians'
> homecoming, and I told him about the way back and requested
> conveyance, again he did not refuse, but granted me passage.

Aeolus gave Odysseus a bag stuffed with all of the winds but one, setting 'the West Wind free to blow me and carry/the ships and the men aboard them on their way; but it was not/so to be, for we were ruined by our own folly.'

With the west wind behind them, Odysseus relates that they

> sailed on, night and day, for nine days,
> and on the tenth day at last appeared the land of our fathers,
> and we could see people tending fires, we were very close to them.
> But then sweet sleep came upon me, for I was worn out
> with always handling the sheet myself, and I would not give it
> to any other countryman, so that we could come home quicker.

Odysseus tells of how 'my companions talked with each other/ and said that I was bringing silver and gold home with me,/given me by great-hearted Aiolos, son of Hippotas'. One of his men suggested to the others:

'Let us quickly look inside and see what is in there,
and how much silver and gold this bag contains inside it.'
    ...
So he spoke, and the evil counsel of my companions
prevailed, and they opened the bag and the winds all burst out.
    Suddenly
the storm caught them away and swept them over the water
weeping, away from their own country. Then I waking
pondered deeply in my own blameless spirit, whether
to throw myself over the side and die in the open water,
or wait it out in silence and still be one of the living;
and I endured it and waited, and hiding my face I lay down
in the ship, while all were carried on the evil blast of the stormwind
back to the Aiolian island, with my friends grieving.

They beached their ships once again on the island of Aeolus, and
after they found water Odysseus and his companions 'soon took
their supper there by the fast ships'. Odysseus, taking two of his men
with him, then went up to see Aeolus, who was having dinner with
his family. The king asked him, 'What brings you back, Odysseus?
What evil spirit has vexed you?/We sent you properly on your way
home, so you could come back/to your own country and house and
whatever else is dear to you.'
Odysseus replied:

'My wretched companions brought me to ruin, helped by the pitiless
sleep. Then make it right, dear friends, for you have the power.'
So I spoke to them, plying them with words of endearment,
but they were all silent; only the father found words and answered:
'O least of living creatures, out of this island! Hurry!
I have no right to see on his way, none to give passage
to any man whom the blessed gods hate with such bitterness.
Out. This arrival means you are hateful to the immortals.'
    ...
So speaking he sent me, groaning heavily, out of his palace,
and from there, grieving still at heart, we sailed on further,
but the men's spirit was worn away with the pain of rowing
and our own silliness, since homecoming seemed ours no longer.
Nevertheless we sailed on, night and day, for six days,
and on the seventh day came to the sheer citadel of Lamos,
Telepylos of the Laestrygonians.

Most writers both ancient and modern have put the
Laestrygonians in Magna Graecia, with Thucydides identifying

them as the first inhabitants of Sicily. A number of modern scholars place them at the eastern tip of Sicily, around the huge sound known as the Stagnone di Marsala, just north of the city of Marsala, the westernmost on the island.

At its northern horn the bay is almost enclosed by the long Isola Grande, whose northern tip was probably joined to the mainland in antiquity, forming a deep natural harbour. This was the site of the Phoenician colony of Motya, founded *c.* 725 BC by settlers who would have sailed directly across the Sicilian Strait from Carthage. Sixteen kilometres to the north looms Mt Eryx (Erice), its peak at about 750 metres a landmark for passing mariners from the time of Odysseus to our own, as I noted when we steamed around the eastern tip of Sicily on an Italian passenger-ship in September 1963, after leaving Palermo en route to the Greek port of Patras.

The historic town of Erice atop the mountain, which still retains fragments of its Phoenician walls, is crowned with a medieval Norman castle built on the ruins of the ancient Roman temple of Venus Ercina, supposedly built by Aeneas. This is the landmark that Odysseus called Lamos when he first spotted the land of the Laestrygonians, unaware that they were lawless giant *anthropophagi*, or cannibals.

He describes 'the glorious harbor, which a sky-towering/cliff encloses on either side, with no break anywhere,/and two projecting promontories facing each other/ran towards the mouth, and there is a narrow entrance'.

Odysseus kept his ship on the outside end of the harbour, tied to the cliff with a cable. He climbed to the top of a rocky prominence to survey the surroundings, but he saw no men nor cattle, only 'smoke going up from the country'. So he sent three of his companions to find out 'what men, eaters of bread, might live here in this country'. His companions walked along a road leading down from the hills to the city and met a girl drawing water, who told that she was the daughter of Antiphates, King of the Laestrygonians, pointing out the house where her family lived. But when they entered the house they found there a woman

> as big as a mountain peak, and the sight of her filled them with
>   horror.
> At once she summoned famous Antiphates, her husband,
> from their assembly, and he devised dismal death against them.
> ...
> He snatched up one of my companions, and prepared him for dinner.
> But the other two darted away in flight, and got back to my ship.
> The king raised the cry through the city. Hearing him the powerful

Laistrygones came swarming from every direction,
tens of thousands of them, and not like men, like giants.

The giants ran to the cliffs above the harbour, where all but one
of the Achaean ships lay tied up side by side, helpless. Only that of
Odysseus was outside the harbour, from where he saw the destruction
being unleashed on his companions by the Laestrygonians. 'These,
standing along the cliffs, pelted my men with man-sized/boulders,
and a horrid racket went up by the ships, of men/being killed and
ships being smashed to pieces. They speared them/like fish, and
carried them away for their joyless feasting.'

Meanwhile, Odysseus drew his sword and cut the cable that tied
his ship to the cliff. He says he

called out to my companions, and urged them with all speed
to throw their weight on the oars and escape the threatening evil,
and to make the water fly, fearing destruction. Gladly
my ship, and only mine, fled out from the overhanging
cliffs to the open water, but the others were all destroyed there.

The next stage of their journey took them to the island of Aiaia,
home of Circe, a goddess *pharmakia*, a witch or sorceress, who was
skilled in the magic process of metamorphosis, or shape-shifting, and
the dark art of necromancy, divination by communicating with the
dead, and in the use of wizard drugs. Her brother Aietes lived on
the isle of Aia, the land of the far east, while Aiaia was thought to
be in the far west, on the boundary between the sea and the River
Oceanos which encircled the earth.

Odysseus says that 'We came to Aiaia, which is an island. There
lived Circe of the lovely hair, the dread goddess who talks with
mortals.' He goes on: 'There we brought our ship into the shore,
in silence,/at a harbor fit for ships to lie, and some god guided us/
in. There we disembarked, and for two days and two nights/we lay
there, for sorrow and weariness eating our hearts out.'

When the third day dawned, Odysseus, armed with his spear
and sword, set out 'to look for some trace of people, listen for some
sound./I climbed to a rocky point of observation and stood there,/
and got a sight of smoke which came from the halls of Circe/going
up from wide-wayed earth through undergrowth and forest.'

All ancient sources, and most modern writers, including Ernle
Bradford, agree in identifying Aiaia as Cape Circeo, the north-
western horn of the Gulf of Gaeta, just to the north beyond the
Gulf of Naples. The promontory, which is also called Monte Circeo,
its peak rising to 541 metres, is connected to the mainland by low

flat land, alluvial earth carried into the sea by the Tiber, so that in antiquity it was probably an island. Strabo says 'The Island of Circe lies between the marshes and the sea, and it really is an island.' Ernle Bradford quotes the *Admiralty Pilot* for the west coast of Italy:

> Promentario or Monte Circeo, of which Cape Circeo is the southwestern extremity, is an isolated rocky mass, which rises steeply, and is covered with sparse vegetation. The promontory is connected with the mainland by low flat land and when seen from north-north-westward, it appears as a high conical and pointed island.

After surveying the island, Odysseus pondered on whether he should go on farther to investigate, but he decided that he would first go back to the ship and arrange dinner for his companions. As he neared the ship 'a great stag with towering antlers' appeared in his path, and Odysseus killed him with his javelin, after which he carried the beast back to his companions, who 'washed their hands and set to preparing a communal high feast'.

They spent the rest of that day 'feasting on unlimited meat and sweet wine', and when night came on they lay down to sleep on the seashore. When the sun rose Odysseus assembled his companions and told them what he had seen in his observation of the island the day before, saying there was no course open to them other than to investigate it further. For they had no idea of where they were and needed to find Circe's dwelling-place, since she was the only one who could help them.

They were all saddened on learning that the island was inhabited, remembering the disasters they had suffered at the hands of the Cyclops and the Laestrygonians. With this in mind, Odysseus divided his companions into two equal groups, he himself heading one, 'while godlike Eurylochos had the other'. They then drew lots in a helmet to see who would go off to make contact with Circe, 'and the lot of great-hearted Eurylochos sprang out. He then/went on his way, and with him two and twenty companions.'

They came upon Circe's house in the forest glen

> and all about it there were lions, and wolves of the mountains,
> whom the goddess had given evil drugs, and enchanted,
> and these made no attack on the men, but came up thronging
> about them, waving their long tails and fawning …
> They stood there in the forecourt of the goddess with the glorious
> hair, and heard Circe inside singing in a sweet voice
> as she went up and down a great design on a loom, immortal

such as goddesses have, delicate and lovely and glorious
their work.

They then called out to Circe, 'and at once she opened the shining
doors, and came out, and invited/them in, and all in their innocence
entered; only/Eurylochos waited outside, for he suspected treachery'.
Circe sat them down 'and mixed them a potion, with barley and
cheese and pale honey/added to Prammeian wine, but put into
the mixture/malignant drugs, to make them forgetful of their own
country'. After they drank the potion

she struck them with her wand and drove them into her pig pens,
and they took on the look of pigs, with the heads and voices
and bristles of pig, but the minds within them stayed as they had
    been
before. So crying they went I, and before them Circe
threw down acorns for them to eat, and ilex and cornel
buds, such food as pigs on the ground always feed on.

Eurylochos fled back to the ship and told his companions what
had happened. Odysseus armed himself with his sword and bow
and told Eurylochos to guide him back to Circe's dwelling. But
Eurylochos begged not to be taken against his will, telling Odysseus
that he and his companions at Circe's house would never return, so
'Let us rather make haste, and with these/who are left, escape, for we
may still avoid the day of evil.'
Odysseus told Eurylochos to remain by the ship, saying that he
himself would go alone. As he was approaching Circe's house, he
met Hermes, in the guise of a young man. Hermes warned Odysseus
that he would never return from Circe's house unless he took the
medicine and advice that he would now give him:

'She will make you a potion, and put drugs in the food, but she will
    not
even so be able to enchant you, for this good medicine
which I give you now will prevent her. I will tell you the details
of what to do. As soon as Circe with her long wand strikes you,
then drawing from beside your thigh your sharp sword, rush
forward against Circe, as if you were raging to kill her.
    ...
she will be afraid, and invite you to go to bed with her.
Do not resist and refuse the bed of the goddess,
for she will set free your companions, and care for you also;
but bid her swear the great oath of the blessed gods, that she

has no other evil that she is devising against you,
so she will not make you weak and unmanned, once you are naked.'
So spoke Agreïphontes, and he gave me the medicine,
which he picked out of the ground, and he explained the nature
of it to me. It was black at the root, but with a milky
flower. The gods call it moly. It is hard for mortal
men to dig up, but the gods have power to do all things.

Ernle Bradford cites R. M. Henry's article on the plant in the *Classical Review* of December 1906 (p. 434) in writing about moly: 'R. M. Henry concluded that the legend of the sacred plant derived from Phoenician or Egyptian sources. Since classical times the name has been applied to a species of garlic (*Allium Moly*) which has yellow flowers.'

Hermes then flew away and Odysseus made his way to Circe's house, where he stood outside and shouted aloud. She immediately opened the doors and invited him in, whereupon, as he says,

and I, deeply troubled in my heart, went in with her.
...
She made a potion for me to drink and gave it to me in a golden
cup, and with evil thoughts in her head added the drug to it.
Then when she had given it and I drank it off, without being
enchanted, she struck me with her wand and spoke and named me:
'Go to your sty now and lie down with your other friends there.'

When she spoke to him, Odysseus responded by doing exactly what he had been advised to do by Hermes:

I, drawing from beside my thigh the sharp sword,
rushed forward against Circe as if I were raging to kill her,
but she screamed aloud and ran under my guard, and clasping both
    knees
in loud lamentation spoke to me and addressed me in winged words:
'What man are you and whence? What are your city and parents?
The wonder is on me that you drank my drugs and have not been
enchanted, for no other man beside could have stood up
under my drugs, once he drank and they passed the barrier
of his teeth. There is a mind in you no magic will work on.
...
You are then resourceful Odysseus. Argeïphontes
of the golden staff was forever telling me you would come
to me, on your way back from Troy with your fast black ship.
Come then, put away your sword in its sheath, and let us

two go up into my bed so that, lying together
in the bed of love, we may then have faith and trust in each other.'

Odysseus, again recalling the advice of Hermes, responded by asking Circe how could he trust her when she had turned his companions into pigs, and might do the same to him once he was naked and helpless. Then he asked her to swear the oath that Hermes had advised:

'I would not be willing to go to bed with you unless
you can bring yourself, O goddess, to swear a great oath
that there is no other evil hurt you devise against me.'
So I spoke, and she at once swore me the oath, as I asked her,
but after she had sworn me the oath, and made an end of it,
I mounted the surpassingly beautiful bed of Circe.

Circe had her maidservants bathe Odysseus and give him food and drink. But nothing seemed to please him, and Circe asked him what was wrong. Odysseus said to her,

Oh, Circe, how could any man right in his mind ever
endure to taste of the food and drink that are set before him,
until with his eyes he saw his companions set free? So then,
if you are sincerely telling me to eat and drink, set them
free, so my eyes can again behold my eager companions.

As soon as he spoke, Circe took up her wand and walked through the palace and opened the doors of the pigsty, where she freed the companions of Odysseus:

They looked like nine-year-old porkers. They stood
ranged and faced her, and she, making her way through their
ranks, anointed each of them with some other medicine,
and the bristles, grown upon them by the evil medicine Circe
had bestowed upon them before, now fell away from them,
and they turned back once more into men, younger than they had been
and taller for the eye to behold and handsomer by far.

The freed companions of Odysseus recognized him at once and clustered around him, clinging to his hand and weeping together with him. Circe was so moved by this that she spoke to Odysseus, telling him to go down to the shore to beach his ship 'and then come back, and bring with you the rest of your eager companions'.

Odysseus did so, and after some resistance from Eurylochos, who feared a trap, they followed him as he made his way back to Circe's palace.

> Meanwhile, inside the house, Circe with loving care bathed
> the rest of my companions, and anointed them well with olive oil,
> and put about them mantles of fleece and tunics. We found them
> all together, feasting well in the halls. When my men
> looked each other in the face and knew one another,
> they burst into an outcry of tears, and the whole house echoed.

Circe then spoke to Odysseus, saying,

> But come now, eat your food and drink your wine, until
> you gather back again into your chests that kind of spirit
> you had in you when first you left the land of your fathers
> on rugged Ithaka. Now you are all dried out, dispirited
> from the constant thought of your hard wandering, nor is there any
> spirit in your festivity, because of so much suffering.

Odysseus says that 'So she spoke, and the proud heart in us was persuaded.' He recites:

> There for all our days until a year was completed
> we sat there feasting on unlimited meat and sweet wine.
> But when it was the end of a year, and the months wasted
> away, and the seasons changed, and the long days were accomplished,
> then my eager companions called me aside and said to me:
> 'What ails you now? It is time to think about our own country,
> if truly it is ordained that you shall survive and come back
> to your strong-founded house and to the land of your fathers.'

Odysseus was persuaded, and after a day of feasting with his companions he pleaded with Circe to keep her promise that she would see him off on his homeward voyage. He says that when they all retired to their chambers, he mounted

> the surpassingly beautiful bed of Circe,
> clasped her by the knees and entreated her, and the goddess
> listened to me, and I spoke to her and addressed her in winged words:
> 'O Circe, accomplish now the promise you gave, that you
> would see me on my way home. The spirit within me is urgent
> now, as also in the rest of my friends, who are wasting
> my heart away, lamenting around me, when you are elsewhere.'

Circe told him that he and his companions need

> no longer stay in my house when none of you wish to.
> ...
> but first there is another journey you must accomplish
> and reach the house of Hades and of revered Persephone,
> there to consult with the soul of Teiresias the Theban,
> the blind prophet, whose senses stay unshaken within him,
> to whom alone Persephone has granted intelligence
> even after death, but the rest of them are flittering shadows.

Odysseus was heartbroken by her response and reduced to tears. Then, when he recovered, he asked the goddess: 'Circe, who will be our guide on that journey? No one/has ever yet in a black ship gone all the way to Hades.' She answered by telling him that he need only set his sail and let the north wind carry him on:

> But when you have crossed with your ship the stream of the Ocean,
> you will
> find there a thickly wooded shore, and the groves of Persephone,
> and tall black poplars growing, and fruit-perishing willows;
> then beach your ship on the shore of the deep-eddying Ocean
> and yourself go forward into the moldering home of Hades.
> There Pyriphlegethon and Kokytos, which is an off-break
> from the water of the Styx, flow into Acheron. There is
> a rock there, and the junction of two thunderous rivers.

Circe then told Odysseus the ritual sacrifices he must perform to attract the souls of the dead. 'The numerous/souls of the perished will come and gather about you./ ... while you yourself, drawing from beside your thigh the sharp sword,/crouch there and do not let the strengthless heads of the perished/dead draw nearer to the blood until you have questioned Teiresias.'

Circe said to Odysseus that Teiresias would then come to 'tell you the way to go, the stages of your journey,/and tell you how to make your way home on the sea where the fish swarm.'

Odysseus says that at dawn, 'I walked all about the house and roused my companions,/standing beside each man and speaking to him in kind words:/"No longer lie abed and dreaming away in sweet sleep./The queenly Circe has shown me the way. So let us go now."'

But the youngest of his men, Elpenor, had fallen asleep drunkenly on the roof of Circe's palace, and when he heard his companions rising, did not climb down the ladder, 'but blundered straight off the edge of the roof, so that his neck bone/was broken out of its sockets, and his soul went down to Hades'.

Odysseus spoke to his men on the way down to their ship, telling them 'You think that you are on your way back now to your own beloved/country, but Circe has indicated another journey/for us to the house of Hades and of revered Persephone/there to consult with the soul of Teiresias the Theban.'

His companions were heartbroken, for they had thought they were at last headed homeward. Odysseus tells them

> When we came down to our fast ship and the sand of the seashore,
> we sat down, sorrowful, and weeping big tears. Circe
> meanwhile had gone down herself to the side of the black ship,
> and tethered aboard it a ram and one black female, easily
> passing by us unseen. Whose eyes can follow the movement
> of a god passing from place to place, unless the god wishes?

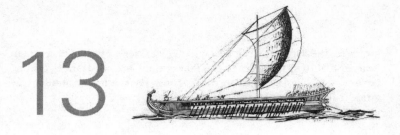

Dialogue with Death

Odysseus and his companions dragged their ship down into the water, set the mast and sail in place, took the sheep aboard, and sorrowfully embarked. 'Circe/of the lovely hair, the dread goddess who talks with mortals', he says,

> sent us an excellent companion, a following wind, filling
> the sails, to carry from astern the ship with the dark prow.
> We ourselves, over all the ship making fast the running gear,
> sat still, and let the wind and the steersman hold her steady,
> all day long her sails were full as she went through the water,
> and the sun set, and all the journeying-ways were darkened.
> ...
> She made the limit, which is of the deep-running Ocean.
> There lie the community and city of Kimmerian people,
> hidden in fog and cloud, nor does Helios, the radiant
> sun, ever break through the dark, to illuminate them with his shining,
> neither when he climbs up into the starry heaven,
> not when he returns again from heaven to earth,
> but always a glum night is spread over wretched mortal.
> Making this point, we ran the ship ashore, and took out
> the sheep, and ourselves walked along by the stream of the Ocean
> until we came to that place of which Circe had spoken.

Writers both ancient and modern, including Ernle Bradford, put Homer's Hades beyond the Pillars of Heracles (Herakles) on the eastern shores of the Atlantic, which in Homeric times would be the all-encompassing river of Ocean. The first Greek geographer, Hecataeus of Miletus, described the bounds of the *oecumenos*, or 'inhabited world', in his *Circuit of the Earth* (*c.* 500 BC), where the limits to the west are the 'Pillars of Herakles'. Pindar, in a poem written *c.* 470–460 BC, calls the Pillars the Gates of Gades (Cadiz), beyond which one comes to the 'gloomy dark which nobody may cross', the Atlantic Ocean.

Robin Lane Fox writes:

> Other travelers, followed by Herodotus, identified them with the Straits of Gibraltar. One pillar, they suggested, was the Rock, while the other was Cueta on the coast of modern Morocco. Heracles, it was said, had either widened the straits to allow a route through to Outer Ocean or had narrowed them so as to block out Ocean's sea-monsters.

The Greeks of Homer's time would have known about the Straits of Gibraltar from the Phoenicians, who by the ninth century BC had established an outpost at what is now Huelva in south-west Spain beyond Cadiz. At that time the Phoenicians erected a temple to their god Melqart, whom the Greeks identified with the hero Heracles. According to Strabo, the two bronze pillars in this temple, each eight cubits high, were believed to be the true Pillars of Heracles.

Homer would have heard of the Pillars of Heracles but he almost certainly would not have seen them. Euripides, writing in the fifth century BC, some three centuries after Homer, says that at the Pillars 'lies the end of voyaging, and the Ruler of Ocean no longer permits mariners to travel on the purple sea', although by then Greek mariners from Phoecea in Asia Minor had sailed out through the straits and founded a colony at Tartessus, in what is now Seville.

The ancient Greeks distinguished between a *katabasis*, an actual journey to the Underworld, such as those of Odysseus and several other Greek and Roman heroes, and a *nekyia*, a ritual in which the participant is able to communicate with the ghosts of the departed, who may be queried about the future, i.e. necromancy. The gods associated with the *nekyia* rite include Hades, his wife Persephone, and Hermes in his role as Psychopompus, the escort of souls to Hades.

There were a number of sites in the ancient Greek world dedicated wholly or in part to the practice of necromancy, usually caverns believed to communicate directly with the Underworld. The most famous of these was the Necromanteion in Ephyra, also known as Kichyros, in what is now Epiros in north-western Greece, the region known to Homer as Thesprotia, on the mainland opposite Ithaca and the other northern Ionian Islands. This site was first mentioned by the traveller Pausanias, writing in the second century AD in his *Description of Greece*: 'Near Kichyros lie an Acherousian lake and a river Acheron, and the detestable stream Kokytos. I think Homer must have seen this region and in his very daring poetry about Hades taken the names of rivers from the rivers in Thesprotia.'

The site of Ephyra has been unearthed ten kilometres south-east of Parga. The Necromanteion is on the hill of Aghios Ioannis near the village of Mesopotamos, 150 metres north of the confluence of the rivers Kokytos and Acheron, which flow to the sea through a marsh which was once the Acherousian lake and the course of the River Pyriphlegethon. As noted earlier, Homer used these names in describing the rivers of Hades, where he has Circe tell Odysseus that 'There Pyriphlegethon and Kokytos, which is an off-break from the water of the Styx, flow into Acheron.'

Excavations on the acropolis of Ephyra have unearthed potsherds of the Bronze Age and the Mycenaean period, as well as votive objects dating to as early as the seventh century BC dedicated to the goddess Persephone, wife of Hades, god of the Underworld. The Necromanteion was excavated in 1958–64 and again in 1967 by the Greek archaeologist Sotirios Dakaris, who found evidences of sacrifices to the dead similar to those that Odysseus was instructed to make by Circe. Dakaris dated the site to the late fourth century BC, though he found votive objects dating back to the seventh century BC, and he concluded that the Necromanteion was destroyed when the Romans conquered Epiros in 167 BC.

When we visited the site in 1988 we walked up the deeply worn stone steps to the Necromanteion, which has been restored to a semblance of its state in the Hellenistic period. As Professor Dakaris describes it, the Necromanteion was built on two levels, the upper floor for those who came to consult the oracle, and the lower for the souls of the dead. Following a cleansing ceremony, the pilgrims were led along a maze of corridors, passing through a series of three iron gates before they came to the room where they consulted the oracle, who would question them and then communicate with the souls of the dead below, passing on their responses.

The Necromanteion at Ephyra is only a short way south of the famous oracle of 'the whispering oak' of Zeus at Dodona, the oldest in the Greek world, surpassed in importance only by the oracle of Pythian Apollo at Delphi. Homer mentions Dodona in Book 14 of the *Odyssey*, in a false story that the disguised Odysseus relates first to the faithful swineherd Eumaeus and then to his wife Penelope, telling them that in Thesprotia he had received word of the real Odysseus, who had been given refuge there by the king. And so, as Pausanias surmised, it would seem that Homer was familiar with the shrines of Thesprotia, modern Epiros, and thus he used his knowledge of the Necromanteion at Ephyra to describe the topography and ritual of Hades for the visit of Odysseus to the Underworld.

When Odysseus arrived in Hades he did exactly what he had been told to do by Circe, thus summoning up the souls of the departed from the Underworld. There were

> brides and young unmarried men, and long-suffering elders,
> virgins, tender and with the sorrows of young hearts upon them,
> and many fighting men killed in battle, stabbed with brazen
> spears, still carrying their bloody armor upon them.
> These came swarming around my pit from every direction
> with inhuman clamor, and green fear took hold of me.
> ...
> Then I encouraged my companions and told them, taking
> the sheep that were lying by slaughtered with the pitiless
> bronze, to skin these, and burn them, and pray to the divinities,
> to Hades the powerful, and to revered Persephone,
> while I myself, drawing from beside my thigh my sharp sword,
> crouched there, and would not let the strengthless heads of the
>   perished
> dead draw nearer to the blood, until I had questioned Teiresias.

But then there appeared before him the soul of his departed companion Elpenor, who had died when he fell from the roof of Circe's palace and had been left behind unburied when they hastily began their voyage to Hades. Odysseus burst into tears when he saw him, saying 'Elpenor, how did you come here beneath the fog and the darkness?/You have come faster on foot than I could in my black ship.'

Elpenor groaned and answered, pleading with Odysseus not to leave him behind unwept and unburied when he leaves Circe's isle again after his return from Hades, 'for fear I might be the god's curse upon you':

> but burn me there with all my armor that belongs to me,
> and heap up a grave mound beside the beach of the gray sea,
> for an unhappy man, so that those to come will know of me.
> Do this for me, and on top of the grave mound plant the oar
> with which I rowed when I was alive and among my companions.
> So he spoke and I in turn spoke to him in answer:
> 'All this, my unhappy friend, I will do for you as you ask me.'

Odysseus stood there for a while talking sadly with the phantom of Elpenor, holding his sword over the pit of blood to keep the ghosts of the dead away, until the soul of his departed mother appeared before him:

> Next there came to me the soul of my dead mother,
> Antikleia, daughter of great-hearted Autolykos,
> whom I had left alive when I went to sacred Ilion.
> I broke into tears at the sight of her and my heart pitied her.
> But even so, for all my thronging sorrow, I would not
> let her draw near the blood until I had questioned Teiresias.

Then the soul of Teiresias appeared, holding

> a staff of gold, and he knew who I was, and spoke to me:
> 'Son of Laertes, and seed of Zeus, resourceful Odysseus,
> how is it then, unhappy man, you have left the sunlight
> and come here, to look on dead men, and this place without pleasure?
> Now draw back from the pit, and hold your sharp sword away from
>   me,
> So that I can drink of the blood and speak the truth to you.'

Odysseus sheathed his sword and Teiresias, after he had drunk the blood, began speaking to him: 'Glorious Odysseus, what you are after is sweet homecoming,/but the gods will make it hard for you. I think you will not/escape the Shaker of the Earth, who holds a grudge against you/in his heart, and because you blinded his dear son, hates you.'

Teiresias tells Odysseus that if he and his companions kill the cattle of Helios, the sun god, 'you will come home in bad case, with the loss of all your companions,/in someone else's ship, and find troubles in your household,/insolent men, who are eating away your livelihood/ and courting your godlike wife and offering gifts to win her.'

Odysseus said in answer: 'All this, Teiresias, surely must be as the gods spun it.' Then he asked Teiresias how he could communicate with his mother, who was sitting beside the pool of blood in silence. Teiresias told him that any of the perished dead whom he allowed to come 'to the blood will give you a true answer, but if you begrudge this/to any one, he will return to the place where he came from'.

Having said this, Teiresias went back into 'the house of Hades', while Odysseus waited patiently until his mother 'came and drank the dark-clouding blood, and at once she knew me,/and full of lamentation she spoke to me in winged words':

> My child, how did you come here beneath the fog and the darkness
> and still alive? All this is hard for the living to look on,

for in between lie the great rivers and terrible waters
that flow, Ocean first of all, which there is no means of crossing
on foot, not unless one has a well-made ship. Are you
come now to this place from Troy, with your ship and your
    companions,
after wandering a long time, and have you not yet come
to Ithaka, and there have you seen your wife in your palace?

Odysseus told her that he had come to Hades to consult the soul of Teiresias, for he had not set foot on Ithaca since he left with Agamemnon in the expedition against Troy. Then he asked her about herself and the rest of his family, particularly his wife Penelope. Antikleia told him that Penelope still awaited his return 'with enduring heart', while his son Telemachus 'administers your allotted lands', while his father Laertes remains on the estate, grieving, 'as he longs for your homecoming, and harsh old age is on him'. Antikleia then told her son that she herself had not died of illness, 'but, shining Odysseus, it was my longing for you, your cleverness/and your gentle ways, that took the sweet spirit of life from me'.

So she spoke, but I, pondering it in my heart, yet wished
to take the soul of my dead mother in my arms. Three times
I started toward her, and my heart was urgent to hold her,
and three times she fluttered out of my hands like a shadow
or a dream, and the sorrow sharpened at the heart within me,
and so I spoke to her and addressed her in winged words, saying:
'Mother, why will you not wait for me, when I am trying
to hold you, so that even in Hades with our arms embracing
we can both take the satisfaction of dismal mourning?
Or are you nothing but an image that proud Persephone
sent my way, to make me grieve all the more for sorrow?'

Antikleia answered him immediately, saying 'this is not Persephone, daughter of Zeus, beguiling you,/but it is only what happens, when they die, to all mortals':

The sinews no longer hold the flesh and the bones together,
and once the spirit has left the white bones, all the rest
of the body is made subject to the fire's strong fury,
but the soul flutters out like a dream and flies away. Therefore
you must strive back toward the light again with all speed; but
    remember these
things for your wife, so you may tell her hereafter.

While Odysseus was talking with Antikleia, Persephone had sent his way the shades of all the noble women in the Underworld, 'all who had been the wives and daughters of princes,/and now they gathered in swarms around the dark blood'. He decided that he 'would not let them all drink the dark blood at the same time./So they waited and came to me in order, and each one/told me about her origin.'

At that point Odysseus interrupted his long tale to Alkinoös and his court, saying that it is time for him to go to sleep. But Alkinoös urged him to go on, saying,

Did you see any of your godlike companions, who once with you
went to Ilion and there met their destiny? Here is
a night that is very long, it is endless. It is not time yet
to sleep in the palace. But go on telling your wonderful story.
I myself could hold out until the bright dawn, if only
you could bear to tell me, here in the palace, of your sufferings.

Odysseus then went on, saying to Alkinoös,

if you insist on hearing me still, I will not begrudge you
the tale of these happenings and others yet more pitiful
to hear, the sorrows of my companions, who perished later,
who escaped onslaught and cry of battle, but perished
all for the sake of a vile woman, on the homeward journey.

Odysseus says that when Persephone dispersed the souls of the women who were still gathered around the pool of blood, 'there came the soul of Agamemnon, son of Atreus,/grieving, and the souls of the other men, who died with him/and met their doom in the house of Aigisthos, were gathered around him'.

He knew me at once, when he had drunk the dark blood, and fell to
lamentation loud and shrill, and the tears came springing,
and threw himself into my arms, meaning so to embrace me,
but there was no force there any longer, nor any juice left
now in his flexible limbs, as there had been in times past.
I broke into tears at the sight of him and my heart pitied him.

Odysseus questioned the shade of Agamemnon, asking him about the circumstances of his death. Agamemnon, answering him, said that he had not died in a storm at sea nor in a battle on land, but that he had been murdered by his wife Clytemestra and her lover Aegisthus, who also killed his companions and Priam's daughter

Kassandra, whom he had taken captive at Troy. He described the gory scene, saying that it was worse than anything Odysseus had observed in battle:

> we lay sprawled by the mixing bowl and the loaded
> tables, all over the palace, and the whole floor was steaming
> with blood; and most pitiful was the voice I heard of Priam's
> daughter Kassandra, killed by treacherous Klytaimestra
> over me; but I lifted my hands and with them beat on
> the ground as I died upon the sword, but the sluttish woman
> turned away from me and was so hard that her hands would not
> press shut my eyes and mouth though I was going to Hades.

Odysseus relates that he stood there for a while talking with the ghost of Agamemnon, exchanging sad words and weeping together. After this they were joined by the souls of Achilles, Patroclus, Antilochus and Telamonian Aias. The first to speak was Achilles:

> The soul of swift-footed Achilleus, scion of Aiakos, knew me,
> and full of lamentations he spoke to me in winged words:
> 'Son of Laertes and seed of Zeus, resourceful Odysseus,
> hard man, who made you think of this bigger endeavor, how could
> you
> endeavor to come down here to Hades' place, where the senseless
> dead men dwell, mere imitations of perished mortals?'

Odysseus answered, telling Achilles that he had come to consult Teiresias about how he 'might come back to rocky Ithaka', for he had not yet returned home. He then said to Achilles that he should not grieve, for he was honoured in death as he had been in life: 'no man before has been more blessed than you, nor ever/will be. Before, when you were alive, we Argives honored you/as we did the gods, and now in this place you have great authority/over the dead. Do not grieve, even in death, Achilleus.'

Achilles answered him in turn: 'O shining Odysseus, never try to console me for dying./I would rather follow the plow as thrall to another/man, with no land allotted him and not much to live on,/ than be a king over the perished dead.'

Achilles then asked Odysseus to tell him anything he may have heard of his son Neoptolemus and his father Peleus. Odysseus said that he had no word of Peleus, but he had much to say of Neoptolemus, whom he praised as one of the greatest of the Achaean heroes at Troy, who had been with him inside the wooden horse when they gained entrance to the citadel. 'So I spoke, and the soul of the swift-footed scion of Aiakos/stalked away in long strides across the meadow of asphodel,/happy for what I had said of his son, and how he was famous.'

Odysseus goes on to tell of how the other souls of the perished dead clustered around, telling him of their sorrows. Only the soul of Telamonian Aias stood apart, still angry over the decision that awarded the armour of Achilles to Odysseus rather than to him. So Odysseus spoke to him now 'in words of conciliation':

'Aias, son of stately Telamon, could you then never
even in death forget your anger against me, because of
that cursed armor? The gods made it to pain the Achaians,
so great a bulwark were you, who were lost to them. We Achaians
grieved for your death as incessantly as for Achilleus ...'
So I spoke. He gave no answer, but went off after
the other souls of the perished dead men, into the darkness.

Odysseus then saw Minos, King of Crete, who was seated 'holding a golden scepter and issuing judgments among/the dead, who all around the great lord argued their cases'. After him, Odysseus says, 'I was aware of gigantic Orion', a hero beloved by the Dawn, set among the stars as a constellation. Then he saw Tityos, 'Earth's glorious son', who because he had 'manhandled Leto', the mistress of Zeus, was condemned to have two vultures, one on either side, eternally tearing out his liver.

Odysseus then saw, in turn, the shades of two other notables, Tantalus and Sisyphus, who were being tormented eternally for having offended the gods.

Tantalus, brother of Niobe and King of Phrygia, was said to be a son of Zeus. He was extremely wealthy and built a palace on Mt Sipylus, where he entertained the gods. But he abused the friendship of his divine guests, stealing nectar and ambrosia from their table and revealing their secrets to men. At one of his feasts he served up to the gods the butchered body of his son Pelops, who was later restored to life and given a kingdom in the Peloponnesos, which was named for him.

The gods punished Tantalus by destroying his palace in an earthquake, after which they confined him to a pit in the Underworld. There he was condemned to an eternity of hunger and thirst, with fresh water and abundant fruit always just beyond his reach, 'tantalizing' him, as Odysseus observes:

And I saw Tantalos also, suffering hard pains, standing
in lake water that came up to his chin, and thirsty

as he was, he tried to drink, but could capture nothing;
for every time the old man, trying to drink, stooped over,
the water would drain away and disappear, and the black earth
showed at his feet, and the divinity dried it away.

Sisyphus, son of King Aeolus of Thessaly, killed travellers and guests in his father's palace, violating the law of hospitality and thus incurring the wrath of the gods, who condemned him to an eternity of frustrating labour, trying to push a huge stone up a steep hill in the Underworld:

Also I saw Sisyphos. He was suffering strong pains,
and with both arms embracing the monstrous stone, struggling
with hands and feet alike, he would try to push the stone upward
to the crest of the hill, but when it was on the point of going
over the top, the force of gravity turned it backward
and the pitiless stone rolled back down to the level.

Odysseus explains that after Sisyphus 'I was aware of powerful Herakles;/his image, that is.' Odysseus goes on to say:

He recognized me at once, as soon as his eyes had seen me.
And full of lamentation he spoke to me in winged words:
'Son of Laertes and seed of Zeus, resourceful Odysseus,
unhappy man, are you too leading some wretched destiny
such as I too pursued when I was still in the sunlight?'

Odysseus adds that Heracles then 'went back into the realm of Hades', but he himself stood where he was, hoping to see if some other

one of the generation of heroes who died before me ...
Perithoös and Theseus, gods' glorious children
but before that the hordes of the dead men gathered about me
with inhuman clamor, and green fear took hold of me
with the thought that Persephone might send up against me
some gorgonish head of a terrible monster up out of Hades.
...
So going back on board my ship, I told my companions
also to go aboard, and to cast off the stern cables;
and quickly they went aboard the ship and sat to the oarlocks,
and the swell of the current carried her down into the Ocean river
with rowing at first, but after that on a fair wind following.

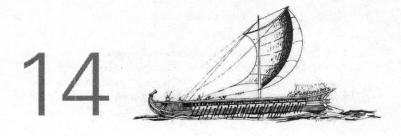

14

Siren Land

When Odysseus and his companions returned to Circe's island it was still night, and so after they ran their ship ashore they 'stepped out onto the break of the sea beach, and there we fell asleep and waited for the divine Dawn'. At daybreak Odysseus sent his companions to Circe's house to bring back the body of Elpenor, which, as he wished, they cremated and covered with a tumulus, and afterwards they 'planted the well-shaped oar in the very top of the grave mound'.

While they were busy at their work Circe arrived with her attendants, who were carrying bread and meat and wine for Odysseus and his companions. Odysseus says that 'Bright among goddesses she stood in our midst and addressed us':

> Unhappy men, who went alive to the house of Hades,
> so dying twice, when all the rest of mankind die only
> once, come then eat what is there, and drink your wine, staying
> here all the rest of the day, and then tomorrow, when dawn shows,
> you shall sail, and I will show you the way and make plain
> all details, so neither by land nor on the salt water
> you may suffer and come to grief by unhappy bad designing.

They then sat there feasting on meat and wine, and at sunset the men lay down to sleep, while Circe took Odysseus by the hand and led him away from his companions, so that she could tell him of the dangers he would encounter on his homeward voyage, beginning with the Sirens.

> You will come first of all to the Sirens, who are enchanters
> of all mankind, and whoever comes their way; and that man
> who unsuspecting approaches them, and listens to the Sirens

singing, has no prospect of coming home and delighting
his wife and little children as they stood about him in greeting.
But the Sirens by the melody of their singing enchant him.
They sit in their meadow, but the beach beside it is piled with boneheaps
of men now rotted away, and the skins shriveled upon them.

Circe then told Odysseus what he and his companions must do
to make their way safely past the deadly lure of the Sirens.

You must drive straight on past, but melt down sweet wax of honey
and with it stop your companion's ears, so none can listen;
the rest, that is, but if you yourself are wanting to hear them,
then have them tie you hand and foot on the fast ship, standing
upright against the mast with the rope's ends lashed around it,
so that you can have joy in hearing the song of the Sirens;
but if you supplicate your men and implore them to set you
free, then they must tie you fast with even more lashings.

According to one version of the myth, the Sirens, known in
Greek as Seirenes, were daughters of the river god Achelous and the
muse Melpome. They were originally handmaidens of Persephone,
daughter of Demeter. When Persephone was secretly kidnapped by
Hades and taken to the Underworld, Demeter gave them the bodies
of birds and sent them to the netherworld of Hades to help in the
search for her daughter.

Some ancient writers, including Strabo, say that the Sirens
were fated to live only till some mariner hearing their song would
pass without being enchanted, as did Odysseus, and thereupon
they plunged into the sea and were transformed into rocks. Strabo
writes:

Surrentum [Sorrento], a city of the Kampanoi [Campania], whence
the Athenaion juts forth into the sea, which some call the Cape of
Seirenoussai ... It is only a short voyage from here to the island of
Kaprea [Capri]; and after doubling the cape you come to desert,
rocky isles, which are called the Seirenes [Sirens].

Ernle Bradford notes that the rocky isles mentioned by Strabo
'should be identified with the Galli islets, which lie at the entrance
to the Gulf of Salerno'. He goes on to write that 'It is about seventy-
five miles from Cape Circeo to the Galli if one sails direct through
the Procid and Capri channels; a little more if, as Ulysses probably
did, one follows the coast along the Bay of Gaeta and round the Bay
of Naples.'

When we first explored this surpassingly beautiful coast, early in the summer of 1963, I had in hand as a companion-guide *Siren Land* (1911) by Norman Douglas, who spent most of his adult life in and around the Bay of Naples, particularly on the Isle of Capri, where he died in 1952. More than any writer, ancient or modern, he evokes the enchanting atmosphere of Siren Land, which he describes from the uplands of Sorrento:

> The eye looks down upon the two gulfs of Naples and Salerno, divided by a hilly ridge; the precipitous mass of Sant' Angelo, stretching right across the peninsula in an easternly direction, shuts off the view from the world beyond. This is Siren Land. To the south lies the islets of the Sirens, nowadays known as the Galli; westwards, Capri, appropriately associated with them from its craggy and yet alluring aspect; Sorrento, whose name has been derived from them … lies on the northern slope. A favoured land, flowing with milk and honey; particularly the former; Saint Noj maintains as proof of its fertility the fact that you can engage wet-nurses there from the ages of fourteen to fifty-five.

After Circe told Odysseus how to escape the Sirens, she instructed him on what he should do to pass between the clashing rocks known as the Rovers, saying that the only ship ever to survive the passage was the famous Argo, carrying Jason and the Argonauts after their visit to Circe's brother Aietes:

> No ship of men that came here ever has fled through,
> but the waves of the sea and storms of ravening fire carry
> away together the ship's timbers and the men's bodies.
> That way the only seagoing ship to get through was Argo,
> who is in all men's minds, on her way home from Aietes;
> and even she would have been driven on the great rocks that time,
> but Hera saw her through, out of her great love for Jason.

Circe tells Odysseus that the passage is made even more perilous because of the two monstrous sea-goddesses Scylla and Charybdis who dwelt on the Rovers, one on either side. She says that Scylla lives in a cave halfway up the higher rock, and that no one, 'not even a god encountering her could be glad at that sight':

> She has twelve feet, and all of them wave in the air. She has six
> necks upon her, grown to great length, and upon each neck
> there is a horrible head, with teeth in it, set in three rows
> close together and stiff, full of black death. Her body

from the waist down is holed up inside the hollow cavern,
but she holds her heads poked out and away from the terrible
    hollow
and there she fishes, peering all over the cliffside, looking
for dolphins or dogfish to catch or anything bigger,
some sea monster of whom Amphitrite keeps so many;
never can sailors boast aloud that their ship has passed her
without any loss of men, for with each of her heads she snatches
one man away and carries him off from the dark-prowed vessel.

Circe then tells Odysseus that Charybdis lives on the smaller of
the two rocks, which lie so close together that 'you could even cast
with an arrow/across':

There is a great fig tree grows there, dense with foliage.
And under this shining Charybdis sucks down the black water.
For three times a day, she flows it up, and three times she sucks it
terribly down; may you not be there when she sucks down water,
for not even the Earth-Shaker could rescue you out of that evil.
But sailing your ship swiftly drive her past and avoid her,
and for Scylla's rock instead, for it is far better
to mourn six friends out of your ship than the whole company.

All ancient sources and most modern writers, including Ernle
Bradford, put the rocks of Scylla and Charybdis as the northern
end of the Strait of Messina, with Scylla on the toe of Italy and
Charybdis at the north-eastern tip of Sicily, separated by about
six kilometres, which Homer has narrowed to a bowshot.

Thus when Odysseus left Circe's isle with his companions he
would have sailed by the Bay of Naples and down the Italian coast,
passing just to the east of the volcanic isle of Stromboli and the
Lipari Islands as he approached the Strait of Messina.

We passed through the Strait of Messina in June 1963 aboard
an Italian passenger ship, bound for Naples, emerging into the
Tyrrhenian Sea just before sunset. A couple of hours later we passed
to the east of Stromboli, whose volcano was glowing in the darkness.
And so once again I crossed the wake of Odysseus, this time going in
the opposite direction.

Thucydides writes:

The Strait in question is the sea that lies between Rhegium [Reggio]
and Messana [Messina], the place where Sicily is the least distance
from the Continent, and this is the so-called Charybdis through
which Odysseus is said to have sailed. It has naturally become

accounted dangerous because of the narrowness and of the currents caused by the inrush of the Tyrrhhenian Sea.

Ernle Bradford quotes the *Admiralty Pilot* regarding the tidal currents and whirlpools in the Strait of Messina, one of the few places in the Mediterranean, the Euboea Channel being another, where such phenomena are observed.

Twice each lunar day the water level has a maximum slope northward through the strait, and twice each lunar day a slope southward. Though the difference of level is small, amounting to less than a foot at springs, it is concentrated into such a short distance that streams with a rate of four knots at springs are generated by it. These springs run with their greatest force where the strait is narrowest and shallowest, viz. between Punta Pezzo and Ganzirri.

Punta Pezzo is on the Italian side of the strait close to the Rock of Scylla, where the village of Scilla bears its name, while the Sicilian village of Ganzirri is three kilometres along the strait from Cape Pesaro, the Rock of Charybdis, where, some two or three hundred metres offshore, there is a powerful whirlpool associated with her name. The *Admiralty Pilot* notes that this whirlpool

is the Charybdis of the ancients; its opposite number Scylla is now very feeble due to changes in the local topography caused by an earthquake in February 1783. There is, however, every reason to suppose that a whirlpool did exist off the town of Scilla and that both it and Charybdis were rather more impressive than they are today.

Circe's remark that Scylla, looking out from her seaside cavern, fishing for dolphins or dogfish or any bigger sea monster, prompted Ernle Bradford to note that this part of the strait 'is also remarkable for its variety of unusual marine creatures, dogfish, octopus, and squid among others'. He quotes from an article by the American biologist Dr Paul A. Zahn in *The National Geographic Magazine* (November 1953), entitled 'Fishing in the Whirlpool of Charybdis'. Because of the topography of the seabed, according to Zahn, during the spring tides,

the surface waters in the Strait of Messina abound with living or half-living creatures whose habitat is normally down where all is black and still ... After a strong onshore wind I have often seen beaches along the Strait of Messina littered with thousands of dead or dying creatures whose strange appearance would make even the artist Dali wince.

After Circe advised Odysseus on how to get past Scylla and Charybdis, she told him what to do when he reached the island of Thrinikia, home of the sun-god Helios. She repeated the advice of Teiresias concerning the cattle of Helios:

> Then, if you keep your mind on homecoming and leave these
>   unharmed,
> you might all make your way to Ithaka, after much suffering;
> but if you do harm them, then I testify to the destruction
> of your ship and your companions, but if you yourself get clear,
> you will come home in bad case with the loss of all your companions.

At the break of day, when Circe had completed her instructions, she returned to her palace, while Odysseus went back and told his companions to board their ship. He says that Circe had sent them a following breeze, and so they 'let the wind and the steersman hold her steady'. He then told his companions about the instructions that Circe had given him to avoid the perils awaiting them, beginning with the Sirens.

While he was speaking the ship was approaching the Sirens' isle, when suddenly the wind dropped, 'and some divinity stilled the tossing/waters'.

The crew took down the sails and stowed them away, while Odysseus took a piece of wax and stopped up their ears, 'and they then bound me hand and foot in the fast ship, standing/upright against the mast with the ropes' ends lashed around it,/and sitting then to row they dashed their oars in the gray sea'. When they came within earshot of the island their ship 'was seen by the Sirens, and they directed their sweet song toward us':

> Come this way, honored Odysseus, great glory of the Achaians,
> and stay your ship, so you can listen here to our singing;
> for no one else has ever sailed past this place in his black ship
> until he has listened to the honey-sweet voice that issues
> from our lips, then goes on, well pleased, knowing more than ever
> he did, for we know everything the Argives and Trojans
> did and suffered in wide Troy through the gods' despite.
> Over all the generous earth we know everything that happens.

Odysseus was sorely tempted by the song of the Sirens, but though he indicated to his companions that he wanted to be freed they tied him to the mast even more securely and rowed on until they were well beyond the island:

> So they sang, in sweet utterance, and the heart within me
> desired to listen, and I signaled my companions to set me
> free, nodding with my brows, but they leaned on and rowed hard,
> and Perimedes and Eurylochos, rising up straightaway,
> fastened me with even more lashings and squeezed me tighter.
> But when they had rowed on past the Sirens, and we could no longer
> hear their voices and lost the sound of their singing, presently
> my eager companions took away from their ears the beeswax
> with which I had stopped them. Then they set me free from my
>   lashings.

Heading south, their next landmark was the volcanic isle of Stromboli, which they passed to their west as they approached the Strait of Messina:

> But after we had left the island behind, the next thing
> we saw was smoke, and a heavy surf, and we heard it thundering.
> The men were terrified, and they let the oars fall out of
> their hands, and these banged all about in the wash. The ship stopped
> still, with the men no longer rowing to keep her on her way.

Odysseus walked fore and aft in the ship, calming his companions and telling them to row on, ordering the steersman to stay clear of the volcanic isle and stay on course for the strait between Scylla and Charybdis.

Odysseus says that 'I put on my glorious armor and, taking up two long/spears in my hands, I stood bestriding the vessel's foredeck/ at the prow, for I expected Skylla of the rocks to appear first/from that direction, she who brought pain to my companions.' And thus they made their way up the strait, with Scylla menacing to the east and Charybdis to the west.

> So we sailed up the narrow strait lamenting. On one side
> was Skylla, and on the other side was shining Charybdis,
> who made her terrible ebb and flow of the sea's water.
> When she vomited it up, like a caldron over a strong fire,
> the whole sea would boil up in turbulence, and the foam flying
> spattered the pinnacles of the rock in either direction;
> but when in turn she sucked down the sea's salt water,
> groaned terribly, and the ground showed at the sea's bottom,
> black with sand; and green fear seized upon my companions.

Odysseus goes on to say that while they were looking to avoid being swallowed up by the sea monster on one side, the one on the other side struck without warning.

> We in fear of destruction on one side kept our eye on Charybdis,
> but meanwhile Skylla out of the hollow vessel snatched six
> of my companions, the best of them for strength and hands' work,
> and when I turned to look at the ship, with my other companions,
> I saw their feet and hands from below, already lifted
> high above me, and they cried out to me and called me
> by name, the last time they ever did it, in heart's sorrow.

Circe had told Odysseus that when he got past Scylla and Charybdis he would come to the isle of Thrinikia, where the sun-god Helios, also known as Hyperion, kept his inviolable cattle. Writers both ancient and modern put Thrinikia off the east coast of Sicily. Ernle Bradford identifies it as Rada di Taormina, a cove off the ancient town of Taormina, 42 kilometres south of Scylla and Charybdis along the Strait of Messina.

Odysseus says that after he and his surviving companions escaped from the dread sea monsters they made their way to the island of Helios.

> While I was on the black ship, still out on the open water,
> I heard the lowing of the cattle as they were driven
> home, and the bleating of sheep, and my mind was struck by the
>   saying
> of the blind prophet, Teiresias the Theban, and also
> Aiaian Circe. Both had told me many times over
> to avoid the island of Helios who brings joy to mortals.

He then passed on these warnings to his companions, saying 'So drive the black ship onward and pass the island.' But Eurylochos objected, saying that they were all worn out and hungry, and should stop on the island and 'make ready our evening meal, remaining close by our fast ship,/and at dawn we will go aboard and put forth into the wide sea'.

The other men agreed with Eurylochos, and so Odysseus reluctantly gave in, but he made them swear an oath that they would not touch the cattle of the sun-god, but would eat 'at your pleasure of the food immortal Circe provided'. They all agreed, but during the night a fierce storm arose from the south, preventing them from leaving the next morning, and so they berthed their ship, 'dragging her into a hollow sea cave/where the nymphs had their beautiful dancing places and sessions'.

But for the next month the winds blew only from the south and east, and since they needed a west wind for their homeward voyage they had to remain on the island. When their supplies ran out 'they turned to hunting, forced to it, and went ranging/after fish and birds, anything they could lay hands on,/and with curved hooks, for the hunger was exhausting their stomachs'.

Odysseus went off by himself to pray to the gods, 'but what they did was to shed a sweet sleep on my eyelids,/and Eurylochos put an evil counsel before my companions'. Eurylochos persuaded his companions, rather than starve to death, to kill the cattle of Helios and sacrifice them to the gods. 'But if, in anger over his high-horned cattle,/he wishes to wreck our ship, and the rest of the gods stand by him,/I would far rather gulp the waves and lose my life in them/once for all, than be pinched to death on this desolate island.'

Odysseus says that when he awakened and headed back to the ship, 'the pleasant savor of cooking meat came drifting around me', and he cried out in grief: 'Father Zeus, and you other everlasting and blessed/gods, with a pitiless sleep you lulled me, to my confusion,/ and my companions staying here dared a deed that was monstrous.'

The nymph Lampetia, daughter of the sun-god, ran swiftly to tell her father that Odysseus and his companions had killed his sacred cattle. Helios then demanded that Zeus punish them, saying that unless they 'are made to give me just recompense for my cattle,/I will go down to Hades and give my light to the dead men'.

Zeus said in answer: 'Helios, shine on as you do, among the immortals/and mortal men, all over the grain-giving earth. For my part/I will strike these men's fast ship midway on the open/wine-blue sea with a shining bolt and dash it to pieces.'

Odysseus goes on to say that for the next six days his companions feasted on the cattle of the sun, and then on the seventh day, the south wind finally stopped blowing, 'and presently we went aboard and put forth on the wide sea,/and set the mast upright and hoisted the white sails on it'.

After they left Thrinikia the sky darkened and suddenly a screaming west wind came upon them and snapped the mast, which struck the steersman on the head and killed him.

Zeus with thunder and lightning together crashed on our vessel,
and, struck by the thunderbolt of Zeus, she spun in a circle,
and all was full of brimstones. My men were thrown in the water,
and bobbing like sea crows they were washed away on the running
waves all around the black ship, and the god took away their
    homecoming.

Odysseus tells of how he survived by lashing together fragments of the broken ship to fashion a raft on which he floated before the howling wind:

> But I went on my way through the vessel, to where the high seas
> had worked the keel free out of the hull, and the bare keel floated
> on the swell, which had broken the mast off at the keel; yet
> still there was a backstay made out of oxhide fastened
> to it. With this I lashed together both keel and mast, then
> rode the two of them, while the deadly stormwind carried me.

The wind then changed direction and began blowing from the south, carrying him back up the Strait of Messina, to Scylla and Charybdis. As his raft was sucked down by the whirlpool under Charybdis, he reached up to grab a fig tree on the rock, holding on to it until the water surged upward, and then he dropped down next to his raft and clambered aboard, paddling away with both hands.

Odysseus now concludes his long recital to King Alkinoös and his court, telling them of how, after his second escape from Scylla and Charybdis, he drifted in his raft until he came to Calypso's isle.

> From there I was carried along nine days, and on the tenth night
> The gods brought me to the island Ogygia, home of Kalypso
> with the lovely hair, dreaded goddess who talks with mortals.
> She befriended me and took care of me. Why tell the rest of
> this story again, since yesterday in your house I told it
> to you and your majestic wife? It is hateful to me
> to tell a story over again, when it has been well told.

Calypso's isle has been identified with a number of places, but the most plausible one is Gozo, the second largest island in the Malta archipelago. A bay on the north coast of the island named Ir-Ramla has long been pointed out as the place where Odysseus landed, and a cavern above the sea there is called Calypso's Cave. Ernle Bradford, who for years lived in Malta, identified this as the place where Odysseus landed, based on the winds and currents of the seaways around Sicily, which he had sailed in both war and peace.

A guidebook to Malta published in 1910, with text by Frederick W. Ryan and paintings by the nineteenth-century Maltese artist Vittorio Boron identifies the cavern at Ramla Bay as Calypso's Cave, where Odysseus was to spend seven long years with the nymph before he was allowed to begin the penultimate stage of his homeward journey. As Ryan writes of Calypso's Cave:

The annalists of the islands have always claimed Gozo as the Ogygia of Homer, where dwelt Calypso when she allured Ulysses. By this statement, no doubt, they wished to secure, like historians of the Middle Ages everywhere, a good place for their own particular country in the geography – whether real or imaginary – of the classic; and in this way, indeed, the fair Calypso has had quite twenty island homes placed at her disposal. Anyway, we find Gozo called by the Maltese the Island of Calypso, and her Grotto may there be admired today by the uncritical.

Return to Ithaca

When Odysseus finished telling his tale to King Alkinoös and the Phaeacean court, 'all of them stayed stricken in silence,/held in thrall by the story all through the shadowy chambers'.

Then Alkinoös assured Odysseus that his homecoming was guaranteed, and he told the Phaeaceans

> Clothing for our guest is stored away in the polished
> chest, and intricately wrought gold, and all those other
> gifts the Phaikian men of counsel brought here to give him.
> Come, let us man by man each one of us give him a great tripod
> and a cauldron, and we will make it good to us by a collection
> among the people. It is hard for a single man to be generous.

The following morning all of the Phaiakian nobles brought the bronze cauldrons they were presenting to Odysseus, and Alkinoös stowed these and other gifts aboard the ship that he had prepared to take their guest home. 'Then all went to Alkinoös' house and made the feast ready.'

> Alkinoös, the hallowed prince, sacrificed an oxen for them
> to Zeus, dark-clouded son of Kronos, lord over all men.
> They burned the thigh pieces and enjoyed feasting on the glorious
> banquet, and among them Demodokos, the divine singer,
> sang his songs and was prized by the people. But now Odysseus
> turned his head again and again to look at the shining
> sun, to hasten its going down, since he was now eager
> to go ...

Odysseus addressed the Phaeaceans, particulary Alkinoös, asking their leave to be sent on his way, thanking them for their hospitality and generous gifts, and wishing them well in the future.

O great Alkinoös, pre-eminent among all people,
make libation and send me on my way untroubled;
and yourselves fare well, for all my heart desired is now made
good, conveyance and loving gifts. May the sky gods make these
prosper for me. May I return to my house and find there
a blameless wife, and all who are dear to me unharmed. May you
in turn, remaining here, bring comfort and cheer to your wedded
wives and your children, and may the gods grant success in every
endeavor, and no unhappiness be found in your people.

He then offered a last libation to Alkinoös' wife, Queen Arete, putting the goblet into her hand, 'and addressed her in winged words, saying':

'Farewell to you, O queen, and for all time, until old age
comes to you, and death, which befall all living creatures.
Now I am on my way, but have joy here in your household,
in your children and your people, and in your king, Alkinoös.'
So spoke great Odysseus, and strode over the door sill,
and great Alkinoös sent his herald to go along with him
and show him the way to the fast ship and the sand of the seashore.
Also Arete sent her serving women with him. One
carried a mantle, washed and clean, and a tunic. Another
one she sent along with him to carry the well-made
chest, and a third went along with them bearing food and red wine.

When they came down to the ship, the crew took the gifts and stowed them away along with the food and drink, after which they spread out a coverlet on the deck at the stern, where he could rest and sleep. The crew then took their places at the oarlocks, slipped the cable and set off for Ithaca.

They bent to their rowing, and with their oars tossed up the sea
    spray,
and upon the eyes of Odysseus there fell a sleep, gentle,
the sweetest kind of sleep with no awakening, most like
death ... while the ship ... ran on ... very steady and never wavering
...
She carried a man with a mind like the gods for counsel, one whose
spirit up to this time had endured much, suffering many

pains: the wars of men, hard crossing of the big waters;
but now he slept still, oblivious to all he had suffered.

They finally reached Ithaca at dawn, when the steersman directed the ship into a sheltered harbour and the oarsmen drove them up onto the beach, which Homer says was named for Phorkys, the Old Man of the Sea. As he describes it, two precipitous promontories jut out to create a sheltered harbour.

At the head of the harbor there is an olive tree with
spreading leaves, and nearby is a cave that is shaded and pleasant,
and sacred to the nymphs ...
There are mixing bowls and handled jars inside it,
all of stone, and there the bees deposit their honey.
And therein also are looms made of stone, very long, where
the nymphs weave their sea-purple webs, a wonder to look on;
and there is water forever flowing.

The ship had been driven ashore with such force that it ran up on the beach for fully half its length, so that the crew were able to disembark directly onto the shore and unload their vessel.

They stepped from the strong-benched ship out onto the dry land,
and first they lifted and carried Odysseus out of the hollow
hull, along with his bed linen and shining coverlet,
and set him down on the sand. He was still bound fast in sleep. Then
they lifted and carried out the possessions, those which the haughty
Phaiakians, urged by great-hearted Athene, had given him, as he
set out for home, and laid them next to the trunk of the olive,
all in a pile and away from the road, lest some wayfarer
might come before Odysseus awoke, and spoil his possessions.
Then they themselves turned back toward home.

And so, after ten years of war and ten more years of perilous wanderings, Odysseus was finally back on Ithaca.

Some modern writers have suggested that the island now know as Ithaca was not the home of Odysseus. Wilhelm Dörpfeld, Schliemann's collaborator, believed that Homeric Ithaca was the island of Leukas, a theory which no modern authority supports. More recently, Robert Bittlestone and his associates have tried to show that Odysseus' home was the Paliki peninsula on Kephallonia. Although Bittlestone has presented a strong case, I still believe that the island that has been called Ithaca throughout historic times was the home of Odysseus.

When we first visited Ithaca we took the ferry from Astakos on the Greek mainland, which weaves around the northernmost isles of the Echinades on its way to Vathi, the capital and principal port of the island. The town is at the inner end of a deeply indented bay at the south-eastern corner of the Gulf of Molo, which almost cuts Ithaca into two parts, with the northern and southern peninsulas of the island connected by a rugged isthmus that narrows to a width of only 620 metres. The peak of the southern peninsula is Mt Petalaiko (671 m), also known as Merovigli, and the summit of the northern one is Mt Neriton (806 m), the Neritos of the *Odyssey*. The isthmus between them is dominated to its south by Aetos, the Eagles' Cliff' which looks out across the Ithaki Strait toward Kephallonia, whose serrated north-western shore is less than four kilometres from the isthmus of Ithaca as the eagle flies, with Leukas visible to the north and Zakynthos to the south.

Ithaca was famous in antiquity as the home of Odysseus, though Strabo comments on some of the geographical inconsistencies in Homer's description of the island and its surroundings. Nevertheless, the very existence of Ithaca was almost forgotten in Europe during the medieval Byzantine era, when the ravages of barbarians and corsairs forced the few surviving islanders to flee or to take refuge in the mountains, where they have left virtually no trace. Ithaca was permanently severed from the Byzantine Empire in 1185, when the island was taken by the Sicilian admiral Margaritone.

Thenceforth the island was held in turn by the Normans (1185–1209), the Venetians (1209–18), the Latin Emperors of Constantinople (1204–61), the Angevins (1267–1404), the Tocco dynasty (1404–79), the Turks (1479–1503), the Venetians (1503–1797), and finally, after brief periods of rule by other powers, it was ruled by the British from 1815 until 1864, when it became part of the modern Greek Kingdom.

When the Venetians regained control of the island in 1503, it was known in the local Greek dialect as Thiaki, as it is still today. The Venetians found it virtually uninhabited, whereupon they invited colonists to settle there with a five-year exemption from taxes.

The first thorough attempt to identify the Homeric sites on the island was by Sir William Gell, whose work on the *Geography and Antiquities of Ithaka* was published in 1807. Byron, who first visited Ithaca three years later, was initially sarcastic about the work of such antiquarians, writing that 'Of Dardan Tours let Dilettanti tell, I leave topography to coxcomb Gell'. But after meeting the author he changed his opinion; as he wrote in the *Monthly Review*. 'That laudable curiosity concerning the remains of classical antiquity, which has of late years increased among our countrymen, is in no traveller or author more conspicuous than in Mr Gell.'

Byron first visited Ithaca in August 1810, crossing over from Kephallonia and staying for eight days as guest of the British Resident, Captain Wright Knox, who showed him the Homeric sites identified by Gell. He returned to Ithaca in 1823, shortly before his death at Mesolongi.

Ithaca was also studied by William Martin Leake, who writes of it in his multivolume *Travels in Northern Greece* (1835). Leake came to Ithaca by caique from Astakos in his search for the Homeric Fountain of Arethusa, 'which by the learned of Vathy is supposed to be the Arethusa of the poet'.

Although Leake, Gell and other scholars had explored the antiquities of Ithaca, the first systematic archaeological excavations were made by Heinrich Schliemann, who visited the island in 1868 and 1878. Wilhelm Dörpfeld also explored the island, beginning in 1900, and his findings convinced him that Leukas was the original Ithaca of the *Iliad*, a theory that he expounded in his *Alt-Ithaka*, published in 1927. That same year the opposing view was presented in two influential books, Victor Bérard's *Ithaca et la Grèce des Achéens* (first volume of *Les Navigations d'Ulysse*), and *Homer's Ithaca* by Rennell Rodd. Rodd subsequently sponsored a research programme by the British School of Archaeology in Athens, which began excavating sites in Ithaca in the early 1930s under the direction of W. A. Heurtley. These excavations, which continue to the present day, show that the island was inhabited continuously from the early Bronze Age down to Roman times; also a number of findings have led most archaeologists and historians to conclude that this is in fact Homeric Ithaca.

This conclusion has been reinforced by the studies of J. V. Luce, who in his splendid *Celebrating Homer's Landscapes* (1998) says that professional bards like Homer travelled just like seers and healers, and that his own detailed topographical study of Ithaca 'is written in the firm belief that Homer was just such a traveller and that his eagle eye and well-stocked mind gave him an accurate and comprehensive grasp of the landscapes in which his epics are set'.

The town of Vathi stretches around the inner end of its harbour, the most spectacular in Greece, measuring 926 metres from its narrow mouth to the inner end of the port, from where the town looks across the gulf to Mt Neriton.

A stele in this memorial courtyard commemorates Byron's two visits to Ithaca, with an inscription recording his first impression of the isle of Odysseus: 'If this island belonged to me, I would bury all my books here and never go away.'

One of the secondary roads going out from Vathi leads to Perapigadia, an offshore islet in a bay that indents the south-eastern corner of the island. Above the bay there are three Homeric sites, identified by both Leake and Gell: Arethusa's Fountain, the Rock of Korax (the Raven), and the House of Eumaeus, the faithful swineherd of Odysseus. These are mentioned in Book 13 of the *Odyssey*, where the disguised Athena instructs Odysseus to seek out Eumaeus before proceeding to his palace.

The main road to the northern peninsula of the island begins at the western end of Vathi's quay. About a kilometre out of town a turn-off on the left is signposted for Spilaio Nymphi, the Cave of the Nymphs, which is some three kilometres inland. But it is unlikely that this is the cavern that Athena describes to Odysseus in Book 13 of the *Odyssey*, for that would have been on or near the shore by the Harbour of Phorkys, the Old Man of the Sea, which Gell and other authorities have identified with Dexia Bay, a cove just to the west of the entrance to Vathi's harbour. Unfortunately, the grotto on Dexia Bay that Gell identified as the Cave of the Nymphs was destroyed during the British Occupation, demolished to make way for the highroad along the shore. According to Gell, this is where the Phaeaceans put the sleeping Odysseus ashore with all of his possessions.

Some three kilometres out of Vathi there is a turn-off on the left that leads to Piso Aetos, a cove that in times past was used as a landing-place for travellers crossing from Kephallonia to Ithaca. As it crosses the saddle the road passes a site known locally as the Kastro tou Odysseus, which Schliemann identified as Alalkomenai, the capital of ancient Ithaca. Since 1930 the site has been under excavation by archaeologists from the British School, who have unearthed there the remains of an archaic temple and both structures and pottery ranging in date from the late Mycenaean period to the imperial Roman era. The earliest structure discovered in these excavations is a sanctuary dated *c.* 1200 BC, around the time that Odysseus would have returned to Ithaca after his long wanderings.

The main highway continues around Aetos Bay and winds up to the spine of the precipitous isthmus that links the southern and northern peninsulas of Ithaca, with a breathtaking view back across the gulf toward the harbour of Vathi. At the northern end of the isthmus the highway passes two turn-offs; the first, on the left, leads down to the coastal hamlet of Agios Ioannis; the second, on the right, winds up around the slopes of Mount Neriton to the mountain village of Anogi and then down to Stavros, the hub of all the roads in north Ithaca.

The countryside at the northern end of the isthmus is known locally as Agros Laertou, the Fields of Laertes. This was so identified by Gell, who believed that he had discovered here 'the site of the gardens of Laertes, to which the father of Ulysses retired during the absence of his son'.

In the centre of Stavros there is a small park with a monument surmounted by a bronze bust of Odysseus, for local tradition holds that his palace was just to the north on the Hill of Pelikata.

Just outside the village, on the road that leads to Exogi, there is a small but interesting archaeological museum with exhibits from sites in the area around Stavros. The most important of these is part of a female face-mask with an inscription recording that it was 'Dedicated to Odysseus'. This ex-voto, which dates from the Roman era, was found in a cave-sanctuary on the Bay of Polis known as Spiliou Louizou. The cave was first excavated in 1930 by archaeologists of the British School, who discovered there sherds ranging in date from the Mycenaean Age down to the Roman period. This led them to conclude that Spiliou Louizou was a *heroon*, or shrine of a deified hero, dedicated to Odysseus, whose memory was celebrated on Ithaca as late as the third century BC in games known as the Odysseia.

Other objects in the Stavros museum are from a site just to the north of the village on the Hill of Pelikata known as Kastro, where excavations by the British School in 1930 uncovered remains dating from the early Bronze Age down to the Mycenaean era. These finds and the geographical position of the site have led a number of authorities to identify this as the ancient capital of Ithaca, rather than Aetos. Those who favour it as the Homeric capital point to the position of the Hill of Pelikata, which has Mt Neriton to its south, Mt Marmarakas to its north-east, and Mt Exogis to its north-west, with the latter two mountains rising from peninsulas that define Phrikes Bay to the east and Aphales Bay to the north. This agrees with the description in the *Odyssey*, where the capital of Ithaca is situated between 'three mountains' and looks out upon 'three seas', the three bodies of water being the two large bays and the Ithaki Strait.

The road divides north of Stavros, with the left fork leading to Exogi and the right going through the village of Platithias and on to Phrikes Bay (Reithron) on the north-eastern coast.

Exogi is one of the oldest villages in Ithaca, and excavations on its eastern side have unearthed both ancient and Byzantine ruins.

Platithias had been inhabited since antiquity, since it is in the centre of a fertile and well-watered area, with easy access to the sea at the bays of Aphales and Phrikas. Ancient remains have been found in the vicinity of Platithias, where excavations have unearthed structures and graves from the Mycenaean period. The only ancient structure that is visible above ground can be seen at Agios Athanasios, a ruined chapel between Platithias and Exogi. All that remains of the structure are some courses of its polygonal wall, which form the foundations of the chapel. The ruins, which local tradition have identified as 'The School of Homer', are thought to be Mycenaean, as evidenced by a few sherds of that period found on the site. Gell agreed with this identification after he visited the site in 1806, and thereafter it became one of the regular stops on the tour of Homeric Ithaca.

When Odysseus finally awakened he did not recognize his own homeland, because Athena had 'poured a mist over all, so she could make him/unrecognizable and explain all the details to him,/to have his wife not recognize him, nor his townspeople/and friends, till he had punished the suitors for their overbearing oppression'.

Then he saw Athena, disguised as a young herdsman, and he went over to ask where he was: 'What land is this, what neighborhood is it, what people live here?/Is it one of the sunny islands, or is it some foreland/slanted out from the generous mainland into the salt sea?' Athena then answered him:

> You are some innocent, O stranger, or else you have come from
> far away, if you ask about this land, for it is not
> so nameless as all that. There are indeed many who know it,
> whether among those who live toward the east and the sunrise,
> or those who live up and away toward the mist and darkness.

The disguised goddess then describes the island to him, saying

> this is a rugged country and not for the driving of horses,
> but neither is it so unpleasant, though not widely shapen;
> for there is abundant grain for bread grown here; it produces
> wine, and there is always rain and the dew to make it
> fertile; it is good to feed goats and cattle; and timber
> is there of all sorts, and watering places good through the seasons;
> so that, stranger, the name of Ithaka has gone even
> to Troy, though they say that is very far from Achaian country.

Athena, having revealed her true identity to Odysseus, then scattered the mist and he finally recognized his homeland. The goddess then helped him hide his possessions in the cave, after which she told him what he should do to take vengeance on the suitors who had been living in his palace and besieging his wife.

She said that he should first make his way to the faithful swineherd
Eumaeus.

> You will find him posted beside his pigs, and these are herded
> near the Rock of the Raven and beside the spring Arethousa,
> to eat the acorns that stay their strength, and drink of the darkling
> water, for these are nourishing for pigs and fatten them.
> There you shall wait, and stay with him, and ask him all questions,
> while I go over to Sparta, the country of lovely women
> and call back Telemachos, your own dear son, Odysseus,
> who went into spacious Lakedaimon to see Menelaos
> and ask him for news of you, and whether you are still living.

When Athena finished speaking she tapped Odysseus with her
wand, whereupon he was transformed from a handsome warrior in
the prime of life to an old man dressed in rags, the disguise he would
assume for most of the time until he had overcome the suitors and
recovered his palace and his family.

After Athena departed Odysseus set out to contact Eumaeus,
whom he found sitting in front of his house, which he had built with
field stones roofed with shrubbery. Within the enclosure there were
a dozen pens each with fifty pigs, guarded by four dogs, looked after
by four swineherds, one of whom had been sent off to the palace
with a pig to be sacrificed for the suitors.

When the dogs spotted Odysseus they came charging at him till
they were called back by Eumaeus, who then spoke to him, saying,

> Old sir, the dogs were suddenly on you and would have savaged you
> badly; so you would have covered me with shame, but already
> there are other pains and sorrows the gods have bestowed upon me.
> For here I sit, mourning and grieving away for a godlike
> master, and carefully raise his fatted pigs for others
> to eat, while he, in need of finding some sustenance, wanders
> some city or countryside of alien-speaking people;
> he still is alive somewhere and looks on the sunlight.
> Come, old sir, along to my shelter, so that you also
> first may be filled with contentment with food and wine, then tell me
> where you come from, and about the sorrows you have been suffering.

The two then spent the night feasting and talking, Odysseus
spinning a tall tale about how he had gone from Crete to fight at
Troy, Eumaeus telling him of how as a boy he had been captured by
Phoenician pirates and then ransomed and brought up in Ithaca by
Laertes, who was still alive and grieving for his lost son.

Meanwhile Telemachus, having eluded an ambush by the suitors, had returned to Ithaca, where he sent his ship on to the city, while he himself set out on foot to the house of Eumaeus, arriving at dawn, just as the faithful swineherd and the disguised Odysseus were stirring the fire and preparing their breakfast. Eumaeus kissed Telemachus, and in a burst of weeping he said to him:

> You have come, Telemachos, sweet light; I thought I would never
> see you again, when you had gone in a ship to Pylos.
> But now come into the house dear child, so that I can pleasure
> my heart with looking at you again when you are inside;
> for you do not come very often to the estate and the herdsmen,
> but you stay in town, since now it seems you are even minded
> to face the deadly company of the lordly suitors.

Telemachus said that he had come to see Eumaeus and to learn from him if his mother 'endures still in the halls, or whether/some other man has married her, and the bed of Odysseus/lies forlorn of sleepers with spider webs grown upon it'. Eumaeus said to him: 'All too much with enduring heart she does wait for him/there in your own palace, and always with her the wretched nights and the days also waste her away with weeping.'

Telemachus then went inside and the disguised Odysseus rose to give him his seat but his son said: 'No, sit, my friend, and we shall find us another seat.' Then, when they had finished feasting, Telemachus questioned Eumaeus: 'Father, where did this stranger come from? How did the sailors/bring him to Ithaka? What men do they claim they are?/For I do not think he could have traveled on foot to this country.' Eumaeus repeated the tall tale that the disguised Odysseus had told him, whereupon Telemachus said that he would certainly receive the stranger as his guest, but he could not bring him to the palace for fear that he would be insulted by the overbearing suitors.

Telemachus then asked Eumaeus to go quickly to the city to inform Penelope that he had returned safely from Pylos, and to ask her to pass on the news to Laertes at his farm. Eumaeus departed, and at that moment Athena appeared to Odysseus and beckoned for him to come outside the wall of the courtyard, where she spoke to him, saying:

> Son of Laertes and seed of Zeus, resourceful Odysseus,
> it is time now to tell your son the story; no longer
> hide it, so that, contriving death and doom for the suitors,

you two may go to the glorious city. I myself shall not
be long absent from you in my eagerness for the fighting.

Athena then tapped Odysseus with her wand and restored his
original appearance, whereupon she disappeared and he returned to
the house. Telemachus was astonished at the change and said to him:
'Surely you are one of the gods who hold the high heaven.' Then in
turn Odysseus answered him:

> No, I am not a god. Why liken me to the immortals?
> But I am your father, for whose sake you are always grieving
> so you look for violence from others and endure hardships.
> So he spoke, and kissed his son, and the tears running
> down his cheeks splashed on the ground. Until now he was always
> unyielding.

At first Telemachus did not believe him, but Odysseus convinced
him that he was his father. Thereupon Telemachus 'folded his great
father in his arms and lamented/shedding tears, and desire for
mourning rose in both of them'.

Then, in answer to his son's questions, Odysseus told him how
he had been brought to Ithaca by the Phaeaceans, and that he had
come here to meet Telemachus and learn about the suitors, to 'decide
whether we two alone will be able to face them/without any help, or
whether we must go looking for others'.

Telemachus told him that the suitors numbered more than a
hundred, and Odysseus asked him if he thought the two of them
would be up to the task if they had the help of Athena and Zeus.
Telemachus said in answer: 'Those indeed are two excellent helpers
you name to me, even/though they sit away high in the clouds, for
they have power/over others besides, over mortal men and the gods
immortal.'

Odysseus told Telemachus that when they met later in his palace
he would again be disguised as an old vagabond. He then instructed
his son on what they would do to take vengeance on the suitors:

> When Athene, lady of many counsels, puts it into
> my mind, I will nod my head to you, and when you perceive it,
> take all the warlike weapons which are stored in the great hall,
> and carry them off and store them away in the inward corner of the
> high chamber ...
> But leave behind, for you and me alone, a pair each
> of swords and spears, and a pair of oxhide shields, to take up
> in our hands, and wield them, and kill these men.

Eumaeus returned to his house that evening and had supper with Telemachus and Odysseus, who by then had been again transformed into an old vagabond by Athena, 'for fear the swineherd/might recognize him, face to face, and go with the message/to circumspect Penelope, and not keep fast the secret'.

Telemachus asked Eumaeus, 'Are the haughty suitors now back from their ambush,/or are they still lying in wait for me on my homeward journey?' Eumaeus said that he had seen a fast ship coming into the harbour with many armed men aboard. 'So he spoke and Telemachos, the hallowed prince, smiled/as he caught his father's eye, but avoided the eyes of the swineherd.'

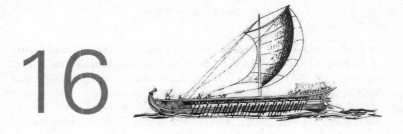

16

Revenge and Reunion

The next day Telemachus set out for the city, a walk of some 20 kilometres, telling Eumaeus to take their guest there later in the day to beg his bread, and the disguised Odysseus agreed. When Telemachus entered the palace he was greeted by his nurse Eurykleia, and soon afterwards his mother Penelope came down from her chamber and embraced him tearfully, questioning him about his journey. Telemachus said that he would tell her all about it later, after he had gone to meet a guest friend whom he had met on his way home, referring to the disguised Odysseus, telling her that he had left him at the home of his trusted companion Piraeus.

Meanwhile Eumaeus and the disguised Odysseus had set out, and were nearing the city when they encountered the goatherd Melanthius who, with two other herdsmen, was driving his finest goats to the palace for the suitors' dinner. Seeing them, Melanthius said: 'See now how the rascal comes on leading a rascal about/ ... Where, you detestable swineherd, are you taking this wretched/ man, this bothersome beggar who spoils the fun of the feasting.' Melanthius then kicked Odysseus, who stood it unshaken, while he considered whether to bludgeon the goatherd with his cudgel, only to remain silent. Eumaeus lifted his hands and prayed aloud to the nymphs of the sacred fountain beside the path, asking them to bring Odysseus home, so that he could deal with Melanthius and the suitors he served. Melanthius said that he would send the stranger off on a ship to be sold as a slave, if only Telemachus was struck down by Artemis or killed by the suitors, 'as surely/as Odysseus, far away, has lost his day of homecoming'.

Melanthius went on ahead of them with his herders and goats, and when they arrived at the palace he went in directly and joined the suitors at their feast, sitting 'opposite Eurymachos, whom he was fondest of'.

When Odysseus and Eumaeus reached the house they could hear the sound of a lyre, as the bard Phemius had begun to sing for the suitors at their feast. Odysseus told Eumaeus to go on inside while he himself waited outside the gate, which he had last walked through when he departed for Troy twenty years before.

As the two of them were conversing with one another, a dog who was lying there raised his head and ears. It was Argos, Odysseus' dog, whom he himself raised, but now, with his master long gone, he was old and neglected and lay, covered with ticks on the deep pile of dung from the mules and oxen outside the gates, so that the servants could take it to the great estate, for manuring.

> Now as he perceived that Odysseus had come close to him,
> he wagged his tail, and laid both his ears back; only
> he now no longer had the strength to move any closer
> to his master, who, watching from a distance, without Eumaios
> noticing, secretly wiped a tear away.

Eumaeus then entered, followed close after by Odysseus. 'But the doom of dark death now closed over the dog, Argos,/when after twenty years had gone by, he had seen Odysseus.'

Eumaeus took a footstool and seated himself at the table opposite Telemachus, while Odysseus, disguised as an old vagabond dressed in foul clothing, sat down inside the doorway. Seeing him there, Telemachus took bread and meat and said to Eumaeus: 'Take all this and give it to the stranger, but also tell him/to go about among the suitors, and beg from all of them./Modesty, for a man in need, is not a good quality.'

Odysseus, sitting on the floor, ate all the food he was given. Athena then appeared to Odysseus,

> and stirred him to go collect bits of bread from the suitors,
> and so learn which of them was fair, which unfair; but even
> so, she would not deliver any of them from disaster ...
> He went on his way, from left to right, so to beg from each man,
> reaching his hand out always, as if for a long time he had been
> a beggar, and they took pity and gave, and they wondered at him;
> they asked each other what man he was, and where he came from.

All of them gave him food, except Antinoös, one of the two leading suitors, who ordered him to stay away from his table. He threw a footstool that hit Odysseus in the back of his right shoulder. Odysseus went back to his place by the door, saying to all assembled, 'if there are any gods or any furies for beggars, Antinoös may find his death before he is married'. Antinoös responded that the stranger should go away 'or else, for the way you talk, the young men might take you and drag you/by hand or foot through the house, and tear the skin on your body'.

When Penelope heard what happened, she implored Eumaeus to summon the stranger so that she could befriend him and obtain news of her husband. Odysseus in response asked Eumaeus to let Penelope know that he would come to her chamber after sunset to answer her questions in private without fear of the suitors. Eumaeus then told Telemachus he was going home to look after his pigs and would return in the morning.

Back in the main hall of the palace a burly beggar named Iros arrived, and Antinoös set him upon the disguised Odysseus, saying that he would reward the victorious beggar with blood and fat pudding. Iros challenged Odysseus, who knocked him down with one light blow and then dragged him out to the gate. Antinoös put the pudding before Odysseus, while Amphinomus, another suitor, gave him two loaves of bread, declaring, 'Your health, father and stranger, may prosperous days befall you/hereafter; but now you are held in the grip of many misfortunes.'

Odysseus, responding to Amphinomus, claimed that the suitors

> show no respect to the wife, and despoil the possessions
> of a man who, I think, will not for long be far from
> his country and friends. He is very close by. But I hope your destiny
> takes you home, out of his way. I hope you never will face him,
> at the time he comes back to the beloved land of his fathers.
> For I believe that, once he enters his halls, there will be
> a reckoning, not without blood, between that man and the suitors.

Athena put it into Penelope's mind 'to show herself to the suitors, so that she might all the more/open their hearts, and so that she might seem all the more precious/in the eyes of her husband and son even than she had before this'. When Penelope did so, after Athena enhanced her surpassing beauty, she came down from her chamber with attendants on either side, fairly bedazzling the suitors: 'Their knees gave way, and the hearts in them were bemused with passion,/and each one prayed for the privilege of lying beside her.'

Her appearance had just the effect that Athena predicted, for 'Each man sent his herald to bring back the presents': Antinoös giving her a beautiful robe, Eurymachus an elaborate gold necklace, Eurydamas a pair of earrings, Peisandrus another necklace. 'Each of the Achaians brought a different beautiful/present; and she, shining among women/went back to her upper room, and her maidservants carried the beautiful presents for her.'

The suitors resumed their feasting and drinking as night came on. Eurymachus began taunting the disguised Odysseus, who responded by calling him a coward, saying that 'if Odysseus were to come back to the land of his fathers,/the gates of the house, although they are very wide, would suddenly/be too narrow as you took flight from the forecourt'. This enraged Eurymachus and he threw a stool at Odysseus, but it hit the cupbearer and knocked him to the ground. This started a tumult among the suitors, which led Telemachus to advise them all to go home, and so 'when they had made libation and drunk as much as they wanted,/then they went home and went to bed, each to his own house'.

After the suitors departed Odysseus remained in the dining hall with Telemachus, and they rehearsed the tactics they would use to slaughter them when the time came, hiding all the weapons except those they would use themselves. Telemachus then went off to bed, leaving his father alone in the great hall, 'pondering,/how, with the help of Athene, he would murder the suitors'.

Then Penelope came down with her handmaidens, who set a chair for her by the fireplace, while they cleaned up after the suitors. Seeing the disguised Odysseus, she said to her housekeeper: 'Eurynome, bring up a chair and put a fleece on it,/so that the stranger can be seated, and tell me his story,/and listen also to what I say. I wish to question him.' After Odysseus was seated opposite her Penelope asked him, 'What man are you and whence? What is your city? Your parents?' Odysseus answered: 'Question me now here in your house about all other/matters, but do not ask who I am, the name of my country,/for fear you may increase in my heart its burden of sorrow.'

Penelope responded by telling him of her sorrows, besieged by a legion of suitors while 'I waste away at the inward heart, longing for Odysseus.' She said that she had put off the suitors by setting up a great loom in the palace and setting out to weave a winding sheet for Odysseus' aged father Laertes, telling them that she could not consider their proposals until she had completed this task, which she worked on during the day, but then secretly undid it at night to prolong the process. But then her maidservants, some of whom were sleeping with the suitors, discovered her secret and scolded her.

So now she could no longer put off her decision, since 'my parents are urgent with me/to marry; my son is vexed as they eat away our livelihood'.

Odysseus, in answer to her question about his origins, spun her a tall tale that he is a grandson of King Minos of Crete, and that he had entertained Odysseus there when he was on his way home from Troy. Penelope tested him by asking about the clothing that her husband wore, and when he described it in precise detail she was convinced that he was telling the truth. He also told her that he had heard from King Phidon of Thesprotia that Odysseus had been there recently and was on his way home to Ithaca. He concluded by telling Penelope that 'Some time within this very year Odysseus will be here,/either at the waning of the moon or at its onset.'

Penelope, nonetheless, still doubted that her husband would ever return. She ordered her maidservants to bathe the stranger and prepare a couch for him in the great hall. But Odysseus told her that he would sleep on the floor in his cloak, and that he had no desire for her maidservants to bathe his feet, 'not unless there is some aged and virtuous woman/whose heart has had to endure as much as mine has./If such a one were to touch my feet, I should not be angry.'

Penelope then called to the old nurse: 'Come then, circumspect Eurykleia, rise up and wash the feet of one who is the same age as your master./Odysseus must by this time have such hands and feet as you do,/for in misfortune mortal men grow old more suddenly.'

As the old woman began washing his feet, Odysseus realized that she might recognize the scar on his knee, incurred in his youth when a boar gored him when he was hunting. Just then Eurykleia saw the scar and realized that the stranger was Odysseus, causing her to drop his foot and knock over the basin of water.

Pain and joy seized her at once, and both eyes
filled with tears, and the springing voice was held within her.
She took the beard of Odysseus in her hands and spoke to him:
'Then, dear child, you are really Odysseus. I did not know you
before, not until I touched my lord all over.'

Eurykleia turned toward her mistress to reveal the stranger's identity, but Athena momentarily distracted Penelope so that she did not notice. Odysseus grabbed his old nurse by the throat, warning her not to identify him, and Eurykleia swore to him that she would be silent, after she refilled the basin and continued washing his feet.

After he had been washed, Odysseus drew his chair closer to the fire, hiding his scar under his ragged clothing, as Penelope addressed him, saying: 'Friend, I will stay here and talk to you, just for a little./

To be sure, it will soon be time for sweet rest,/for once delicious sleep takes hold of you, although he may be/sorrowful. The divinity gave me grief beyond measure.'

She went on to tell him of two dreams that she had, asking him if he could interpret them. The first involved her geese, twenty in number, which in her dream were killed by a great eagle who swept down upon them from the mountain, leaving their dead bodies lying around the palace. The eagle came back and perched on the roof of the palace, speaking to her in a human voice:

> Do not fear, O daughter of far-famed Ikarios.
> This is a blessing real as day. You will see it
> done. The geese are the suitors, and I, the eagle, have been
> a bird of portent, but now I am your own husband, come home,
> and I shall inflict shameless destruction on all the suitors.

Odysseus spoke in turn, interpreting Penelope's dream: 'Lady, it is impossible to read this dream and avoid it/by turning another way, since Odysseus himself has told you/its meaning, how it will end. The suitors' doom is evident/for one and all. Not one will avoid his death and destruction.'

She then told him her second dream, which she said was a strange one, asking him to put it away in his heart:

> This dawn will be a day of evil name, which will take me
> away from the house of Odysseus; for now I will set up a contest;
> those axes which, in his palace, he used to set up in order
> so that, twelve in all, they stood in a row, like timbers
> to hold a ship. He would stand far off, and send a shaft through
>   them.
> Now I will set these up as a contest before my suitors,
> and the one who takes the bow in his hands, strings it with the
>   greatest
> ease, and sends an arrow clean through all the twelve axes
> shall be the one I will go away with, forsaking this house
> where I was a bride, a lovely place and full of good living.
> I think that even in my dreams I will not forget it.

Odysseus spoke in turn, interpreting her dream by telling her to go ahead with this contest:

> O respected wife of Odysseus, son of Laertes,
> do not put off this contest in your house any longer.
> Before these people can handle the well-wrought bow, and manage

to hook the string and bend it, and send a shaft through the iron,
Odysseus of the many designs will be back here with you.

Penelope responded by saying that if he was willing to sit there
and entertain she would listen to him all night, but drowsiness had
come upon her and she felt the need to sleep:

'So I shall now go back again to my upper chamber,
and lie on my bed, which is made a sorrowful thing now, always
disordered with the tears I have wept, ever since Odysseus
went away to that evil, not-to-be-mentioned Ilion.
There I must lie, but you can sleep here in the house, either
bedding down on the floor, or else they can make a bed for you.'
So she spoke, and went back to her shining chamber,
not alone, since others, her women, went to attend her.
She went back to the upper story with her attendant women
and wept for Odysseus, her beloved husband, until
gray-eyed Athene cast sweet slumber over her eyelids.

The next day was a public festival, and so Telemachus rose early
and went down to the great hall, where the servants were preparing
a feast for the suitors. Eumaeus came 'driving in three porkers, which
were the best in his keeping'. The swineherd then looked around the
palace and, seeing the disguised Odysseus, spoke to him affectionately,
'Friend, have the Achaians been giving you more regard, or/do they
slight you still in the halls, as they did earlier?' Odysseus responded
by saying 'How I wish, Eumaios, the gods would punish the outrage/
these men do in the violence of their reckless designs, here in/the
house of another man. They have no gift of modesty.'
   While they were speaking, the goatherd Melanthius entered the
hall, followed by two other herdsmen driving the goats selected for
the suitors' feast. Melanthius tethered the goats, 'and he himself now
spoke to Odysseus, in terms of revilement':

'Stranger, are you still to be here in the house, to pester
the gentlemen with your begging? Will not you take yourself outside
and elsewhere? I think that now you and I can no longer
part, until we have tried our fists. There is nothing orderly
about you begging. And other Achaians are feasting elsewhere.'
So he spoke. Resourceful Odysseus gave him no answer,
but shook his head in silence, devising evils.

Then the oxherd Philoitius entered, 'driving in for the suitors a
barren cow and fat goats'. He asked Eumaeus who the stranger was,

saying that 'he is like a king and a lord in appearance'. He went over and offered his right hand to the stranger and welcomed him, saying that he mourned for Odysseus, 'now dead and gone to the house of Hades', who in his youth had put him in charge of all the oxen. He would have long ago escaped and gone to another country, he said, but he still thought that his lord might return and drive away the suitors. The disguised Odysseus spoke to him in turn, swearing that: 'Odysseus will come home again, while you are still here/in the house, and with your own eyes, if you desire to,/you can watch him killing the suitors, who are supreme here.'

Meanwhile the suitors gathered in the great hall for the feast, and Telemachus seated his disguised father at a poor chair and little table by the threshold, setting food and wine before him. Seeing the stranger there, Ktesippus of Same (Kephallonia) threw an ox-head that just missed him and hit the wall. Telemachus said it was fortunate for otherwise he himself would have killed Ktesippus.

Meanwhile Athena had put Penelope in mind of the contest she had spoken of to her disguised husband, and she went to the storeroom to get his bow and quiver of arrows, which her maids carried down to the great hall, where she addressed the suitors:

> Hear me now, you haughty suitors ... since here is a prize set out
>   before you;
> for I shall bring you the great bow of godlike Odysseus.
> And the one who takes the bow in his hands, strings it with the
>   greatest
> ease, and sends an arrow clean through all the twelve axes,
> shall be the one I go away with, forsaking this house.

Telemachus set up the twelve axes so that the holes in their handles were all in a straight line, after which he tried out the bow, saying that if he won the contest his mother would remain with him in the palace, which he would take over as his father's heir. So saying, Telemachus took up the bow and tried to string it, but though he made the attempt three times he failed, and though on the fourth try he was on the point of doing so, Odysseus made a gesture with his head for him to stop.

Telemachus then put down the bow and invited the suitors to try their hand, and Antinoös said to them: 'Take your turns in order from left to right, my companions/all, beginning from the place where the wine is served out.'

The first to try was Leodes, son of Oinops, who had divinatory powers. When he tried to string the bow and failed he spoke to the other suitors, prophetically, advising them to give up their hopeless wait for Penelope, which would cost all of them their life, and instead 'court some other fair-robed Achaian woman'.

Antinoös was outraged, saying that although Leodes was a weakling and could not bend the bow, 'presently the other lordly suitors would string it'. He then ordered the goatherd Melanthius to light a fire in the fireplace 'and bring out from the inside stores a great wheel of tallow, so that we young men, having heated the bow and rubbed it/with fat, can then attempt to bend it, and finish the contest'.

Melanthius did as he was told and then 'The young men heated the bow and tried it, but were not able/to string it. They were not nearly strong enough. All this time/Antinoös still held back, as did godlike Eurymachos,/those lords of the suitors, out and away the best men amongst them.'

The swineherd Eumaeus and the oxherd Philoitius went outside the house together into the courtyard, followed close behind by Odysseus. He asked them what they would do if their old master suddenly returned, 'Would you fight for the suitors, or would you fight for Odysseus?' The two of them swore that they would fight for Odysseus, whereupon he revealed his true identity to them, revealing the scar on his knee. They then embraced and kissed one another, after which Odysseus revealed to them his plan to take revenge upon the suitors.

He said that when he asked for the bow and quiver Eumaeus should carry them to him despite the objections of the suitors, after which he should tell the women to bar the doors to the hall and remain quiet. He then told Philoitius that 'your task is to make fast the courtyard/door with the bolt, and tie the fastening bolt quickly upon it'.

Odysseus went back inside the palace and sat in the chair from which he had risen, followed soon afterwards by Eumaeus and Philoitius. Eurymachus by now had taken up Odysseus' bow, 'turning it round and round by the blaze of the fire, but even/so he could not string it, and his proud heart was harrowed./Deeply vexed he spoke to his great-hearted spirit':

Oh, my sorrow. Here is a grief beyond all others;
it is not so much the marriage I grieve for, for all my chagrin.
There are many Achaian women besides, some of them close by
in sea-girt Ithaka, and some in the rest of the cities;
but it is the thought, if this is true, that we come so far short
of god-like Odysseus in strength, so that we cannot even
string his bow. A shame for men unborn to be told of.

Antinoös responded in turn, saying that they would not give up but simply postpone the contest to the morrow, when, after sacrificing the goats they would feast on, 'to the glorious archer/we can attempt the bow and finish the contest'. This pleased the suitors, and the heralds were called to bring wine so that they could resume their drinking. When they had drunk their fill Odysseus spoke up, addressing his words in particular to Eurymachus and Antinoös:

> Let the bow be for the time being, give it over to the divinities,
> and tomorrow the god will give success to whomever he wishes;
> but come now, give me the well-polished bow, so that among you
> I may try out my strength and hands, to see if I still have
> force in my flexible limbs as there has been in times past,
> or whether my wandering and lack of good care have ruined me.

The suitors were wildly indignant, and Antinoös warned him not to touch the bow, telling him to be quiet and 'and drink your wine, nor quarrel with men who are younger than you are'. Penelope said to him in response:

> Do you imagine that if this stranger, in the confidence
> of hands and strength, should ever string the great bow of Odysseus,
> that he would take me home with him and make me his wife? No,
> he himself has no such thought in the heart within him.
> Let none of you be sorrowful at heart in his feasting
> here, for such a reason. There is no likelihood of it.

Eurymachus answered her, saying that they had no fear that the stranger would take her away. But they were ashamed to face the talk of those who would say that, while he and the other suitors were unable to do so, 'another, some beggar man, came wandering in from somewhere/and easily strung the bow, and sent a shaft through the iron./So they will speak, and that would be a disgrace on all of us.'

Penelope told Eurymachus that there could in any case be no glory 'for those who eat away and dishonor/the house of a great man. Why be concerned over reproaches?'

Telemachus then said to Penelope that he alone had authority over the bow and could give it to the stranger if he so decided, after which he ordered his mother to return to her chamber with her handmaidens,

> 'For mine is the power in this household.'

Penelope went back inside the house, in amazement,

for she laid the serious words of her son deep away in her spirit;
and she went back to the upper story with her attendant women,
and wept for Odysseus, her beloved husband, until
gray-eyed Athene cast sweet slumber over her eyelids.

Eumaeus now took the bow to carry it to Odysseus, but the suitors raised such an outcry that he put it back on its place. But Telemachus ordered him to go on and give the bow to the stranger, saying that if he himself were stronger he would drive all the suitors out of his house. 'So he spoke, and all the suitors laughed happily at him,/and all gave over their bitter rage against Telemachos./The swineherd took up the bow and carried it through the palace,/and stood beside the wise Odysseus, and handed it to him.'

Eumaeus then told the nurse Eurykleia to bar the door to the inner palace, and to remain there with the other women in silence. At the same time Philoitius left the hall silently and locked the doors of the outer courtyard, after which he returned to his seat, 'looking toward Odysseus, who by now was handling the bow, turning it/ all up and down, and testing it from one side and another to see if worms had eaten the horn in the master's absence'.

As the suitors observed Odysseus, one of them remarked disdainfully that 'This man is an admirer of bows, or one who steals them.' Another said he hoped that the stranger's ill fortune was a measure of his ability to string the bow. While they talked,

without any strain, Odysseus strung the great bow.
Then plucking it in his right hand he tested the bowstring,
and it gave him back an excellent sound like the voice of a swallow.
A great sorrow now fell upon the suitors, and all their color
was changed, and Zeus showing forth his portents thundered
    mightily.

Hearing the sound, Odysseus chose an arrow that lay on the table beside the quiver, where the other arrows were stored, and then he began.

Taking the string and the head grooves he drew to the middle
grip, and then from the very chair where he sat, bending the bow
before him, he let the arrow fly, nor missed any axes
from the first handle on, but the bronze-weighted arrow passed
    through
and out the other end.

Addressing his son, Odysseus said: 'Telemachos, your guest that sits in your hall does not then/fail you; I missed no part of the mark, nor have I made much/work of stringing the bow; the strength is still sound within me, and/not as the suitors said in their scorn, making little of me.'

He then nodded to Telemachus, who 'put his sharp sword about him/and closed his own hand over his spear, and took his position/close beside him and next the chair, all armed in bright bronze':

> Now resourceful Odysseus stripped his rags from him, and sprang
> up atop the great threshold, holding his bow and the quiver
> filled with arrows, and scattered out the swift shafts before him
> on the ground next his feet, and spoke his word to the suitors:
> 'Here is a task that has been achieved without any deception.
> Now I shall shoot at another mark, one that no man yet
> has struck, if I can hit it and Apollo grants me the glory.'

He spoke and aimed at Antinoös, who was on the point of drinking wine from a two-handled golden goblet, shooting an arrow clean through his throat, killing him instantly so that he fell to the floor, dropping the goblet and knocking over the table and scattering all the food on the ground. The suitors all sprang up from their seats and looked around the room for weapons so that they could defend themselves, 'but there was never a shield there nor any strong spear for them'.

They shouted at Odysseus, saying that because he had struck down the greatest youth of Ithaca his 'sudden destruction is certain'. Odysseus answered, 'looking darkly upon them':

> You dogs, you never thought that I would any more come back
> from the land of Troy, and because of that you despoiled my
>   household,
> and forcibly took my serving women to sleep beside you,
> and sought to win my wife while I was still alive, fearing
> neither the immortal gods who hold the wide heaven,
> nor any resentment sprung from men to be yours in the future.
> Now upon all of you the terms of destruction are fastened.

The suitors were terrified, and each of them looked around for a way to escape death. Only Eurymachus spoke up to answer, saying that Odysseus, if it was truly he, was justified in taking revenge for what the suitors had done, but he blamed it all on Antinoös, who intended to kill Telemachus and set himself up as king of Ithaca. Eurymachus said that he and the other suitors would compensate

Odysseus 'for all that has been eaten and drunk in your halls ... Till then we cannot blame you for being angry.'

Odysseus rejected the offer, telling Eurymachus that he would not stop the slaughter 'until I had taken revenge for all the suitors' transgression./Now the choice has been set before you, either to fight me/or run, if any of you can escape death and its spirits./But I think that not one man will escape from sheer destruction.'

Eurymachus then shouted to the other suitors, telling them to draw their swords and use their tables as shields, to make a rush against Odysseus so that they could push him back from the threshold to raise a hue and cry in town. Having spoken, he drew his sword and charged against Odysseus, who shot him dead with an arrow through the chest. Amphinomus then sprang forward with his sword and made a rush against Odysseus, but Telemachus cast his spear skewering him from behind, after which he ran to join his father at the threshold:

'Father, now I will go and bring you a shield, and two spears,
and a helmet of bronze fitting close to your temples.
I too will go out in armor, and give the swineherd
and oxherd more to wear. It is better for us to be armored.'
Then in turn Odysseus spoke to him in answer:
'Run and fetch them, while I have arrows still to defend me,
or else, while I am alone, they might force me from the doorway.'

Odysseus kept killing suitors with every shot as long as his arrows lasted, after which he took up his oxhide shield and donned his crested helmet, arming himself with two powerful bronze spears. He told Eumaeus to guard the side door to the outer alley, which could be attacked by only one suitor at a time. Agelaus cried out to the other suitors, suggesting that one of them slip through the side door and raise the alarm in town, but the goatherd Melanthius told him that it would be difficult to get through and that, instead he would get into the inner chambers of the palace where he believed the arms were hidden. Melanthius climbed in through the vents in the great hall and brought back a dozen shields and spears for the suitors, who began arming themselves.

Odysseus was dismayed when he saw this and spoke to Telemachus, telling him to have the swineherd check on who was smuggling out the arms. Just then Eumaeus saw Melanthius sneaking back into the chamber, and he asked what he should do with the goatherd, kill him or bring him back captive. Odysseus said that if he and Philoitius caught Melanthius they should bind him securely with a rope and hoist him upward to the roof beams, where he would remain and suffer until they had time to deal with him. They did as they were told, after which they armed themselves and rejoined Odysseus and Telemachus, the four of them facing the hostile suitors.

Just then Athena appeared in the form of Mentor, close friend of Odysseus, who knew it was the goddess in disguise and asked for help. The suitors cried out, warning Mentor that they would kill him if he sided with Odysseus, which angered Athena, who now, 'likening herself to a swallow in their sight, shot up/high aloft, and perched on a beam of the smoky palace'.

Agelaus now urged on five other suitors, the best of those who still survived, saying that all six of them should hurl their spears at Odysseus simultaneously, adding that 'We care nothing about the others, once this man has fallen.' They then threw their spears, but Athena deflected them so that they missed their target, whereupon Odysseus and his companions hurled their spears, killing four of the suitors.

The other suitors withdrew to a corner of the palace, whereupon Odysseus and his comrades rushed in to retrieve their spears from the bodies of those they killed. The suitors returned to hurl another volley of spears, slightly wounding Telemachus and Eumaeus, after which Odysseus and his company hurled their spears and killed four more suitors. Odysseus and Telemachus then charged with their long spears and killed another two suitors, Agelaus and Leocritus, after which the bewildered survivors 'stampeded about the hall, like a herd of cattle'.

Then the slaughter really began, as Odysseus and his comrades, 'sweeping about the palace, struck down/the suitors, one man after another; the floor was smoking/with blood, and the horrible cries rose up as their heads were broken'.

The diviner Leodes grabbed the knees of Odysseus and begged for clemency, claiming that he only prophesied for the suitors and did nothing wrong. Odysseus responded by saying that Leodes often must have prayed that he would never return so 'that my dear wife would go off with you, and bear you children. So you cannot escape sorry destruction'. Odysseus then picked up the sword that Agelaus had dropped when he was killed, cutting through the neck of Leodes, whose head 'dropped in the dust while he was still speaking'.

The only ones given clemency were the singer Phemius and the herald Medon, who were spared when Telemachus told his father that they had been forced to serve the suitors. Odysseus told both of them to sit outside in the courtyard 'so that I can do in the house the work that I have to'.

Odysseus looked about the great hall to see if any of the suitors had escaped him, 'but he saw them one and all in their number, lying fallen in their blood and in the dust ... piled on each other'. He then had Telemachus summon the nurse Eurykleia, whom he told to 'assemble here the women who are in the palace,/both those who have done me no honor, and those who are innocent'. She informed him that of the fifty maidservants, 'twelve in all have taken to immorality. They pay no attention to me, or even to Penelope'.

Odysseus had the twelve unfaithful women brought out and put to work, first carrying the bodies of the suitors out to the courtyard and piling them up in the portico, then cleaning up the great hall. Odysseus had ordered that when the unfaithful women finished their work they should be put to the sword. But Telemachus, speaking to Eumaeus and Philoitius, said 'I would not take away the lives of these creatures by any/clean death, for they have showered abuse on the head of my mother,/and on my own head too, and they have slept with the suitors.'

Telemachus first took a ship's cable and fastened it between a tall pillar and another structure in the courtyard, after which he strung up the women 'so their heads were all in a line, and each had her neck caught/fast in a noose, so that their death would be most pitiful./They struggled with their feet for a little, not for very long'.

Next they dealt with Melanthius, pulling him down from the rafters where he had been hanging and dragging him out to the courtyard, where 'They cut off, with the pitiless bronze, his nose and his ears,/tore off his private parts and gave them to the dogs to feed on/raw, and lopped off his hands and feet, in fury of anger.'

After they had washed their hands and feet they rejoined Odysseus, who spoke to the nurse Eurykleia: 'Bring me brimstone, old dame, the cure of evils, and bring me/fire, so I can sulfur the hall, and tell Penelope/to come here now, together with her attendant women,/and tell all the servant maids to come here to the palace.'

Eurykleia 'brought him out the fire and brimstone; and then Odysseus/cleaned his palace, house and courtyard alike, with sulfur', while she went to summon the faithful maid-servants to gather in the great hall.

> They came from the main house, and in their hands held torches,
> and all the serving women clung to Odysseus, and greeted him,
> and made much of him, and kissed him on his head and his shoulders
> and hands, admiring him, and sweet longing for lamentation
> and tears took hold of him. He recognized all these women.

Eurykleia had in the meantime gone to wake Penelope and tell her that the stranger-guest was her beloved Odysseus, who had killed all the suitors, and was now waiting to see her in the great hall. Penelope refused to believe the old nurse, but nevertheless accompanied her down to the hall, pondering 'whether to keep away and question her dear husband,/or to go up to him and kiss his head, taking his hands'.

> But then, when she came in and stepped over the stone threshold,
> she sat across from him in the firelight, facing Odysseus,
> by the opposite wall, while he was seated by the tall pillar,
> looking downward, and waiting to find out if his majestic
> wife would have anything to say to him, now that she saw him.
> She sat a long time in silence, and her heart was wondering.
> Sometimes she would look at him with her eyes full upon him,
> and again would fail to know him in the foul clothing he wore.

Telemachus scolded his mother for her hesitance, and Penelope explained to him in response:

> My child, the spirit that is in me is full of wonderment,
> and I cannot find anything to say to him, nor question him,
> nor look him straight in the face. But if he is truly Odysseus,
> and he has come home, then we shall find other ways, and better,
> to recognize each other, for we have signs that we know of
> between the two of us only, but that are secret from others.

Odysseus smiled and assured his son: 'Telemachos, leave your mother to examine me in the palace/as she will, and presently she will understand better; but now I am dirty and wear foul clothing upon me,/she dislikes me for that, and says I am not her own husband.'

He went on to insist that they must make plans, for the suitors' families would soon learn of the deaths of their sons and would be seeking revenge. His instructions were that they should all wash and get dressed, and have the singer Phemius play his lyre as if they were celebrating a wedding. 'Let no rumor go abroad in the town that the suitors/have been murdered, until such time as we can make our way/out to our estate with its many trees, and once there/see what profitable plan the Olympian shows us.'

The housekeeper Eurynome bathed Odysseus and anointed him with olive oil, after which she dressed him in a beautiful mantle and tunic. 'Then, looking like an immortal, he strode forth from the bath,/and came back then and sat on the chair from which he had risen, opposite his wife, and now he spoke to her, saying':

> You are so strange. The gods, who have their homes on Olympos,
> have made your heart more stubborn than the rest of womankind.

No other woman, with spirit as stubborn as yours, would keep back
as you are doing from her husband, who, after much suffering,
came at last in the twentieth year back to his own country.
Come then, nurse, make me up a bed, so that I can use it
here; for this woman has a heart of iron within her.

Penelope answered:

You are so strange. I am not being proud, nor indifferent,
nor puzzled beyond need, but I knew very well what you looked like
when you went in the ship with the sweeping oars, from Ithaka.
Come then, Eurykleia, and make up a firm bed for him
outside the well-fashioned chamber: that very bed that he himself
built. Put the firm bed here outside for him, and cover it
over with fleeces and blankets, and with shining coverlets.

Odysseus revealed that his heart was deeply hurt by her response,
for he had built their bed around the bole of an olive tree growing in
the courtyard and laid out their chamber about it. After describing
its structure in great detail he said: 'There is its character, as I tell
you; but I do not know now,/dear lady, whether my bed is still in
place, or if some man/has cut underneath the stump of the olive, and
moved it elsewhere.'

So he spoke, and her knees and the heart within her went slack
as she recognized the clear proofs that Odysseus had given;
but then she burst into tears and ran straight to him, throwing
her arms around the neck of Odysseus, and kissed his head saying:
'Do not be angry with me, Odysseus, since, beyond other men,
you are the most understanding ...
Then do not be angry with me or blame me, because
I did not greet you, as I do now, at first when I saw you.
For always the spirit deep in my very heart was fearful
that some one of mortal men would come my way and deceive me
with words. For there are many who scheme for wicked advantage.'

Odysseus also wept as he held Penelope, 'and she could not let
him go from the embrace of her white arms'. When he could bring
himself to speak he said: 'But come my wife, let us go to bed, so
that at long last/we can enjoy the sweetness of slumber, sleeping
together'. She in turn promised: 'You shall have your going to bed
whenever the spirit/desires it, now that the gods have brought about
your homecoming/to your own strong-founded house and to the
land of your fathers.'

While they were talking, Eurykleia and Eurynome made up
their bed. Eurykleia then went to her own bed, while Eurynome, as
mistress of the chamber, conducted Odysseus and Penelope to their
bedchamber. When Eurynome departed, they 'gladly went together
to bed, and to their old ritual'. Then, 'When Penelope and Odysseus
had enjoyed their love-making, they took pleasure in talking, each
one telling his story.'

Penelope told Odysseus of all she had endured in the palace at
the hands of the suitors, and then he related to her the long story of
the misery 'he had toiled through. She listened to him with delight,
nor did any/sleep fall upon her eyes until he had told her everything.'

When they awoke the next morning, Odysseus spoke to Penelope
and told her that that he was going out to their estate to see his father
Laertes, instructing her as to what she should do in his absence.

'Presently, when the sun rises, there will be a rumor
about the men who courted you, whom I killed in our palace.
Then go to the chamber with your attendant women,
and sit still, looking at no one, and do not ask any questions.'
He spoke, and put his splendid armor over his shoulders,
and wakened Telemachos and the oxherd and the swineherd,
and told them to take up in their hands their warlike weapons;
nor did they disobey him, but armed themselves in the bronze, then
opened the doors and went outside, and Odysseus led them.
By now the light was over the earth, but Athene, hiding
these men in darkness, guided them quickly out of the city.

The Odyssey Continues

The twenty-fourth and last book of the *Odyssey* begins as Hermes summons the souls of the departed suitors and conducts them 'along down moldering pathways' to Hades: 'They went along, and passed the Ocean Stream, and the White Rock,/and passed the gates of Helios the Sun, and the country/of dreams, and presently arrived in the meadow of asphodel./This is the dwelling place of souls, images of dead men.'

There they found the souls of Achilles, Patroclus, Antilochus, Telamonian Aias and Agamemnon. The first to speak was Achilles, who addressed Agamemnon, saying that they all thought that he was particularly favoured by Zeus, and 'yet it was to you that the destructive spirit/would come to early, but no man who is born escapes her'.

> How I wish that, enjoying that high place of your power,
> you could have met death and destiny in the land of the Trojans.
> So all the Trojans would have made a mound to cover you,
> and you would have won great glory for your son hereafter.
> In truth you were ordained to a death most pitiful.

The soul of Agamemnon responded, telling the shade of Achilles the circumstances of his burial on the Trojan plain:

> For ten and seven days, alike in the day and the night time,
> we wailed for you, both mortal men and the immortals.
> On the eighteenth day we gave you to the fire, and around you
> slaughtered a great number of fat sheep and horn-curved cattle

...

But after the flame of Hephaistos had consumed you utterly,
then at dawn we gathered your white bones, Achilleus

...

Around them then, we, the chosen host of the Argive
spearmen, piled up a grave mound that was both great and perfect,
on a jutting promontory there by the wide Hellespont,
so that it can be seen afar from out on the water
by men now alive and those to be born in the future.

While the spirits of Achilles and Agamemnon were conversing
with one another, Hermes arrived at the gates of Hades, 'leading
down the souls of the suitors killed by Odysseus'. The soul of
Agamemnon recognized 'Amphimedon, the dear son of Melaneus,/
who in his home in Ithaka had once been his guest friend.'

The first of the two to speak was the soul of Agamemnon, saying:
'Amphimedon, what befell you that you came under the dark earth,/
all you choice young men of the same age, nor could one, gathering/
the best men out of all a city have chosen otherwise.'

The soul of Amphimedon answered Agamemnon, telling him
that he and the others had been courting the wife of Odysseus, who
had been long gone and presumed to be dead. But Odysseus finally
returned, in the guise of an old vagabond, and killed them all in his
palace:

So, Agamemnon, we were destroyed, and still at this moment
our bodies are lying uncared for in the halls of Odysseus;
for our people in the house of each man know nothing of this,
they who would have washed away from our wounds the dark blood,
and laid us out and mourned us; for this is the right of us perished.

The soul of Agamemnon answered him in turn, saying how
fortunate Odysseus was to have a faithful wife like Penelope, while
he himself had an evil spouse who 'killed her wedded lord'.

Meanwhile Odysseus and his companions had reached the
estate of his aged father Laertes, who was looked after by an old
Sicilian women, along with his servant Dolius and his son and other
workmen. There Odysseus had a word with his companions:

Go now, all of you, inside the strong-fashioned building,
and sacrifice the best of the pigs for our dinner
presently; but I myself will make trial of my father,
to see whether he will know me and his eyes recognize me,
or fail to know me, with all this time that has grown upon me.

Odysseus went off to the orchard, where he found Laertes working alone, dressed like a simple workman. He spoke to his father, pretending to be a traveller from abroad who had entertained Odysseus and was now hoping to see him again. The old man questioned him closely about his identity, asking him when he had seen Odysseus, and when he said that it was five years ago 'a black cloud of sorrow closed on Laertes':

> In both hands he caught up the grimy dust and poured it
> over his face and grizzled head, groaning incessantly.
> The spirit rose up in Odysseus, and now in his nostrils.
> There was a shock of bitter force as he looked on his father.
> He sprang to him and embraced and kissed and then said to him:
> 'Father, I am he, the man whom you asked about. I am
> here, come back in the twentieth year to the land of my father.
> But stay now from your weeping, shedding of tears, and outcry.
> For I tell you this straight out, the need for haste is upon us.
> I have killed the suitors who were in our palace, avenging
> all their heart-hurting outrage and their evil devising.'

Laertes answered him in turn, saying: 'If in truth you are Odysseus, my son, who have come back/here, give me some unmistakable sign, so that I can believe you.'
Odysseus first showed Laertes the scar that the wild boar had inflicted on his knee, after which he looked around at the trees and vines in the orchard where his father was working:

> Or come then, let me tell you of the trees in the well-worked
> orchard, which you gave me once. I asked you of each one,
> when I was a child, following you through the garden. We went
> among the trees, and you named them all and told me what each one
> was, and you gave me thirteen pear trees, and ten apple trees,
> and forty fig trees; and also you named the fifty
> vines you would give. Each of them bore regularly.

His words convinced the old man that the stranger who was speaking to him was his long-lost son, now returned as if from the dead:

> He threw his arms around his dear son, and much-enduring
> great Odysseus held him close, for his spirit was fainting.
> But when he had got his breath back again, and the spirit gathered
> into his heart, once more he said to him, answering him:
> 'Father Zeus, there are gods indeed upon tall Olympus,

if truly the suitors have had to pay for their reckless violence.
But now I am terribly afraid in my heart that speedily
the men of Ithaka may come against us here, and send out
messages everywhere to the Kephallenian cities.'

They then returned to the house, where Telemachus and the herdsmen had prepared dinner, while the old Sicilian woman bathed and anointed Laertes. They were about to eat when they were joined by the aged Dolius and his sons, who were invited to the table by Odysseus. Dolius recognized Odysseus at once and ran straight to him and kissed his hand, while the old man's sons came to shake hands with him, after which they went back to sit by their father.

Meanwhile rumour had spread through Ithaca and Kephallonia about the death of the suitors

and the people as they heard it came, from their several places,
to gather, with groaning and outcry, before the house of Odysseus.
They carried the corpses out of the house, and each one buried
his own, and sent back all who had come from the other cities,
giving them in charge of fishermen to take in their fast ships.

The mourners then assembled and were addressed by Eupeithes, father of Antinoös, the first of the suitors slain by Odysseus. Weeping as he spoke, Eupeithes reminded the assembly of the evils visited upon them by Odysseus:

Friends, this man's will worked great evil upon the Achaians.
First he took many excellent men away in the vessels
with him, and lost the hollow ships, and lost all the people,
and then returning killed the best men of the Kephallenians.
Come then, before he can make his way quickly over to Pylos,
or else to shining Elis, where the Epeians are lord, let us
go, or else we shall then be shamed forever; all this
shall be a disgrace, even for the men hereafter to hear of,
if we do not take revenge on the murderers of our brothers
and sons; for there would be no pleasure in my heart to go on
living, but I would wish to die and be with the perished.
So let us go, before they cross the sea, and escape us.

Just then they were joined by Medon the herald and Phemius the singer. Medon addressed the assembly and told them that Odysseus '"devised what he did, not without the consent of immortal/gods. I myself saw an immortal god who was standing/beside Odysseus ..."' So he spoke and the green fear took hold of all of them.'

They were then addressed by the aged warrior Halitherses, who 'alone saw what was before and behind him'. He told them that they would not listen to him nor to Mentor,

> when we told you to make your sons give over their senseless
> mood; for they, in their evil recklessness, did a great wrong
> in showing no respect to the wife, despoiling the possessions,
> of a lordly man. They thought that he never would be coming
> home. Now let it be thus. Hear me and do as I tell you.
> Let us not go there. He who does might incur some evil.

More than half of the assembly, those who disagreed with Halitherses, sprang to arms and followed Eupeithes, as he led them toward the estate of Laertes to take revenge on Odysseus. Seeing this from Olympos, Athena questioned Zeus, asking him: 'What does your mind have hidden within it?/Will you first inflict evil fighting upon them, and terrible/strife, or will you establish friendship between the two factions?'

Zeus answered Athena by reminding her that it had been her own intention to allow Odysseus to return home and punish the suitors, and he told her what he thought would be the proper outcome:

> Do as you will; but I will tell you how it is proper.
> Now that noble Odysseus has punished the suitors, let them
> make their oaths of faith and friendship, and let him be king
> always; and let them forget the death of their brothers
> and sons, and let them be friends with each other, as in the times past,
> and let them have prosperity and peace in abundance.

Meanwhile, at the house of Laertes, they had finished feasting when Odysseus said to them: 'Let someone go out now and see if they are approaching.' Dolius' son went out and saw the fathers and brothers of the slain suitors approaching, whereupon he returned and spoke to Odysseus: 'Here they are, coming close to us, so let us arm quickly.'

> So he spoke, and they sprang up and put on their armor,
> Odysseus with his three, and the six sons of Dolios;
> and with them Dolios and Laertes put on their armor,
> gray though they were, but they were fighters perforce. And now,
> when all of them in shining bronze had shrouded their bodies,
> they opened the doors, and went outside, and Odysseus led them.

Athena appeared and spoke to Laertes, 'and breathed into him enormous strength', whereupon he hurled his spear and struck

Eupeithes, killing him instantly. Odysseus and Telemachus fell upon their opponents in the front line, striking with their swords and stabbing with their spears, and they would have killed them all were it not for the intervention of Athena, who 'cried out in a great voice and held back all the company:/"Hold back men of Ithaka, from the wearisome fighting,/so that most soon, and without blood, you can settle everything."'

> So spoke Athena, and the green fear took hold of them,
> and in their terror they let fall from their hands their weapons,
> which fell on the ground at the cry of the goddess speaking.
> Striving to save their lives, they turned in flight toward the city.
> With a terrible cry, much enduring Odysseus, gathering
> himself together, made a swoop, like a high-flown eagle.

But Zeus threw down a thunderbolt, which landed in front of Athena, who then spoke to Odysseus, saying:

> 'Son of Laertes and seed of Zeus, resourceful Odysseus,
> hold hard, stop this quarrel in closing combat, for fear
> Zeus of the wide brows, son of Kronos, may be angry with you.'
> So spoke Athene, and with happy heart he obeyed her.
> And pledges for the days to come, sworn to by both sides,
> were settled by Pallas Athene, daughter of Zeus of the aegis,
> who had likened herself in appearance and voice to Mentor.

Thus ends the twenty-fourth and last book of the *Odyssey*. Modern readers often are left feeling that the ending is too abrupt, for nothing is said of the remainder of Odysseus' life and those of Penelope and Telemachus. Also it leaves unsettled the order given to Odysseus in Hades by the seer Teiresias, who also prophesied the circumstances of his death:

> But after you have killed these suitors in your own palace,
> either by treachery, or openly with the sharp bronze,
> then you must take up your well-shaped oar and go on a journey
> until you come where there are men living who know nothing
> of the sea, and who eat food that is not mixed with salt, who never
> have known ships whose cheeks are painted purple, who never
> have known well-shaped oars, which act for ships as wings do.
> And I will tell you a very clear proof, and you cannot miss it.
> When, as you walk, some other wayfarer happens to meet you,
> and says you carry a winnow-fan on your bright shoulder,
> then you must plant your well-shaped oar in the ground, and render

ceremonious sacrifice to the lord Poseidon
... Death will come to you from the sea, in
some altogether unwarlike way, and it will end you
in the ebbing time of a sleek old age. Your people
about you will be prosperous. All this is true that I tell you.

This mysterious prophecy, left unfulfilled in the *Odyssey*, led post-Homeric writers to compose works in which Odysseus goes off on further travels in Greece and Italy, fathering sons who in foundation myths became local rulers. He is also credited with fathering sons with the nymphs Circe and Calypso.

The best-known of these post-Homeric works is the *Telegony*, a lost Greek epic poem sometimes attributed to Eugammon of Cyrene and dated to the sixth century BC. The *Telegony* is the last part of the Epic Cycle, the series of poems that together tell the story of the Trojan War and the events leading up to and following the *Iliad*, chronologically coming immediately after the *Odyssey*.

All but two lines of the original text of the *Telegony* have been lost, but the story survives in a summary of the myth in the *Chrestomathy* of Proclus.

Later Greek and Roman poets continued to write about the legendary Odysseus, known in Latin as Ulysses, until the end of the Graeco-Roman world. The writers who succeeded the epic poets felt free to add episodes or interpretations of their own, though they always kept Homer's poem in mind. Poets from the fifth century BC onwards tended to emphasize the craftiness and deviousness of Odysseus rather than his heroism and nobility of character. W. B. Stanford writes that Pindar, referring in his *Nemean Odes* to the contest for the arms of Achilles between Odysseus and Telamonian Aias, calls Odysseus 'a devisor of craftiness, an insinuator of mischievous calumnies, always attacking the illustrious and exalting the ignominious'. He notes also that 'The dramatic poets of the fifth century [BC], both tragic and comic, found an inexhaustible source of interest in the complexities of Ulysses' character', for the most part portraying him in negative terms.

Plato was one of the very few writers of the classical Greek era who wrote of Odysseus sympathetically, as he did in the Vision of Er in the last book of the *Republic*, where the shades of the Homeric heroes gather to choose an identity for their reincarnation. As Stanford describes the scene: 'Last of all comes the soul of Ulysses. After his varied experience of men and monsters he has come to realize the futility of all ambition. What he seeks now is the life of some quiet humble citizen unburdened with public affairs.'

Later, through the influence of the Cynic and Stoic philosophers, Odysseus became an allegorical figure, an Everyman 'making his way with fortitude and resourcefulness through the trials and tribulations of human life … who has travelled widely and who regards all mankind as his fellows'.

Among the Roman writers influenced by the Greek Stoics, Horace particularly admired Ulysses, describing him as a 'Choice pattern of the manly and the wise', though elsewhere he describes him as 'two-faced' and 'avaricious'. Seneca, in his philosophical works, praised Ulysses as a man 'unconquered by labours', 'scorning pleasures', and 'victorious in all lands'. But in his tragic drama the *Trojan Women*, he condemned him as 'an artist in crime' because of his deceitfulness and cunning.

Virgil's *Aeneid* is the myth that Aeneas became a prince of the Latin people who ultimately founded Rome, and so the Romans thought of themselves as descendants of the Trojans and enemies of the Greeks. Thus in Virgil's account of the sack of Troy in Book 1 of the *Aeneid*, Ulysses is described as 'harsh', 'dreadful', 'a coiner of smooth talk', and a 'deviser of crime'. But these statements were all made by Ulysses' enemies and not by Virgil himself, who elsewhere in the *Aeneid* writes sympathetically of his sufferings.

Stanford points out that in the second century AD second-rate Roman writers began producing new versions of the story of the Trojan War, which were particularly popular in Latin-speaking Europe. The two best-known of these authors, who called themselves 'Dictys the Cretan' and 'Dares the Phrygian',

> depreciated the heroes whom Homer admired and gave prominence to minor figures like the Trojan Troilos, famous after Homer's time for his tragic love for Cressida. As a result of wide belief in their forgeries, the Homeric portrait of Ulysses as a prominent and honoured hero among the Greeks at Troy came to be discredited.

During the early medieval era, when western Europe was overrun by 'barbarian' tribes, knowledge of ancient Greek disappeared almost entirely except in the Byzantine Empire, where the tradition of classical learning was kept alive, though at times it was nearly extinguished even in Constantinople. Knowledge of classical Latin almost disappeared in western Europe during the Dark Ages, except for a few scholars, most notably Boethius (*c*. 480–524), whose *De consolatione philosophiae* (The Consolation of Philosophy) is considered to be the last great work of classical scholarship.

Thus in medieval Europe, as Stanford points out,

the Ulysses of popular literature was the despicable, or at any rate dubious figure of the spurious accounts of the Trojan War concocted by 'Dictys of Crete' and 'Dares the Phrygian'. And the fact that some of the rulers of Western Europe claimed descent from Trojan princes helped to increase chauvinistic prejudice against Ulysses as the destroyer of Troy.

But, as Stanford writes, 'The earlier Fathers of the Christian Church on the whole accepted Ulysses as a morally commendable person in so far as any pagan could be so.' He notes that Basil of Cappadocia thought that 'the purpose of Homer's poems was to praise virtue'.

The first significant book on the Trojan War in a language other than Greek and Latin, Benoit de Sainte-Maure's *Roman de Troie* (*c.* 1160), gave rise to vernacular translations in Germany, Italy and the Netherlands, England, Scotland and Spain. The depiction of Ulysses in these versions is on the whole negative, following the model of Dictys, Dares and Virgil, although Benoit sometimes portrays him more sympathetically, writing of his physical beauty and eloquence, beloved by his wife and son and loyal people.

The revival of Greek studies in the Renaissance led Petrarch and Boccacio to have their Greek teacher Leontius Pilatus translate Homer's epics into Latin, a task he completed in 1369. The first printed text of the *Iliad* and *Odyssey* in the original Greek was edited in Florence by the Athenian scholar Demetrius Chalcocondylas, and printed there by the Cretan Antonios Damilas in 1488 in two volumes, which led to numerous translations into Latin and the vernacular languages of Europe.

The first notable English translation of the *Iliad* and the *Odyssey* was by George Chapman in the years 1598–1615. As Stanford notes: 'Chapman adored "divine Homer" and idolized Ulysses as "the much-sustaining, patient, heavenly man" and ... "the wise and God-observing man".'

This translation inspired one of the most memorable poems of Keats, his sonnet *On First Looking Into Chapman's Homer* (1817). There the narrator compares his own poetic journey to the wanderings of Odysseus, having 'many goodly states and kingdoms seen' on his travels 'round many western islands', but when he came upon Chapman's translation,

> Then felt I like some watcher of the skies
> When a new planet swims into his ken;
> Or like stout Cortez when with eagle eyes
> He star'd at the Pacific – and all his men

> Look'd at each other with a wild surmise –
>   Silent, upon a peak in Darien.

Alexander Pope's very popular translation of the *Iliad* and the *Odyssey* in 1716 did much to restore the ancient reputation of Odysseus as a true hero. As Standford notes, Pope rejected the criticism of Odysseus' character by Alexandrian critics and European writers in the sixteenth and seventeenth centuries.

> Instead of judging the manners and morals of Ithaca by those of Versailles or Windsor, Pope made a genuine effort to understand them in the perspective of their own era ... His footnotes frequently defend Ulysses from charges of immodesty or incivility and they show a sensitive appreciation of the nuances of Ulysses' character and conduct.

The notion that Odysseus would leave his home in Ithaca to go travelling once more was revived by Tennyson in his beautiful poem *Ulysses* (1842), inspired by the death of his best friend Arthur Hallam in 1833. Here the aged Ulysses, bored with life on Ithaca and remembering his exploits in the Trojan War, attempts to convince his companions to accompany him on one last voyage:

> 'Tis not too late to seek a newer world.
> Push off and sitting well in order smite
> The sounding furrows; for my purpose hold
> To sail beyond the sunset, and the baths
> Of all the western stars, until I die.

James Joyce's *Ulysses* (1922) and Nikos Kazantzakis' *The Odyssey: A Modern Sequel* (1938) are the two modern works which, according to Stanford,

> offer by far the fullest and most detailed portrayal of Odysseus, much fuller even than Homer's. (The account of Ulysses in the *Iliad* and *Odyssey* amounts to about 100,000 words, Joyce's to over 250,000, Kazantzakis' to over 350,000 in its translation by Kimon Friar.) They are remarkable too, in the candour and fairness of their portraits of Ulysses ... In Joyce and Kazantzakis we find both his virtues and his faults fully displayed and explored to a depth quite unparalleled in any of the earlier tradition. Perhaps no other ancient hero has been so fully and elaborately reincarnated in modern times as in these books by an Irish and a Greek author.

During the interval from Tennyson to Joyce to Kazantzakis the new science of archaeology enabled Frank Calvert, Heinrich Schliemann, Wilhem Dörpfeld, Carl Blegen, Sir Arthur Evans and others to unearth and identify the remains of the Homeric world, while historians have tried to separate myth from history and writers have brought the spirit of Odysseus back to life, as Stanford writes in his final chapter:

> Finally there is the sheer vitality of his personality as a constant source of inspiration for writers and artists alike – and even for imaginative scientists too, as when the command module of the lunar exploration spacecraft, Apollo 13, in 1970 was named *Odyssey* (and there is an *Odysseus* among the minor planets). Every year Ulysses is re-created in some book, or play, or film, or painting, or statue, not as a mere figure of antiquity, but as a contemporary personality. In fact the quest for Ulysses is essentially a quest for a deeper understanding of man's ever-voyaging indomitable spirit. It will never be concluded as long as there are writers and artists and thinkers who share in the aim of Tennyson's Ulysses: 'To strive, to seek, to find, and not to yield'.

The Hellespontine shores were once again the scene of a great war in 1915–16, some three millennia after the siege of Troy. The Ottoman Empire entered World War I in 1914 on the side of Germany, and on 18 March of the following year the Allied navy tried to force its way through the Narrows of the Dardanelles. That assault was a total failure, with two British battleships and a French dreadnought sunk by Turkish shore batteries and underwater mines, as well as two other Allied battleships put out of action. A total of 2,750 Allied sailors lost their lives within a few hours. One of the Allied warships that escaped damage was the British battleship HMS *Agamemnon*, whose name resonated with the epic battle that had taken place on the Hellespontine shore some four millennia before.

The Allied high command had already decided that the straits could not be forced by a fleet alone, and they had been planning for a large-scale amphibious landing at the Aegean end of the Dardanelles, the main thrust to be made on the European side, at the end of the Gallipoli peninsula at Cape Helles. The initial landings took place on 25 April 1915, the beginning of an eight-month battle in which more than 100,000 men of the Allied forces lost their lives fighting over a few square kilometres of barren ground at the western end of the Thracian Chersonnese. The Allies eventually evacuated their troops from the Gallipoli peninsula early in 1916, leaving the Turks in control of the Dardanelles.

On the same day that the main landings took place on the European side of the strait, 25 April 1915, the Russian cruiser *Askold* bombarded the fortress of Kumkale on the Asian side for several hours, after which a regiment of French Senegalese infantry fought their way ashore. The Senegalese captured the fortress and held it against seven counterattacks by the Turks. They then went on the offensive and moved out on to the Trojan plain, establishing a perimeter that extended from the tumulus of Telamonian Aias on the Dardanelles to the tumuli of Achilles and Patroclus on the Aegean. This was the same ground that the Achaeans had taken when they began their siege of Troy three millennia before. But then the Allied high command ordered the Senegalese to withdraw from their beach-head, for the attack on Kumkale was only a diversionary action, masking the main invasion across the strait. So the French evacuated their forces, having buried the 500 Senegalese soldiers killed in the assault, after which the Turks reoccupied Kumkale and interred their own dead in the same blood-drenched ground. This incident is a haunting reminder of a scene in Book 7 of the *Iliad*, where the Trojans and Achaeans agree on a brief truce to bury their dead, 'whose dark blood has been scattered beside the fair waters of Skamandros'. Priam led the Trojans in their grim task, after which the Achaeans performed their funeral rites, as they 'piled their slain upon a pyre, with their hearts in sorrow,/and burned them upon the fire, and went back to their hollow vessels'.

Those who made the first landings on Cape Helles on 25 April on the converted collier *River Clyde* came under heavy fire from the Turkish defenders, and few of them survived. One of those who survived the landing, Lieutenant-Colonel H. E. Tizard of the Munster Fusiliers, later wrote that 'The water by this time all along the shore and around the boats was red with blood.'

We were at Cape Helles on 25 April 1965, just fifty years to the day from the first landing there. We watched as a party of Allied veterans of the Gallipoli campaign came ashore in a small boat, in a reenactment of their original landing. This time they found waiting for them on the shore only a handful of aged Turkish veterans, and the old men embraced and wept on the same beach where they had tried to kill one another in the flower of their youth. And now they are all gone, as the living memory of Gallipoli passes into what Homer called 'the country of dreams', along with the Trojan War.

Nine months later, during the winter holiday, we spent a few days on Marmara Island, Greek Proconnesos, in the middle of the Sea of Marmara, which links the Bosphorus with the Hellespont. After we booked into a very simple hotel, the children went out to explore the village, which clustered around a small square shaded by an ancient plane tree. In the lobby we met a very friendly middle-aged woman who introduced herself as Evelyn Lyle-Kalchas, who told us that she had first come to Turkey from Australia ten years before, to cover the fortieth anniversary of the Gallipoli landings for newspapers in Australia and New Zealand, and there she met and married Homer Kalchas, a Greek from the ancient town of Silivri who had graduated from Robert College, the American school in Istanbul where I was teaching. 'There he is now', she said, gesturing to a white-haired bespectacled gentleman sitting on a marble slab beneath the plane tree, talking to our children. I went out to say hello, and as I approached he stood up and held out his hand, saying 'Let me introduce myself, sir, my name is Homer. I've been telling your children about Odysseus and the Trojan War.'

And so the Odyssey continues.

Source Notes

Note from the Author

'the man of many ways', *Odyssey*, 1.1

Chapter 1 The Homeric World

'We have no record ...', Thucydides, 1.3

'was after the Trojan ...', Herodotus, 2.145

'four hundred years ...', Ibid., 2.53

'in the third generation ...', Ibid., 7.171

'far the greatest ...', *Iliad*, 1.91

'in the next generation ...', Herodotus, 1.2

'first to kill ...', *Iliad*, 4.457

'the Asian meadow...', Ibid., 2.461

'the country now ...', Thucydides, 1.2

'the period of shifting ...', Ibid.

'Nestor had a certain ...', Latacz, *Homer: His Art and His World*, p. 62

'Starting from the very ...', Nagy, p. 84

'But some say ...', quoted in ibid., p. 83

'How, then, shall I ...', Hesiod, p. 327

'And you, O lord Apollo ...', Ibid., p. 335

'And now may Apollo ...', Ibid., p. 337

Chapter 2 The Catalogues of Ships and Trojans

'Zeus bids you ...', *Iliad*, 2.28–30

'run away with ...', Ibid., 2.140–1

'There she came to Odysseus ...', Ibid., 2.169–71

'So he went through ...', Ibid., 2.207–8

'so of these ...', Ibid., 2.464–8

'Who then of all those ...', Ibid., 2.487

'I will tell you the lords ...', Ibid., 2.493

'far the greatest ...', Ibid., 1.91

'Of these there were ...', Ibid., 2.509–10

'offers a truthful ...', Page, p. 122

'But Odysseus led ...', *Iliad*, 2.631–7

'lord of many islands ...', Ibid., 2.108

'They who hold Argos ...', Ibid., 2.559–63

'But the men who held Mykenai ...', Ibid., 2.569–80

'They who held the swarming ...', Ibid., 2.581–90

'They who dwelt about Pylos ...', Ibid., 2.591–692

'Out of Salamis ...', Ibid., 2.557–8

'Swift Aias, son of ...', Ibid., 2.527–35

'They who held Euboia ...', Ibid., 2.536–45

'Prothoös son of Tenthredon was ...', Ibid., 2.756–9

'Idomeneus the spear-famed ...', Ibid.,
2.645–52

'They who held Nisyros ...', Ibid.,
2.676–80

'Herakles' son Tlepolemos ...', Ibid.,
2.653–8

'Nireus from Syme ...', Ibid., 2.671–5

'Sea-girt Rhodes, child ...', quoted
in Freely, *The Western Shores of
Turkey*, pp. 257–8

'the Trojan Catalogue ...', Leaf, p. 13

'It would seem to follow ...', Ibid.

'Tall Hektor of the shining ...', *Iliad*,
2.816–21

'They who dwelt in Zeleia ...', Ibid.,
2.824–7

'They who held Adresteia ...', Ibid.,
2.828–34

'They who dwelt in the places above
Perkote ...', Ibid., 2.835–9

'Hippothoös led the tribes ...', Ibid.,
2.840–3

'These four lines ...', Leaf, p. 270

'Akamas led the men of Thrace ...',
Iliad, 2.842–50

'an easy day's sail', Leaf, p. 271

'Hebros, loveliest of rivers ...',
Lattimore, p. 43

'separated them from ...', Leaf,
p. 272

'Pylaimenes the wild heart ...', *Iliad*,
2.851–7

'This part of the coast ...', Leaf, p.
291

'The silver mines of the Taurus ...',
quoted in ibid., p. 291

'Chromis, with Ennomos ...', *Iliad*,
2.856–66

'held sway for two and twenty ...',
Herodotus, 1.7

'The Karians of the outland ...', *Iliad*,
2.867–77

Chapter 3   The Anger of Achilles

'Sing, goddess, the anger ...', *Iliad*,
1.1–7

'still sat in anger ...', Ibid., 2.488–92

'She spoke, nor did ...', Ibid., 2.807–9

'to fight together ...', Ibid., 3.70

'fight alone for the sake ...', Ibid.,
3.91–5

'Menelaos the warlike ...', Ibid.,
3.136–7

'as cicadas', Ibid., 3.151

'Surely there is no blame ...', Ibid.,
3.156–60

'Come over where ...', Ibid., 3.162–5

'Listen to me, O Trojans ...', Ibid.,
3.456–60

'on that day ...', Ibid., 4.543–4

'wall, subdued by terror ...', Ibid.,
6.74–6

'and lay it along ...', Ibid., 6.92–5

'planned that the Trojans ...', Ibid.,
7.21

'whose dark blood ...', Ibid., 7.329

'that we may not ...', Ibid., 7.343

'So he spoke, and all the kings ...',
Ibid., 7.343

'I refuse, straight ...', Ibid., 7.362–4

'looking out over ...', Ibid., 8.52

'they dashed their ...', Ibid., 8.61–5

'A thousand fires ...', Ibid., 8.562–5

'Come then, do as ...', Ibid., 9.26–8

'Here is the night ...', Ibid., 9.78

'since those who have ...', Ibid., 9.204

'if I stay here ...', Ibid., 9.412–16

'He will fight again ...', Ibid., 9.702–3

'So he spoke, and all ...', Ibid.,
9.711–13

'after they had bathed ...', Ibid.,
10.577–9

'And the men, like ...', Ibid., 11.67–71

'foam ran down ...', Ibid., 11.282–3

'let him give you ...', Ibid., 11.797–8

'fought on like ...', Ibid., 12.40

'Everywhere the battlements ...', Ibid.,
12.430–1

'Whirling, he called out ...', Ibid.,
12.467–72

'came on after Hektor ...', Ibid.,
13.40–5

'we might haul ...', Ibid., 14.79–80

'and in the heart ...', Ibid., 14.151–2

'So speaking, the son of Kronos ...',
Ibid., 14.346–50

'remembered once again ...', Ibid.,
    14.441
'left the Achaian people ...', Ibid.,
    15.218–19
'and stood by him ...', Ibid., 16.3
'For all those ...', Ibid., 16.23–4
'so perhaps the Trojans ...', Ibid.,
    16.41
'each man looked ...', Ibid., 16.283
'within the broad countryside ...',
    Ibid., 16.683
'three times Phoibos Apollo ...', Ibid.,
    16. 703
'hit him between the shoulders ...',
    Ibid., 16.807
'thunderously, to the horror ...', Ibid.,
    16.822
'raging to cut ...', Ibid., 17.8
'carried the dead ...', Ibid., 17.735–6
'Patroklos has fallen ...', Ibid.,
    18.20–1
'He spoke, and the dark ...', Ibid.,
    18.22–7
'set him upon ...', Ibid., 18.233–6
'led the thronging ...', Ibid., 18.316
'I will not bury ...', Ibid., 18.334–5
'walked along by ...', Ibid., 19.40–1
'leaning on spears ...', Ibid., 19.49–53
'we will let all this ...', Ibid., 19.65
'Go now and take ...', Ibid., 19.275
'I shall stay ...', Ibid., 20.22–5
'shining in all ...', Ibid., 20.46
'gods went on to ...', Ibid., 20.75–6
'gathering the fury ...', Ibid., 20.381–
    2
'But Phoibos Apollo ...', Ibid.,
    20.443–4
'harrying them as they ...', Ibid.,
    20.494
'split them and chased ...', Ibid.,
    21.3–4
'Hera let fall ...', Ibid., 21.6–7
'the water was reddened ...', Ibid.,
    21.21–2
'the loveliness of ...', Ibid., 21.218–21
'until he has killed ...', Ibid., 21.226
'Phoibos Apollo went ...', Ibid.,
    21.515–20
'all this time ...', Ibid., 21.606–11

'the shivers took hold ...', Ibid.,
    22.136–8
'went straight for him ...', Ibid.,
    22.143–56
'Now though he ...', Ibid., 22.364–6
'Bury me as quickly ...', Ibid.,
    23.70–1
'Therefore, let one single ...', Ibid.,
    23.91–2
'Good-bye, Patroklos, I hail you ...',
    Ibid., 23.179
'and a huge inhuman ...', Ibid., 23.214
'And I would have you ...', Ibid.,
    23.245–8
'scattered to go away ...', Ibid.,
    24.1–6
'So be it ...', Ibid., 24.139–40
'which might soften ...', Ibid., 24.147
'you killed a few days since ...', Ibid.,
    24.500–6
'So he spoke, and stirred ...', Ibid.,
    24.507–12
'If you are willing ...', Ibid., 24.660–7
'Then all of this ...', Ibid., 24.669–70
'Priam and the herald ...', Ibid.,
    24.673–6
'in his heart ...', Ibid., 24.680–1
'He spoke, and the old ...', Ibid.,
    24.689–91
'Nine days/they spent ...', Ibid.,
    24.783–7
'and thereafter the brothers ...', Ibid.,
    24.792–7
'they piled up the grave-barrow ...',
    Ibid., 24.799–804
'In fact, Achilleus ...', Ibid., p. 17

Chapter 4 Mixed Multitudes and the Great Migration

'the period of shifting ...', Thucydides,
    1.2
'mixed multitudes', Freely, *The
    Western Shores of Turkey*, p. 320
'The Pamphylians ...', Herodotus,
    7.91
'It is said that Kalchas ...', Hesiod,
    p. 267

'there to consult ...', *Odyssey*,
10.488–95
'The largest and best ...', Strabo,
13.3.6
'it is not agreed ...', Ibid.
'But, as for Homer ...', Hesiod, p. 567
'Muse, sing of Artemis ...', Ibid., p. 435
'the first settled ...', quoted in Freely,
The Western Shores of Turkey,
p. 197
'I myself have seen ...', Pausanias, vol.
1, p. 59
'But she remembered ...', *Iliad*,
24.613–17
'from Lykia far ...', Ibid., 2.877
'first he sent him away ...', Ibid.,
6.179–95
'Olympos, a large city ...', Strabo,
14.3.8
'In Lycia ... we have ...', quoted
in Freely, *The Western
Mediterranean Coast of Turkey*,
p. 287
'the founder Kalchas ...', Freely, *The
Eastern Mediterranean Coast of
Turkey*, p. 59
'it was founded by Achaeans ...',
Strabo, 14.5.8
'Amphilochus was killed ...', Hesiod,
p. 271
'Nicator also settled ...', Strabo,
14.5.12

Chapter 5 Troy After the Fall

'I, Herodotus of Halicarnassus ...',
Herodotus, 1.1
'Mardonius brought with him ...',
Ibid., 6.43
'having fought very ingloriously',
Ibid., 6.45
'a vast and well-equipped ...', Ibid.,
6.95
'After the subduing ...', Ibid., 7.20
'On learning this, Xerxes ...', Ibid.,
7.35
'I say he climbed ...', Ibid., 7.42
'When he saw all ...', Ibid., 7.44–6

'When the sun rose ...', Ibid., 7.54–6
'Philip and his descendants',
Hammond, *A History of Greece
to 322 BC*, p. 572
'not much more ...', Arrian, 1.11
'They who held Phylake ...', *Iliad*,
2.695–701
'Alexander's purpose in performing
...', Arrian, 1.11
'It is generally believed ...', Ibid.
'Once ashore he traveled ...', Ibid.
'One account is that ...', Ibid., 1.12
'From Troy Alexander ...', Ibid., 1.13
'Arsites escaped to Phrygia ...', Ibid.,
1.14
'But after his [Alexander's] death ...',
Strabo, 13.1.26
'He walked around ...', Lucan,
Pharsalia, p. 97
'the beginning of a new ...', Leaf, p.
124
'The Romans for many ...', Ibid., pp.
124–5
'a sanctuary of Hector ...',
Schliemann, *Ilios*, p. 181
'What is there unbecoming ...', Ibid.
'He also most willingly ...', Ibid., pp.
181–2
'One statistic is provided ...', Cook,
The Troad, p. 161

Chapter 6 The Rediscovery of Ancient Troy

'Sultan Mehmed walked around ...',
Kritoboulos, p. 181
'sought locations in the interior ...',
Cook, *The Troad*, p. 20
'By an early application ...', Ibid., p. 7
'ancient citadel on its ...', quoted in
Michael Wood, p. 43
'he concluded that ...', Cook, *The
Troad*, p. 38
'advanced the claims ...', Ibid., p. 33
'After carefully examining ...', quoted
in Michael Wood, p. 44
'The site fully agrees with ...', Ibid.,
p. 34

'The accumulation of debris ...',
Blegen, pp. 27–8
'a most important link ...', quoted in
Michael Wood, pp. 45–6
'House of the City King', Ibid., p. 46
'I hoped to discover ...', Ibid., p. 65
'During the last few ...', Ibid., p. 90
'In broader terms ...', Blegen, p. 30
'With Troy VIIb2 ...', Ibid., pp. 31–2
'Whatever the precise ...', Ibid., p. 161
'the cumulative evidence ...', Ibid., pp.
161–2
'The people of Troy I ...', Korfmann
and Mannsperger, p. 29
'The southeast and ...', Ibid., pp. 31–3
'A completely new princely ...', Ibid.,
p. 34
'That was the horse ...', Blegen, p.
113
'Its existence has long ...', Korfmann
and Mannsperger, p. 38
'The remains of houses ...', Ibid., p.
40
'the mostly abandoned site ...', Ibid.,
p. 42
'Remains of the Troia ...', Ibid., p. 42
'Of this monument ...', Ibid., p. 43
'It is of course premature ...', Michael
Woods, pp. 256–7

Chapter 7 Troy and the Troad

'lovely waters', *Iliad*, 21.354
'blossoming meadow', Ibid., 2.467
'swift-flowing', Ibid., 2.545
'Turkish workmen were not ...',
quoted in Michael Wood, p. 67
'owing to the various ...', Ibid.
'The Harbour of the Achaeans ...',
Strabo, 13.1.31
'This is called the Trojan Plain ...',
Ibid., 13.1.34
'When the city was ...', Ibid., 13.1.42
'a low-lying shore ...', Ibid., 13.1.30
'a mutilated statue ...', Schliemann,
p. 103
'When the city was wiped out ...',
Strabo, 13.1.42

'Near by [to Rhoetium] is ...', Ibid.,
13.1.29
'First of all Zeus ...', *Iliad*, 29. 215–18
'... the lord of men ...', Ibid., 6.33–5
'Altes, lord of the ...', Ibid., 21.86–8
'On Lectum is to be seen ...', Strabo,
13.1
'Offshore there's a long ...', *Aeneid*,
2.5
'now is the moment ...', Alcaeus,
quoted in Freely, *Turkey Around
the Marmara*, p. 259
'and Phoibos Apollo ...', *Iliad*, 1.457
'All day long ...', Ibid., 1.472–4
'Lordly Ilium had fallen ...', *Aeneid*,
3.2
'a masterpiece of military ...', Blegen,
p.
'wonderfully built palace ...', Ibid.,
6.242

Chapter 8 The Heroes Return

'Tell me, Muse ...', *Odyssey*, 1.1–14
'wise Odysseus/unhappy man', Ibid.,
1.48–9
'straining to get sight ...', Ibid.,
1.58–9
'Odysseus the godlike', Ibid., 1.65
'It is the Earth-Encircler ...', Ibid.,
1.68–9
'But come, let all ...', Ibid., 1.75–6
'and put some ...', Ibid., 1.89
'oar-loving Taphians', Ibid., 1.181
'on a sea-washed island', Ibid., 1.196
'forever one in mind ...', Ibid.,
3.128–9
'But after we had sacked ...', Ibid.,
3.130–6
'so as to soften ...', Ibid., 3.145–6
'sacrifice to the immortals', Ibid.,
3.159
'went back, bringing ...', Ibid., 3.164
'It was the fourth day ...', Ibid., 3.180
'by hearsay, sitting ...', Ibid., 3.186
'holy Sounion, the cape ...', Ibid.,
3.277–80
'for he is newly ...', Ibid., 3.318

Chapter 9   Leaving Calypso's Isle

'astride one beam ...', Ibid., 5.371
'Then he was driven ...', Ibid.,
    5.388–93
'stayed his current ...', Ibid., 5.451–3
'took it back ...', Ibid., 5.462
'Odysseus staggered from ...', Ibid.,
    5.462–3
'Odysseus buried himself ...', Ibid.,
    5.491–3
'they lifted the wash ...', Ibid., 6.91–2
'big pebbles up on ...', Ibid., 6.95
'Then they themselves ...', Ibid.,
    6.96–101
'and from the dense foliage ...', Ibid.,
    6.127–30
'blandishingly and full of craft ...',
    Ibid., 6.148
'I am at your knees ...', Ibid., 6.149–
    61
'along from the island Ogygia ...',
    Ibid., 6.172–5
'Show me the way ...', Ibid., 6.178–9
'and since he must have ...', Ibid.,
    6.190
'Stand fast, girls ...', Ibid., 6.199–210
'and laid out for him ...', Ibid.,
    6.214–16
'in the presence of lovely-haired ...',
    Ibid., 6.222
'he went a little aside ...', Ibid., 6.236
'A while ago he seemed ...', Ibid.,
    6.242–7
'Rise up now, stranger ...', Ibid.,
    6.255–7
'if she has thoughts ...', Ibid., 6.313–
    15
'he came to Arete ...', Ibid., 7.141–5
'Arete, daughter of godlike ...', Ibid.,
    7.146–52
'sat down beside ...', Ibid., 7.153–4
'and after that ...', Ibid., 7.191–4
'splendid/clothes which she ...', Ibid.,
    7.234–5
'Stranger and friend ...', Ibid.,
    7.237–9
'It is a hard thing ...', Ibid., 7.241–3
'Then I was aware ...', Ibid., 7.290–7
'being the man you are ...', Ibid.,
    7.312–14

'Alkinoös alone understood ...', Ibid.,
    8.92–3
'Now let us all go outside ...', Ibid.,
    8.100–3
'Come now, you also ...', Ibid.,
    8.145–6
'shrank down against ...', Ibid.,
    8.191–3
'Now reach me that mark ...', Ibid.,
    8.202–6
'do your dance ...', Ibid., 8.251–5
'for Demodokos, who moved ...',
    Ibid., 8.262–5
'stamped out the time ...', Ibid.,
    8.380
'Wonder takes me ...', Ibid., 8.384
'Euryalos shall make amends ...',
    Ibid., 8.396–7
'Farewell, father and stranger ...',
    Ibid., 8.408–11
'Farewell also to you ...', Ibid.,
    8.413–15
'gazed upon Odysseus ...', Ibid.,
    8.459–62
'Nausikaa, daughter of great-hearted
    ...', Ibid., 8.464–8
'in the middle of the ...', Ibid., 8.473
'the stratagem great Odysseus ...',
    Ibid., 8.494–5
'Ever since we ate ...', Ibid., 8.539–41
'So do not longer ...', Ibid., 8.548–57
'I am Odysseus son of Laertes ...',
    Ibid., 9.19–28
'But come, I will tell ...', Ibid., 9.36–7

Chapter 10 Across the Wine-dark
Aegean

'From Ilion the wind ...', *Odyssey*,
    9.39–44
'But meanwhile the Kikonians ...',
    Ibid., 9.47–9
'Both sides stood ...', Ibid., 9.54–61
'He gave me seven ...', Ibid., 9.262–5
From there we sailed ...', Ibid., 9.
    62–3
'drove the North Wind ...', Ibid.,
    9.67–75

'scuttled away in fear', Ibid., 9.396

'Why, Polyphemos, what do ...', Ibid.,
9.401–6

'Good friends, Nobody is ...', Ibid.,
9.408

'If alone as you are ...', Ibid., 9.410–14

'spreading his arms ...', Ibid., 9.417–
19

'I had them in threes ...', Ibid.,
9.429–36

'hastened out of the ...', Ibid.,
9.437–40

'Meanwhile their master ...', Ibid.,
9.440–5

'sheep on board ...', Ibid., 9.470

'Cyclops, in the end ...', Ibid.,
9.475–9

'He broke away ...', Ibid., 9.481–6

'Cyclops, if any mortal ...', Ibid.,
9.502–5

'I only wish ...', Ibid., 9.523–5

'I am your son ...', Ibid., 9.529–31

'feasting on unlimited ...', Ibid., 9.557

'lay down to sleep ...', Ibid., 9.559

'and sitting well in order ...', Ibid.,
9.564–7

'I uprooted Antaeus ...', Ovid,
Metamorphoses 9.183

Chapter 12 The Witch's Palace

'floating island', *Odyssey*, 10.3

'six of them daughters ...', Ibid.,
10.6–13

'We came to the city ...', Ibid.,
10.13–18

'the West Wind free ...', Ibid., 10.25–7

'sailed on night and day ...', Ibid.,
10.28–33

'my companions talked ...', Ibid.,
10.34–6

'Let us quickly ...', Ibid., 10.44–5

'So he spoke, and the evil ...', Ibid.,
10. 46–55

'soon took their supper ...', Ibid.,
10.57

'What brings you back ...', Ibid.,
10.64–6

'My wretched companions ...', Ibid.,
10.68–9

'So I spoke to them ...', Ibid., 10.70–5

'So speaking he sent me ...', Ibid.,
10.76–80

'Nevertheless we sailed on ...', Ibid.,
10.80–3

'the glorious harbor ...', Ibid.,
10.85–9

'smoke going up ...', Ibid., 10.99

'what men, eaters ...', Ibid., 10.101

'as big as a mountain ...', Ibid.,
10.113–15

'He snatched up ...', Ibid., 10.116–20

'These, standing along ...', Ibid.,
10.121–4

'called out to ...', Ibid., 10.28–32

'We came to Aiaia ...', Ibid., 10.135–6

'There we brought ...', Ibid., 10.140–3

'to look for some place ...', Ibid.,
10.147–50

'The island of Circe ...', Strabo, 1.171

'Promontorio or Monte Circeo ...',
Bradford, p. 90

'a great stag ...', *Odyssey*, 10.158

'washed their hands ...', Ibid., 10.182

'feasting on unlimited ...', Ibid.,
10.184

'while godlike Eurylochos ...', Ibid.,
10.205

'and the lot of great-hearted ...', Ibid.,
10.207

'and all about it ...', Ibid., 10.212–15

'They stood there ...', Ibid., 10.22–4

'and at once she ...', Ibid., 10.230–2

'and mixed them ...', Ibid., 10.234–6

'she struck them ...', Ibid., 10.238–43

'Let us rather ...', Ibid., 10.268–9

'She will make ...', Ibid., 10.290–5

'she will be afraid ...', Ibid., 10.296–
301

'So spoke Agreïphontes ...', Ibid.,
10.302–6

'R.M.Henry concluded ...', Bradford,
p. 97

'and I, deeply troubled ...', *Odyssey*,
10.313

'She made me ...', Ibid., 10.316–20

'I, drawing from ...', Ibid., 10.321–4

'O shining Odysseus ...', Ibid.,
11.488–91

'So I spoke, and the soul ...', Ibid.,
11.538–40

'in words of conciliation', Ibid.,
11.552

'Aias, son of stately Telamon ...',
Ibid., 11.553–7

'So I spoke. He gave ...', Ibid.,
11.563–4

'holding a golden ...', Ibid., 11.569–
70

'I was aware ...', Ibid., 11.572

'Earth's glorious son', Ibid., 11.576

'had manhandled Leto ...', Ibid.,
11.579

'And I saw Tantalos ...', Ibid.,
11.582–7

'Also I saw Sisyphos ...', Ibid.,
11.593–7

'I was aware of powerful ...', Ibid.,
11.601–2

'He recognized me ...', Ibid., 11.
615–19

'Son of Laertes, unhappy ...', Ibid.,
11.615–19

'went back into the realm ...', Ibid.,
11.626

'one of the generation ...', Ibid.,
11.629–35

'So, going back ...', Ibid., 11.636–40

Chapter 14 Siren Land

'stepped out onto ...', *Odyssey*,
12.6–7

'planted the well-shaped ...', Ibid.,
12.15

'Bright among goddesses ...', Ibid.,
12.20

'Unhappy men, who went ...', Ibid.,
12.21–7

'You will come first ...', Ibid.,
12.39–46

'You must drive straight on ...', Ibid.,
12.47–54

'Surrenton [Sorrento], a city of ...',
Strabo, 5.4.8

'should be identified ...', Bradford, pp.
120–1

'It as about seventy-five ...', Ibid., p.
121

'The eye looks down ...', Douglas,
p. 13

'No ship of men ...', *Odyssey*,
12.66–72

'not even a god ...', Ibid., 12.88

'She has twelve feet ...', Ibid., 12.89–
100

'you could even cast ...', Ibid.,
12.102–3

'There is a great fig-tree ...', Ibid.,
12.103–10

'The Strait in question ...',
Thucydides, 4.24

'Twice each lunar day ...', Bradford,
pp. 144–5

'is the Charybdis ...', Ibid., p. 150

'is also remarkable ...', Ibid., p. 147

'the surface waters ...', Ibid.

'Then, if you keep ...', *Odyssey*,
12.137–41

'let the wind ...', Ibid., 12.152

'and some divinity ...', Ibid., 12.169–70

'and they then bound ...', Ibid.,
12.176–9

'was seen by the Sirens ...', Ibid.,
12.180

'Come this way, honored Odysseus
...', Ibid., 12.184–91

'So they sang ...', Ibid., 12.192–200

'But after we had left ...', Ibid.,
12.201–5

'I put on my glorious armor ...', Ibid.,
12.228–31

'So we sailed up ...', Ibid., 12.234–43

'We in fear of destruction ...', Ibid.,
12.244–59

'While I was on the black ...', Ibid.,
12.264–9

'So drive the black ship ...', Ibid.,
12.276

'make ready our evening meal ...',
Ibid., 12.292–3

'at your pleasure ...', Ibid., 12.302

'dragging her into ...', Ibid., 12.316–
17

'they turned to hunting ...', Ibid.,
  12.330–3
'but what they did ...', Ibid., 12.338–9
'But if, in anger ...', Ibid., 12.348–51
'the pleasant savor ...', Ibid., 12.369
'Father Zeus, and you ...', Ibid.,
  12.371–3
'are made to give ...', Ibid., 12.382–3
'Helios, shine on ...', Ibid., 12.385–8
'and presently we went aboard ...',
  Ibid., 12.401–2
'Zeus with thunder...', Ibid., 12.415–
  19
'But I went on ...', Ibid., 12.420–5
'From there I was carried ...', Ibid.,
  12.447–53
'The annalists of the islands ...',
  Adam and Boron, pp. 8–9

Chapter 15 Return to Ithaca

'all of them stayed ...', *Odyssey*,
  13.1–2
'Clothing for our guest ...', Ibid.,
  13.10–15
'Then all went ...', Ibid., 13.23
'Alkinoös, the hallowed ...', Ibid.,
  13.24–31
'O great Alkinoös ...', Ibid., 13.38–46
'and addressed her in winged ...',
  Ibid., 13.58
'Farewell to you, O queen ...', Ibid.,
  13.59–62
'So spoke great Odysseus ...', Ibid.,
  13.63–9
'They bent to their rowing ...', Ibid.,
  13.78–92
'At the head of the harbor ...', Ibid.,
  13.102–9
'They stepped from the strong-
  benched ...', Ibid., 13.116–25
'of Dardan tours ...', quoted in Freely,
  The Ionian Islands, p. 131
'That laudable curiosity ...', Ibid.
'which by the learned ...', Ibid., p. 135
'is written in the firm ...', Luce, p. 19
'If this island belonged ...', quoted in
  Freely, *The Ionian Islands*, p. 134

'the site of the gardens ...', Ibid., p.
  138
'Dedicated to Odysseus', Ibid., p. 140
'three mountains' ... 'three seas', Ibid.,
  p. 141
'poured a mist ...', *Odyssey*, 13.190–3
'What land is this ...', Ibid., 13.233–5
'You are some innocent ...', Ibid.,
  13.237–41
'this is a rugged country ...', Ibid.,
  13.242–9
'You will find him ...', Ibid., 13.407–
  10
'There you shall wait ...', Ibid.,
  13.411–15
'Old sir, the dogs ...', Ibid., 14.37–44
'Come, old sir ...', Ibid., 14.44–7
'You have come, Telemachos ...',
  Ibid., 16.23–9
'endures still in the halls ...', Ibid.,
  16.33–5
'All too much ...', Ibid., 16.37–9
'No, sit, my friend ...', Ibid., 16.44
'Father, where did this stranger ...',
  Ibid., 16.37–9
'Son of Laertes ...', Ibid., 16.167–71
'Surely you are ...', Ibid., 16.183
'No, I am not a god ...', Ibid.,
  16.187–91
'folded his great father ...', Ibid.,
  16.214–15
'decide whether we two ...', Ibid.,
  16.238–9
'Those indeed are two ...', Ibid.,
  16.263–5
'When Athene, lady ...', Ibid.,
  16.282–97
'for fear the swineherd ...', Ibid.,
  16.457–9
'Are the haughty suitors ...', Ibid.,
  16.462–3
'So he spoke, and Telemachos ...',
  Ibid., 16.476–7

Chapter 16 Revenge and Reunion

'See now how ...', *Odyssey*, 17.217–
  20

'as surely/as Odysseus ...', Ibid., 17.253–4

'opposite Eurymachos, whom ...', Ibid., 17.257

'Now, as he perceived ...', Ibid., 17.301–5

'But the doom ...', Ibid., 17.326–7

'Take all this ...', Ibid., 17.347–9

'and stirred him to go ...', Ibid., 17.362–4

'He went on his way ...', Ibid., 17.365–8

'if there are any gods ...', Ibid., 17.475–6

'or else, for the way ...', Ibid., 17.479–80

'Your health, father ...', Ibid., 18.122–3

'show no respect ...', Ibid., 18.144–50

'to show herself ...', Ibid., 18.160–2

'Their knees gave way ...', Ibid., 18.212–13

'Each of the Achaians brought ...', Ibid., 18.301–3

'if Odysseus were to come back ...', Ibid., 18.383–5

'when they had made libation ...', Ibid., 18.427–8

'pondering/how, with the help ...', Ibid., 19.32–3

'Eurynome, bring up ...', Ibid., 19.97–9

'What man are you ...', Ibid., 19.105

'Question me now ...', Ibid., 19.115–17

'I waste away ...', Ibid., 19.136

'my parents are urgent ...', Ibid., 19.158–9

'Some time within ...', Ibid., 19.306–7

'not unless there is ...', Ibid., 19.346–8

'Come then, circumspect Eurykleia ...', Ibid., 19.357–60

'Pain and joy ...', Ibid., 19.471–5

'Friend, I will stay ...', Ibid., 19.506–12

'Do not fear ...', Ibid., 19.546–50

'Lady, it is impossible ...', Ibid., 19.555–8

'This dawn will be ...', Ibid., 19.571–81

'O respected wife ...', Ibid., 19.583–7

'So I shall now ...', Ibid., 19.594–9

'So she spoke, and went ...', Ibid., 19.600–4

'driving in three ...', Ibid., 20.163

'Friend, have the Achaians ...', Ibid., 20.166–7

'How I wish, Eumaios ...', Ibid., 20.169–71

'and he himself now spoke ...', Ibid., 20.177

'Stranger, are you still ...', Ibid., 20.178–84

'driving in for the suitors ...', Ibid., 20.186

'he is like a king ...', Ibid., 20.194

'now dead and gone ...', Ibid., 20.208

'Odysseus will come home ...', Ibid., 20.232–4

'Hear me now, you haughty ...', Ibid., 21.68–77

'Take your turns ...', Ibid., 21.141–2

'court some other ...', Ibid., 21.160

'presently the other lordly ...', Ibid., 21.174

'and bring out from ...', Ibid., 21.178–80

'The young men heated ...', Ibid., 21.184–7

'Would you fight ...', Ibid., 21.197

'your task is to make ...', Ibid., 21.240–1

'turning it round ...', Ibid., 21.246–8

'Of, my sorrow ...', Ibid., 21.249–55

'to the glorious archer ...', Ibid., 21.267–8

'Let the bow ...', Ibid., 21.279–84

'and drink your ...', Ibid., 21.319

'Do you imagine ...', Ibid., 21.314–19

'another, some beggar man ...', Ibid., 21.327–9

'for those who eat away ...', Ibid., 21.332–3

'For mine is the power ...', Ibid., 21.353

'Penelope went back inside ...', Ibid., 21.354–8

'So he spoke, and all ...', Ibid., 21.376–9

Chapter 17 The Odyssey Continues

'killed her wedded lord ...', Ibid., 24.200

'Go now, all of you ...', Ibid., 24.214–18

'black cloud of sorrow ...', Ibid., 24.315

'In both hands he ...', Ibid., 24.316–19

'He sprang to him ...', Ibid.,24.320–6

'If in truth you are ...', Ibid., 24.328–9

'Or come then ...', Ibid., 24.336–42

'He threw his arms ...', Ibid., 24.347–55

'and the people ...', Ibid., 24.415–19

'Friends, this man's will ...', Ibid., 24.426–37

'devised what he did ...', Ibid., 24.444–50

'alone saw what was before ...', Ibid., 24.452

'when we told you ...', Ibid., 24.457–62

'What does your mind ...', Ibid., 24.474–6

'Do as you will ...', Ibid., 24.481–6

'Let someone go out ...', Ibid., 24.491

'Here they are ...', Ibid., 24.495

'So he spoke and they sprang ...', Ibid., 24.496–501

'and breathed into him ...', Ibid., 24.520

'cried out in a great voice ...', Ibid., 24.530–2

'So spoke Athena, and the green ...', Ibid., 24.533–8

'Son of Laertes and seed ...', Ibid., 24.542–8

'But after you have killed ...', Ibid., 11.119–37

'a devisor of craftiness ...', quoted in Stanford and Luce, p. 139

'The dramatic poets ...', Ibid.

'Last of all comes ...', Stanford and Luce, p. 143

'making his way ...', Ibid., p. 144

'Choice pattern of the ...', quoted in Stanford and Luce, p. 164

'two-faced' and 'avaricious', Ibid.

'unconquered by labours', 'scorning pleasures', 'victorious in all lands', quoted in Stanford and Luce, p. 166

'harsh', 'dreadful', 'a coiner of smooth talk', and 'a devisor of crimes ...', Ibid., p. 168

'depreciated the heroes ...', Stanford and Luce, p. 168

'the Ulysses of popular literature ...', Ibid., p. 177

'The earlier Fathers ...', Ibid.

'the purpose of Homer's poems ...', Ibid.

'Chapman adored "divine Homer" ...', quoted in Stanford and Luce, p. 191

'many goodly states ...', 'round many western islands', 'On First Looking into Chapman's Homer', Keats

'Then felt I like ...', Ibid.

'Instead of judging ...', Stanford and Luce, p. 204

''Tis not too late ...', Tennyson, pp. 141–5

'offer by far the fullest ...', quoted in Stanford and Luce, p. 220

'Finally there is ...', Stanford and Luce, p. 230

'whose dark blood ...', *Iliad*, 7.329

'The water by this time ...', quoted in Freely, *Turkey Around the Marmara*, p. 121

'the country of dreams', *Odyssey*, 24.13–14

Bibliography

Arrian, *The Campaigns of Alexander*, translated by Aubrey De Sélincourt, Harmondsworth and New York, 1971

Aşkin, Mustafa, *Troy, A Revised Edition*, Istanbul, 2005

Augustinos, Gerasimos, *The Greeks of Asia Minor: Confession, Community and Ethnicity in the Nineteenth Century*, Kent, Ohio, 1992

Bean, George E., *Aegean Turkey, An Archaeological Guide*, London, 1966

———, *Turkey's Southern Shore*, London, 1968

———, *Lycian Turkey*, London, 1971

———, *Turkey Beyond the Maeander*, London, 1971

Bérard, Victor, *Les Navigations d'Ulysse*, 4 vols, 1927–9

Bittlestone, Robert, with James Diggle and John Underhill, *Odysseus Found: The Search for Homer's Ithaca*, Cambridge, 2005

Blegen, Carl W., *Troy and the Trojans*, New York, 1995

Bowra, C. M., *Greek Lyric Poetry*, Oxford, 1961

Bradford, Ernle, *Ulysses Found*, New York, 1963

Burgess, Jonathan S., *The Tradition of the Trojan War in Homer and the Epic Cycle*, Baltimore, 2001

Chandler, Richard, *Travels in Asia Minor 1764–1765*, edited and abridged by Edith Clay, London, 1971

Cook, J. M., *The Troad: An Archaeological and Topographical Study*, Oxford, 1973

———, *The Persian Empire*, New York, 1983

Cressman, Edmund D., 'Beyond the Sunset', *The Classical Journal* 27.9, June 1932, pp. 669–74

Davis, Jack L. (editor), *Sandy Pylos: An Archhaeological History from Nestor to Navarino*, 2nd edition, Princeton, 2008

Douglas, Norman, *Siren Land*, London, 1911

Dowden, Ken, 'The Epic Tradition in Greece', in Fowler, pp. 188–205

Drews, Robert, *The End of the Bronze Age, Changes in Warfare and the Catastrophe ca. 1200 B. C.*, Princeton, 1993

Fowler, Robert (editor), *The Cambridge Companion to Homer*, Cambridge, 2004

Fox, Robin Lane, *Travelling Heroes: Greeks and their Myths in the Epic Age of Homer*, London, 2009

Freely, John, *The Aegean Coast of Turkey*, Istanbul, 1996

——, *The Black Sea Coast of Turkey*, Istanbul, 1996

——, *The Western Mediterranean Coast of Turkey*, Istanbul, 1997

——, *The Eastern Mediterranean Coast of Turkey*, Istanbul, 1998

——, *Turkey Around the Marmara*, Istanbul, 1998

——, *The Western Shores of Turkey: Discovering the Aegean and Mediterranean Coasts*, London, 2004

——, *Crete: Discovering the 'Great Island'*, London, 2008

——, *The Ionian Islands: Corfu, Cepahlonia, Ithaka and Beyond*, London, 2008

——, *Children of Achilles: The Greeks in Asia Minor Since the Days of Troy*, London, 2010

Geisthövel, Wolfgang, *Homer's Mediterranean: From Troy to Ithaca, Homeric Journeys*, translated by Anthea Bell, London, 2008

Grimal, Pierre, *The Dictionary of Classical Mythology*, translated by A. R Maxwell-Hyslop, Oxford and New York, 1985

Gurney, O. R., *The Hittites*, London, 1990

Hall, Edith, *The Return of Ulysses: A Cultural History of Homer's Odyssey*, London, 2008

Hamilton, William J., *Researches in Asia Minor, Pontus and Armenia*, 2 vols, London, 1842

Hammond, N. G. L., *A History of Greece to 322 B. C.*, Oxford, 1952

Hammond, N. G. L. and H. H. Scullard (editors), *The Oxford Classical Dictionary*, 2nd edition, Oxford, 1970

Herodotus, *The History*, translated by David Grene, Chicago and London, 1987

Hesiod, *Hesiod, The Homeric Hymns and Homerica*, translated by Hugh G. Evelyn-White, Cambridge, Mass., 1954

Homer, *The Iliad*, translated by Richmond Lattimore, Chicago, 1951

——, *The Odyssey*, translated by Richmond Lattimore, New York, 1965

How, W. W., and J. Wells, *Commentary on Herodotus*, 2 vols, Oxford, 1912

Huxley, G. L., *The Early Ionians*, London, 1966

Joukowsky, Martha Sharp, *Early Turkey, Anatolian Archaeology from Prehistory through the Lydian Period*, Dubuque, Iowa, 1996

Joyce, James, *Ulysses*, London, 1955

Kazantzakis, Nikos, *The Odyssey: A Modern Sequel*, translated by Kimon Friar, New York, 1958

Keats, John, *The Poetical Works of John Keats*, London, 1912

Korfmann, Manfred and Dietrich Mannsperger, *A Guide to Troia*, Istanbul, 2001

Korfmann, Manfred et al., *Troy: Journey to a City Between Legend and Reality*, Istanbul, 2002

Kritoboulos of Imbros, *History of Mehmed the Conqueror*, translated by Charles T. Riggs, Princeton, 1954

Latacz, Joachim, *Homer: His Art and His World*, translated by James P. Holoka, Ann Arbor, Michigan, 1998

——, *Troy and Homer: Towards a Solution of an old Mystery*, translated by Windle and Rosh Ireland, Oxford, 2004

Lattimore, Richmond (translator), *Greek Lyrics*, 2nd edition, Chicago, 1960

Leaf, Walter, *Troy, A Study in Homeric Geography*, London, 1912

Lefkowitz, Mary R., *The Lives of the Greek Poets*, London, 1981

Lloyd, Seton, *Ancient Turkey: A Traveller's History of Turkey*, London, 1989

Lucan, *Pharsalia*, translated by Robert Graves, Harmondsworth, 1957

Luce, J. V., *Homer and the Heroic Age*, New York, 1975

——, *Celebrating Homer's Landscapes: Troy and Ithaca Revisited*, New Haven, 1998

Macqueen, J. G., *The Hittites and their Contemporaries in Asia Minor*, London, 1986

Miller, William, *The Latins in the Levant: A History of Frankish Greece (1204–1566)*, London, 1908

Nagy, Gregory, *Homeric Questions*, Austin, Texas, 1996

Nicoll, Allardyce (editor), *Chapman's Homer: The Iliad, The Odyssey, and the Lesser Homerica*, 2 vols, New York, 1956

Oliva, Pavel, *The Birth of Greek Civilization*, translated by Urwin Levitova London, 1981

Ovid, *Metamorphoses*, translated by Horace Gregory, New York, 1958

Page, Denys L., *History and the Homeric Iliad*, Berkeley and Los Angeles, 1959

Pausanias, *Guide to Greece*, 2 vols, translated with an introduction by Peter Levi, Harmondsworth and New York, 1971

Pindar, *Nemean Odes*, translated by Richmond Lattimore, Chicago, 1957

Pliny, *Natural History*, vol. 3, translated by H. Rakham, Cambridge, Mass., 1963

Porter, James I., 'Homer, the history of an idea', in Fowler, pp. 324–43

Rodd, J. R., *Homer's Ithaca: A Vindication of Tradition*, London, 1927

Ryan, Frederick W. and Vittorio Boron, *Malta*, London, 1910

Sandars, N. K. *The Sea Peoples: Warriors of the ancient Mediterranean 1250–1150 BC*, London, 1978

Schliemann, Heinrich, *Ithaque, le Péloponnèse et Troie*, London, 1869

——, *Troy and its Remains: A Narrative of Researches and Discoveries on the Site of Ilium and in the Trojan Plain*, London, 1875, reprint New York, 1976

——, *Ilios, the city and country of the Trojans, the results of Researches and Discoveries on the site of Troy and Throughout the Troad in the Year 1871, 72, 73, 78, 79, including an Autobiography of the Author*, London, 1881, reprint New York, 1996

Sperling, Jerome W., 'Kumtepe in the Troad, Trial Excavation, 1934', *Hesperia*, vol. 45, No. 4, Oct.–Dec. 1976, pp. 305–64

Stanford, W. B. and J. V. Luce, *The Quest for Ulysses*, New York and Washington, 1974

Stoneman, Richard, *A Literary Companion to Travel in Greece*, Harmondsworth and New York, 1984

——, *Across the Hellespont: Travellers in Turkey from Herodotus to Freya Stark*, London, 1987

——, *Land of Lost Gods: The Search for Classical Greece*, London, 1987

Strabo, *The Geography*, 8 vols, translated by Horace Leonard Jones, Cambridge, Mass., 1970

Tennyson, Alfred Lord, *A Selected Edition*, edited by Christopher Ricks, London, 1989

Thucydides, *History of the Peloponnesian War*, translated by Rex Warner, Harmondsworth, 1987

Traill, David, *Schliemann of Troy: Treasure and Deceit*, London, 1995

Wolf, Armin and H.-H. Wolf, *Die wirkliche Reises des Odysseus. Zur Reconstruction des Homerischen Weltbildes* [The Real Journey of Odysseus] Vienna, 1990

Wood, Michael, *In Search of the Trojan War*, New York, 1996

Index

Editorial Note: In a number of cases I have written names in a somewhat different form than those of Richmond Lattimore, whose translations of the *Iliad* and the *Odyssey* I have used throughout. For example, where he has called the hero of the *Iliad* Achilleus, I have used the more familiar Achilles.